LIVING AT THE EDGE OF THE WORLD:

IN THE CENTER OF OUR OWN STORY

By

Andrew Steed

To Janet and John,

Wonder well + Wonder well

Andrew.

Introduction

This book was written over many years of connecting deeply with the land. Like any good broth it has been stirred in the cauldron, marinated by walking and talking listening and witnessing a remarkable life. The story rich because of meanderings along the cliffs of Cornwall, by the ebb and flow of the crest capped tide in Merlin's Cave, kissed by the wind on the Hill of the Hag of Ireland's lush green soil, the dragons of Wales have breathed their flames of power into the word magic of my soul as the mountains of Snowdonia have sang their song into my heart and Scotland's rich heritage has added flavors to entice and delight a wanderer from every direction as I have traveled into the center of Sovereignty, developed authentic relationships with beings seen and unseen in this remarkable adventurous journey called life!

As I have gathered the treasures of the story I have come into awareness that whatever we are doing we are doing it anyway. This simple phrase reminds me to be present in all aspects of my life. I can moan and complain about washing dishes or I can rock and groove to some music whilst I clean up my mess for I am washing dishes anyway!

I am well aware that I am a tad crazy, to live a remarkable life means that you are crazy for I constantly color outside the lines and listen to the laughter and playfulness of my own soul. What I recently became aware of is that if we choose to live an unremarkable life we are totally insane. So the choice is be crazy or insane! I have also adopted a saying that is we are either adding to the picture of life or taking away there is no in between. So I say add!!!

The pages in this book hold deep mystery, profound healing, laughter tears and authentic questions to challenge us all to be the authors of our stories. I live on the edge and I have stepped inside my center. As you travel through this Celtic path of writings I encourage you to sit with the meaning of the ancient tales in your life. Stories belong to the community and some of these tales are thousands of years in the telling. The land is older and its wisdom echoes off the paper and an open heart will receive gifts to last a lifetime.

I am eternally indebted to the land for sharing its heartsong with me. By far she has been my greatest teacher and I would be amiss for not mentioning those who have helped me along this road of self-discovery. This book would not have yet been manifested if John Cameron had not been my accountability partner for a year and a day. Thanks to Sue Petersen for hours upon hours of editing. The two-legged teachers Peggy Dylan of Sundoor, Tom Cowan, Brooke Medicine Eagle, JoAnn Ramsey, Charla and Tarwater and others who have shared their wisdom with me along the way. To my Spirit Guides for your patience and insight. To Tom at Valiant Tattoos in Dover PA for being a medicine man and marking my body with parts of the Celtic story that carries me.

I am thankful on my two children Christy & Aylish who chose me as their father and came to teach me the meaning of this and to their mother Karen Colbert for she is the Goddess who birthed them. To the community at Walking Winds in PA who have encouraged me to go deeper. To the countless pilgrims who have traveled with me and who have given me inspiration and the means to travel beyond the horizon into the mysteries of the veil. My Mum and Dad who love me and encouraged me to be true to my journey. To my new friend Kat Naslas who is an old friend a wise sage who encourages me to be the best I can be in every moment. To Susie Faucon for guiding me into my own heart so I could celebrate my own laughter and not hide.

To Pat Ives my old drama teacher who walks in Spirit now and believed in me. Angela Morgan and Caroline Orris who taught me to dance. To Cathy Harner who first invited me to lead a pilgrimage. Yes to all of these people and to all of you who have touched my heart, who have come in and out of my life for you all left an impression and helped me to be who I am this day.

Without further ado I invite you to peel back the pages and begin a quest of discovery into travel, 'storical interest, wisdom teachings, ancient magic, the fae and the land which I lovingly call the Isles.

This book is dedicated to

Christy & Aylish Steed

bringing the best Dad out of me

that I know to be.

Chapter 1

THE RAINBOW BRIDGE

The rich flow of the Celtic story has always bubbled in my veins, seeped through my pores, and lingered on my tongue. As a wee boy, sauntering through the woods and connecting with the land, with faerie, was as natural to me as splashing through puddles with my wellies on. I talked openly with Spirit, and I danced with the echoes of the ancestors by my side. I yearned for magic, to be the mystery, to be a spiral dancer, entering the veil as a mist walker, and it took leaving the land I love, to understand this, and to experience the depth of the dance.

At Cockley Cley, Swaffham, in Norfolk, lies a reconstruction of an Iceni village, a stronghold of the Celtic tribe led by the legendary Queen Boadicea, a powerful role model for all feminines. Her name means victory. Triumphantly she led the Iceni against the might of the Roman invaders and occupiers of Britain in 61 AD sacking Colchester and St. Albans, before going on to torch and capture the capital London. She incited a frenzied revolt that decimated a large part of the Roman IX Legion, before she was finally defeated by the XX and XIV Legions under the command of Suetonius Paulinus. To this day Boadicea's name conjures a fearlessness, an intrepid spirit amongst us Brits, and I yearned to know her story, to suck the marrow from the wild and wonderful tales of the Blessed Isle of the Dead, but instead, my early education in school focused on the industrial revolution and the Romans.

The British Isles and Ireland ooze stories, the very trees, rivers, stones, and earth whisper their tales to those who will listen. The legacy of our past is woven into the magical tapestry of the legends, the myths, and the story. What is history anyway? A perspective, translated simply as his story, so there also is a herstory, an honoring of the feminine story, for until the Goddess and God walk side by side, we will always be in the shadow battles of superiority and deferment. As a young boy, the establishment tried to knock the Celt out of me by ignoring the heritage of Britain, of Bridget, the goddess that is the land, for to walk upon her spine, is undoubtedly to stroke the backbone of Bridget herself. So my direct elders focused on the Roman invasion, rather than the Celtic occupation. In doing so, many of my brothers and sisters are still lost in the mist, denying their connection to the mystical roots of oak knowledge, the sap of wisdom, that flows from heart, to heart, and is part of the ever lasting Celtic knot that connects all beings to the infinite. So in honor of the fertile land that Boadicea's blood and bones enriched, let me share the 'Man from Swaffham's' journey, which has given me great insight into my own.

The Man from Swaffam

There was a peddler who lived in an old rickety shack on the outskirts of Swaffham. Every day he would push open his squeaky door, traipse past the ancient oak, at the end of his drive, and trudge to the butter market in Swaffham, his little white dog scampering at his heels. If he did well at market, he would eat, if he did very well, the dog would eat too, and on this day, he sold and traded nothing. So with a heavy heart he hobbled home. The oak tree was starting to shed its leaves, soon it would be winter, and the drafty shack provided poor shelter from the Calliach's wrath. That night, tired and hungry, the Peddler from Swaffham drifted into his dreams. It was closing in on Samhain, where the veil is at its thinnest, and the Peddler found himself in the betwixt and between of dreamland. He felt himself sliding down the roots of a gnarled oak tree, into a luminous chamber, where the Fata Morgana, Queen of the Fay, penetratingly looked into his eyes, as if her breath caressed his soul, she whispered,

"Go stand on London Bridge, that's where you'll find your fortune."

With a start the Peddler awoke. He jumped to his feet spluttering

"I say dog, I had the weirdest dream, come on we'd better go there's work to be done."

Off to market they went, at a forced march. to keep warm, past the ancient oak, to trade and sell his wares. That day was better, and on returning to his shack, he gobbled down bread and cheese, throwing the scraps to the dog. That night in the warmth and comfort of his dreams, blow me down, he saw her again, the Fata Morgana. Her words shrill, piercing his mind, "Go stand on London Bridge, that's where you'll find your fortune".

With a start and a shake, a rattle and a jig, the peddler was on his feet, heading past the old oak, to market. That day he did splendiferous. The dog was in her element, gorging on a sumptuous feast, the man from Swaffham, stuffed as a goose at Yuletide, snuggled in for the night in glorious satisfaction. A heaped plate of steaming vittles sat on the doorstep, an offering for faerie, and the wandering creatures of the night.

Dreamland came swiftly, and the contented couple, master and friend, snored long into the night. As darkness made way for a brand new dawn, the shape-shifting shadows, that penetrate the veil, cackled eerily through the last vestiges of Samhain eve. And so it was the Fata Morgana loomed forebodingly into the Peddler's view. Shimmering in her glory, she tickled the Peddler's mind, toying with him a luscious, coaxing, melodic, chant emanated from her lips, "Go stand on London Bridge, that's where you'll find your fortune."

The Peddler felt his loins stir, his heart skipping wildly to her rhythmic beauty, his mouth opened to kiss her, and she swallowed him, chewed him up, and swallowed him. Was it his piercing screams that reverberated through the air, or the Faerie Queen's demonic laughter? The screaming intensified as he both watched himself, and felt himself being pushed out of the Mother of the Faeries womb, a rip roaring wrenching screech, that pierced through the worlds and he awoke with a start.

It was with a sense of urgency that the Peddler strutted past the oak tree his dog left his heel to head to market, and had bounded several steps before she realized that the man from Swaffham had taken the London road. It took several days, and frosty nights until the 80 odd miles were worn from the leather of his shoe, and he came to stand upon London Bridge.

For three nights and three days, the pair of them stood, like the Queen's guards, not flinching, not pacing, a silent quest, where both endured the elements, and expanded their vision. A cold damp drizzle provided a constant companion, and the wind whistled across the Thames. It was on the third day, as a mist crept steadily towards them that one of the market traders curiosity finally got the better of him.

"Hey Mate, what are you doing? You've been standing in the bleeding cold for days. What the blooming heck for?"

The man from Swaffham broke his silence looking deeply into his eyes, the window of the man's soul, as he remarked liltingly, "This will probably sound strange, I am here because of a dream. My dream told me to come stand on London Bridge, because that is where I'd find my fortune."

The market trader, spluttered in disbelief, shook his head, then raised his chin into the thickening air, and roared with laughter. "Gather round people, and witness a loon, a man off his bleeding rocker, he's been standing in the cold and rain for three nights and days because of a flaming dream. Man, if I was to believe my dreams, I dreamt last night of a place I've never ever heard of, a town called Swaffham. Now apparently at this Swaffham, there is a beaten down old shack, with a huge oak tree standing in the garden and under this oak tree is a whopping chest of gold. What do you think I'm going to do, go to Swaffham and dig under all the oak trees looking for it?"

"No, I don't expect you will," said the Peddler from Swaffham, "Thank you, I think I should be going home now." With a joyful heart he returned to his humble abode, and sure enough, planted under the oak tree outside his shack, was a large chest of gold!

Treasure of the Tale

This timeless wisdom begs the question, "the grass is always greener?"... I wonder how many people are ingrained with the response, "On the other side." The grass is always infinitely greener where we water it. As Voltaire said, "Cultivate your own garden." He wasn't talking about growing tomato plants! He was challenging himself and others to look after and nurture the sovereignty of the soul. Where are we when it comes to living in Sovereignty? What does living in Sovereignty mean in a Celtic context? The ancient leaders were asked to make oaths on how they would live their lives so the tribe would prosper. When living in Sovereignty we move away from living in 'dominion over'. In the Celtic world Sovereignty is the ancient goddess, made up of all parts, earth, air, fire and water bringing the gifts of the elements into the center, into the heart. She is the fabric of the land, and our relationship with ourselves our planet, our community, all beings and all of our ancestors is either in a respectful dance, whereby we honor all of the parts being as important as each other, or it is in 'dominion over', whereby we feel we are better than and need to horde, own, destroy and be the 'Mistress' or 'Master' over our Universe. When we live and speak from our truth with gentleness and strength, when we connect to the passion of our own fire, when we are in the roots of our own earth, when the waters that run through us are vibrantly clear and not clogged with sludge, the baggage of our repressed past, then we can spread our wings as lightworkers and fly high through the air with a freedom of purpose to unite, connecting and weaving the threads of oneness, to our center, to our heart, to sovereignty.

The Peddlers tale, as all stories, holds many truths on many levels if we have the patience to delve into their secret chambers with careful mindfulness. I have shared this story countless times. It has become the established climax at the integration circle, on the last day of the many pilgrimages that I continue to facilitate in the British Isles and Ireland. The ancestors have gathered on the hill of Dunadd, on the Burren, at Dinas Emrys, Woodhenge and Stonehenge to encourage us to sink further into the strands that connect us to universal truth. Each time I caress the words and flow into the feelings of each character, embodying the intricacies of each moment, I gain new insight, new understanding, and just when I think I comprehend the fullness of the gift I fall into a new canyon of discovery.

Only recently I was leading a shamanic group and I wanted to find out about each person's travels since our last gathering, so I invited a journey into the Peddler's tale to find the three most significant treasures that each of us had gathered through the three previous Celtic seasons of Samhain, Imbolc, and Beltane and share them as our harvest, the first harvest, known as Lughnasadh. As I explored the story before class I experienced the sleeping and dreaming of the Peddler as shamanic work, entering a 'cave' as the 'shack' and going to bed hungry as fasting to receive a vision. Meeting the faerie queen who tells him to go stand on London Bridge. To stand in a place that is betwixt and between, for that is what a bridge is, am I on the water, over it, in it?

And what is a bridge anyway? Is it not a place that bridges it, isn't he being asked to go to Bridget!

He goes on a journey passing the oak tree.   Druid means Oak knowledge and Bridget of Kildaire means exalted one of the church of oaks. Many people enter the underworld through the roots of trees, and our peddler connects with the ancient oak to journey to London. Again he is fasting for a vision standing in the mist and rain on the 'bridge' for three nights and three days. He is finally challenged by the market trader who acts as a kind of trickster to help the Peddler to the truth of where he carries, stores and hides his gifts, in his own backyard all of the time.

In my journeying, this trickster, the trader, became Lugh, the counterpart of Bridget. The sun god in the west who encourages us to walk into our vision, as Bridget the goddess in the east encourages us to embrace the abundance and prosperity of the east and share it with ourselves and our community. Lugh is a trickster, in Irish tradition he is known today in the guise of the

Leprechaun. So often in life I am unable to see clearly when someone points out the obvious to me, and yet when it is hidden for me to make my own connection, truth comes flooding in as a tidal wave. So Lugh shares with the Peddler a version of the dream:

"if I was to believe my dreams, I dreamt last night of a place I've never ever heard of, a town called Swaffham, now apparently at this Swaffham, there is a beaten down old shack, with a huge oak tree standing in the garden, and under this oak tree is a whopping chest of gold. What do you think I'm going to do, go to Swaffham and dig under all the oak trees looking for it?"

Sugar coated in faerie honeycomb, delicious droplets of wisdom are consumed by the peddler who is able to celebrate the authenticity of understanding as his own. It is fascinating to explore the roots of the Leprechaun We search somewhere over the rainbow to find the pot of gold, or as the song goes,'*Somewhere over the rainbow skies are blue and the dreams that you dare to dream really do come true.*'

Like Dorothy from the Wizard of Oz, the Peddler follows the path of light to find his way home. So do we all journey to seek the Wizard, the trader, Lugh, the Leprechaun in search of the treasure, which ultimately resides in our home, in our heart.

How many of us have dreamed of meeting a Leprechaun and discovering their pot of gold?

The Leprechaun is none other than Lugh Lamhfhada, Lugh Longhand, the sun god skilled in all of the arts, which is translated as Lugh Samildanach. This venerated god of light is diminished to Lugh Chromain, which means 'Little Stooping Lugh' as the Tuatha De Dannan went into the mist of the mounds and the old gods and goddesses became the faerie folk who the Christian Church in their fear tried to water down and destroy. However, the people kept the candles burning and the memories of the old ways are kept alive in the stories and in the magic of the land. It is impossible to extinguish the flames of the sun, of Lugh. His bright fire continues to illuminate and he is remembered today in the guise of the Leprechaun. It is said if you catch a Leprechaun they will offer you a piece of silver which when you put it in your pocket will immediately return to their purse. If pressed they will offer you a piece of gold that will crumble into dust when you let them go. Each of us is reminded of this magic when the sun shines on the cleansing waters and a rainbow dances across the sky. There is a sense of awe and the child in each of us jumps for joy, don't you agree? And as we gaze in wonder of the bright colors that arc before our eyes we only get a glimpse of the picture.

We can try our whole lives to find the pot of gold at the end of the rainbow, but the truth is that a rainbow has no end. Rainbows are a circle. They appear to be a multi colored arch because we see them only as far as the horizon. In expanding our horizons, like the rainbow, we will find all things are connected, there is no beginning, there is no end. So again Lugh plays a visual trick with us, and invites seekers of gold to understand the true nature of the treasure. The pot of gold is the sun, our radiance, if we try to steal the gold, the light, it disappears, crumbles to dust, we put out our own flame and flounder in the darkness of self obsessed greed.

When we remember that home is where the heart is and the greatest treasures is within us and not outside of us, then our fire, our passion feeds and nurtures all. We are connected to our heartsong and the peddler, the wandering spirit inside of us makes merry, for we are spiritual millionaires!

Recognizing our own magic, our own inner wizard is an art and an adventure in itself. As I wrote this chapter the connection to the Wizard of Oz was continually echoing in my ear, that night as I sat down and flicked through the channels of the television the vivid colors leapt from the screen as my eyes settled on Judy Garland skipping down the yellow brick road. These magical moments are our confirmation that we are walking our path.

As I feasted upon the story that illuminated my childhood Christmas', it was one of the shows guaranteed to be on every yuletide!, I had a revelation connecting me to my Celtic roots and the Peddler's story. The Scarecrow is searching for his brains, his cauldron of wisdom. The Tin Man is searching for his heart, the cauldron of calling, his passion, his heart song and the Lion is seeking his courage to be in this world, the cauldron of warming, the place where I am, I exist. These three cauldrons are the Celtic energy centers that when fully activated allow us to be, to act, and to know ourselves at our core, and in so doing we are home, we are our true nature.

Dorothy takes the yellow brick road which is a symbol of the sun, the path of light, the pot of gold. When she takes the ruby red slippers off the Wicked Witch of the East, the East represents abundance, prosperity and community. She learns to dance, walk, stand on her own two feet and own her power as she moves through the south to celebrate her story. The South connects us to the poetry, the song, the dance, the music and the laughter. We are taken into the vision of the West by taking on the Wicked Witch of the West. It is not until she speaks her truth in the North and clicks the heels of the ruby slippers three times, as is the Celtic way, that the shoes which have carried her on her journey are revealed as the symbol of her having had the answers all of the time.

The relationships continue as these sparkling 'sun' red slippers are connected to Lugh, who as the Leprechaun is the maker of shoes!!! The Peddler has also used his feet to walk for three days into his vision. He has the courage to follow his own path, as kooky as it may seem to others. He dares to believe in the power of his dreams and in so doing he finds his authentic voice and the magic to celebrate in his own backyard, his own body and soul. This Universal story invites us to explore ourselves and if we have the courage of the Lion, the heart of the Tin Man and the Wisdom of the Scarecrow, we will click our heels and live by a creed that for me calls, 'To be present, to live in the roots of my being, to speak and sing the truth of my heart and to know beyond all knowledge that I am and I act what I think to be true!'

The Tale and the Land

Both the Peddler and Dorothy had to travel away from home to discover that they had everything they needed within them. In these stories I also recognized my own journey of emigration. When I flew from Heathrow to JFK airport in 1993, I began a rekindling relationship with my homeland, my ancestry became of utmost importance, and I realize now, some 17 years later that I have indeed transformed. I have kissed the Fata Morgana, Mother of the Faeries, been reborn, in yet another life death, rebirth ritual, and I understand that the fullness of my treasure is well and truly in my own back yard. We go on a sacred pilgrimage to connect with what we have always had, and the deeper I know this the more my life's spirit unfolds, to dance soulfully between, and within the worlds.

One of my earliest recollections in the so called 'New World', was an ancient tribal gathering of the First People of the USA, a Pow Wow, where the drum beat, heart beat, of the mother penetrated deep into her belly, and saturated her womb with the primordial cries of original song. I felt in that moment that I'd come home. There is a rhythm deep in the earth, that calls us, and when heard, felt, tasted, smelt, sensed within our energetic field, gives us no choice but to surrender, and dance, for that song, is who we are, a part of each and every one of us. It is a vibration that permeates our soul, connecting us to all that has gone before, to all that is yet to come. I believe that each of us is born with this rich sound inside of us, and if we listen to nature's calling, the essence of our being is stimulated to twirl, jump, sway, and slide into an alert stillness, the power of the present moment. Celebrating all that we can be, and all that we truly are.

High up on a green hillside in central Pennsylvania, my body responded to the spirit of the deer, her taut skin singing to the honor beats, as drummers connected in perfect unison. This was the spring of 1994, and I entered through a gateway onto the sacred red road I had found my ruby slippers to take me home. I had wanted to know the story of the land in the USA. It was important to me to experience and understand the place that I was now calling home. Many people would say to me, "We are a young country, just over 200 years old, not like the British Isles," and I would think, this land is as old as Bridget, with as many tales to share. So I called to the elders, and a pathway graciously unfolded before me. Within a couple of months I was attending my first sweat lodge, and within a couple of years I was dancing through the night on Sacred Cherokee land, and stepping into the darkness of the night on vision quest. It has been a feast of indigenous authenticity, and I am so very grateful, to the teachers and the ancestors, who kept the story and the medicine of this land alive, and to the spirit guides who walk by my side with encouragement and guidance.

The more I delved into the ways of the red road, the more evident my own indigenous roots became as they thread into the fabric of my journey, an eternal knot work of fluid curvature. I am a Celt, I am indigenous and I, like many of my brother and sister Celts forgot. It took leaving the Isles to connect with what I always had inside of me. The Celts also went on Vision Quest. We smudged with juniper, danced to the beat of cow hides and goat skin drums, and gathered for sweatlodges. Our medicine wheel is the sacred weave, and the honoring of the directions. We do not call it a medicine wheel, yet I journey to work with our totem animals, the ingredients of the cardinal points, the sacred treasures, and the divine center, sovereignty within my relationship to self, and the land. We have kept our magic alive in the stories, and I was grateful to emigrate when my son was two and my daughter one, for the old tales of their birth land were essential to bathe in, to stir the memories in the fiber of our collective beings, and to celebrate our poignant heritage. I am a wanderer, a gypsy at heart, a lover of life, a traveler with a flair for the dramatic, and as my children say, "Dad you are a rock star," which is so very Celtic. I love to wear bright clothes that dazzle and stir a resplendency in my soul, I dye my hair and am unabashedly proud of it, I wear it long, and revel in being a non-conformist. The more I live my life, the more Celtic I feel. They too were known as the glam rockers of their age.

In delving into the poetry of our people, feasting on the legends, myths, and marvels of Bardic treasure, lyrical enchantments that capture the attention of vibrant minds, I groomed myself for my role as a Seanachie also known as a storyteller or bearer of "old lore." In 1996 I left the comfort of a regular wage, with great benefits, to travel the highways and byways, at festivals, in schools, corporations, and colleges, to be a full time British bard. Looking back I had the courage and recklessness of my ancestors. Like on the battlefields of old, as the naked men and women screamed passionately in the Celtic charge, their long hair flying in the wind, their faces and bodies streaked in blue wode, wild and triumphant, I charged into self employment on a $75 contract, knowing that I would carve such a majestic pattern on the battlefield of life, that my story would be told. It was blind faith and an absolute belief in spirit to guide and direct my life. By 1998 another slice of magic would illuminate my pathway, when helping out a friend at a spiritual expo, I struck up a conversation with a clairvoyant who led sacred site tours to Greece.

"Have you ever thought of taking people to the British Isles?" I innocently asked, and the veil in the gloaming opened up deliciously for me to walk through. For she looked into my eyes and it was if she crooned her response

"Not until now, will you be the guide?"

So in May 1999 I embarked on a quest to discover the hidden gems of Cornwall, to walk the trails of my childhood family holidays, to plan holy days for pilgrims anon. It was a hop, skip and a jump to Glastonbury, Avebury and Stonehenge. In those early years I traveled a familiar path, one recognizable to many seekers, and this in turn led me to more obscure sites, off the beaten track, where magic hangs in the air, undisturbed by the masses. Some of these magical sites are: The Cave of the Dead on the craggy coast of Mull, Alsia well with the guardian Hare a stones throw from the enchanting Rosemerryn, the dank darkness of Boleigh Fogou, St. David's well protected by the dragon in a wooded grove near Kenmore, Moel Ty Uchaf, hidden in the hills of North Wales, and the Owenygat Cave, nestled under a hawthorn tree in the expansive lands of Mebh (Maeve), near Tulsk in Ireland. I rejoice in the continued opportunity to kiss the sensual goddess and make love to the land. My travels have invited a special relationship with the sidhe, a connection to the memory strands of the ancients and many warm friendships with both pilgrims and locals alike. I encourage all to walk gracefully, with purpose, and tread in the footsteps of Rhiannon, Arthur, Lugh, Bridghid, and Biera, and to enter Sancreed Well, Ailwee Caves, Barclodiad Y Gawres, and the Cave of the Nuns on Carsaig Bay. These are among many of the dazzling riches that await an intrepid traveler who listens with an open heart, and squishes her/his toes into the fertile soil.

All these and more are nemetons, places of rich spiritual power, that reveal parts

of the Oran Mor, the original story of the Celts, the deepest note of being, a place where

we remember to remember to remember, and in so doing we understand ourselves, and our ancestors, the shining ones, and all beings in new mysterious ways. What is a nementon? What is the Oran Mor? Who am I? What is the meaning of the Grail? As E.E. Cummings so eloquently said, "Always the beautiful answer who asks a more beautiful question."

Life invites us to ask authentic questions, and so I shall, and in so doing I will look to answer these and more, and I trust I will understand myself more honestly, more authentically, and mayhap you will too!

Chapter 2

WHAT'S IN A NAME?

In Welsh tradition from the Mabinogian, the story of Lleu Llaw Gyffes, the bright one struck with a deft hand, his mother Arianrhod places a tynged on him, this is the Welsh equivalent of the Irish Geas, a fate, destiny, something that has to be followed, an absolute. In the case of Lleu's story, the tynged is that only Arianrhod can name her son, the boys uncle, Gwydion, tricks Arianrhod into believing he is a shoe salesman, and she watches a young boy shoot down a golden wren. Her exclamation in seeing this radiant youth's skill is instinctive. She calls his name onto the winds, and he now exists. Lleu is the sun god, and his name in Welsh means lion or shining one, in Irish Lugh means oath. Amongst its many insights, this story reflects the ancient rites of passage of a mother's right to name the child. Only by giving the child a name does he/she exist.

I have already referred to Britain as Bridget, the Celtic Saint, who is the great pagan goddess, she who bridges it, from the neolithic to the pagan, from the pagan to Christianity and beyond. Her name means exalted one, her festival is Imbolc, the time of birthing, of spring, and this is the time in the Celtic year when names are giving. Across the sea Ireland is also named after a goddess, Eire, she is a goddess who didn't want to be named after a country. No, she demanded a country be named after her! Hence the country is known as Eire land, or Ireland. Carved through her flesh and bones are many mountains, rivers, hills, caves, waterfalls, forests, a luscious natural landscape, forged with markings of the ancestors, our brothers and sisters, all carrying names, stories, wisdom, the land is alive and they carry their names for they too exist.

Origin Stories

Although the Celts have no original story for the conception of us two- leggeds, I am rather fond of the many stories regarding Beira, the old hag who is also known by the names of Cerridwen, Calliach and Bone Mother who while shaking out her apron, upsets her creel, and hits the earth with her hammer to make the mountains and shape them and she milked the goats to make the rivers. My absolute favorite is her interaction with the Dagda the Celtic father figure and protector of the tribe, the good god. So breath in the fleshy fruits of the following tale;

Making Love to the Land

The Dagda's whopping penis was so gargantuan and cumbersome that he had to remove his genitals so he could push and stuff his flaccid member and engorged testicles into a rickety old wheelbarrow allowing him to walk upon the earth without getting tangled up in the lush green vegetation of Ireland. On a Beltane morn with the dew splashed copiously upon the meadow, the Dagda picked up his load and heaved his way through some sloppy mud ploughing his way through marshy bog land. All of a sudden the wheel caught fast in the slurping sludge and with all of his might he rammed his way forward. The wheel spun furiously into the soft gooey soil, churning and turning, whirling and twirling, revealing a moist wet opening in the earth's crust. As he stared panting at the dank dark crevice that invitingly opened before his bulbous eyes, his penis twitched, his heart raced and his mind conjured sweet images of entering the oozing soggy gash and pumping his sperm deep within the sopping juices of Erin's fertile earth. His quivering tool sprang to life, stiffening with expectant pleasure. His hands groped for his erect throbbing shaft and he jammed it on to his thrusting pelvis. With unabated glee he slid his length into the gaping flowering lotus and humping and bumping, grinding and sliding, squirting and spurting he erupted in screams of ecstasy. His body jerked in uncontrollable spasms as he shot his warm milky seed into the mushy slit of the earth's mound.

Wasted and worn he eased his dangling penis from the cozy crevice. His appetite fully satisfied he swayed at half mast gently disengaging from his limp wand. Marveling at the last dustings of magic sticking to his hands he grabbed his testicles and puffed them up as soft pillows to rest his weary head. Grabbing his thick foreskin, he wrapped himself up in his soft floppy package and slipped contentedly into dreamtime.

And all the while the Calliach was watching. She crawled out of her cavern and hovered above the Dagda's sleeping form. As the memories of his shattering climax tickled her fancy, she caressed her hardening nipples, pinching and tweaking, flicking and seeking the intense pleasure of multiple orgasms. Swiftly rubbing her weathered wrinkly hand over her leathery skin, deftly searching for her moist honey pot the nectar of her womb. Parting the craggy flaps that sheltered her fertile garden she exposed her labia and stroked and massaged, polished and brushed, enticingly stimulating her engorged clitoris. As the waves of shimmering bliss burned and bubbled her blood, pulsating through her veins in a glorious tempest, her back arched and her body convulsed in ecstatic glory as fluids gushed from her birthing canal. Streams and seas, lakes and rivers flowed copiously onto the earth, as her muscles tightened around her genitals the surging tingling contracting multiple release of cum spattered pebbles and rocks, boulders and sparkling gemstones forming hills and cliffs, mountains and mounds throughout the Emerald Isle. Tasting the vibrancy of her juice the Calliach drifted blissfully into the bowels of the earth. Sitting satiated she stirred her cauldron and cackled euphorically as the Dagda gently dozed.

As the dreamtime faded the Dagda awoke fully rested from the exertions of spilling his seed, he shook off the sleeping dust and stuffed his bedding into his barrow and once again pushed his penis through the newly birthed land. He hadn't gone far before his mind remembered the warm wet opening, his loins stirred with the pleasure of remembrance and his eyes avidly scanned the land for a moist orifice so he could plough and scatter, furrow and spurt making delicious love to the land.

I have heard the Dagda's name pronounced as written with a hard 'g' and also as Dada. The Dagda is the father of the gods and his name has transferred into our language today. A child looks up at its father and calls out dada!

The Calliach is known as Cerridwen in Wales, Biera in Scotland and Beara in parts of Ireland. In County Cork I have sat beside the Calleach Beara at Gortagarriff on the Beara Penninsula where we have both gazed out over Coulagh Bay. The hag is said to be transfixed in stone waiting for Manannan god of the sea to return. She is the shaper of the land, the goddess who is an aspect of sovereignty. Who Donald Alexander McKenzie, in Wonder Tales from Scottish Myth and Legend, gives voice to as the mother of all the gods and goddesses in Scotland. In myth the Hawk of Achill and Fintan the Wise acknowledge her as outliving them and refer to her as the grandmother who ate the apples in the beginning. She is in the land, referenced many times throughout Scotland and Ireland.

Near Oldcastle in County Meath she is known as Slieve na Calliach, the hags mountain, where the largest complex of passage graves can be found in the whole of the Emerald Isle. Way atop the highest hills in this area, reputing to overlook 17 counties, affording spectacular views of the land and lakes of Ireland are several cairns the most notable being cairn T. As you approach the ridge there is a flat slab bed stone known as the Hags Chair. My first visit to this majestic mound left me initially both awed and frustrated. The main cairn had a padlock forbidding entrance to its passageways and hidden mysteries. I sauntered over to the ruins of another cairn that no longer has its roof intact and I sat watching the weather change from bright sunshine to clouds and rain, back to bright sunshine again, a sweeping wind cleansing, shifting magically changing rapidly and drastically within in a fifteen minute period. In gratitude I made an offering of Guinness to the land and I sang. As my song flowed through the air and hung around me long after I had finished singing, I breathed in the power of place. Knowing that this was a hallowed site that I would return to many times with many pilgrims I lifted myself up and retraced my steps to descend the steep slope to the car park. I glanced over at the main cairn and zeroed in on the gate, no padlock was fastened to it. The gate was closed and bolted, but the large lock barring my way had magically disappeared. I crept quietly towards the entrance, my ears keen to pick out any sounds and my eyes alert, my heart racing.

Inside all was still, deathly quiet and then I saw a light, a torch flickering within and two voices echoed off the ancient walls in reverend whispers, as if through the annals of time, discussing the symbolic carvings that swirl across the rock face within the sanctity of the inner chamber. No padlock meant I was invited, so as in entering a sweatlodge, I crawled on hands and knees into the cairn. Two archeologists swung their faces to greet me with warm smiles and sensing the present moment we all sat in silence honoring our ancestors, the land and our selves. After we had crawled into the sunlight and they had locked the gate once more, they shared with me where I could pick up the key for future visits. With great thankfulness to them for sharing I bade farewell and I did a little jig down the steep incline lined by hawthorn trees to visit the key holders at Loughcrew Garden Visitor Center who at the time of my writing release the key from 10am until around 4pm each day. In honor of the ancestors and spirits of place I have returned to sing and pray inside this womb on many an occasion.

The seventh pilgrimage I offered to this holy hill of the hag provided yet another opportunity to revel in magic. The pilgrims were circling the main cairn three times in reverence, as they sauntered gently on their way a young man climbed the height of the tor and approached the gate to the cairn. I watched him breath in the endless view his eyes alight in wonder and a beaming smile emanating a reveling joy. He gushed some words in eager awe looked at the thick bars and locks adorning the door of the cairn and sighed

"The only thing that would top this is we could find the key to the chamber." With twinkling eyes and a mischievous grin I pulled the key from my pocket and chuckled, "Would you like to go in?"

So it was that a man named Hugh from North America crawled into the shadowed womb to experience himself. I explained to him that the pilgrims and I would be coming into the cairn to sing, listen, pray and share stories in due course and he was welcome to visit before and after our time and if he chose to stay with us in the burial chamber and we would appreciate him honoring the work that we were going to do. He decided to stay and by the time we had scattered offerings of whisky and chocolate at the threshold of the Calliach's crotch he had settled in the Northern passage of this cross shaped grave. As if answering our calls and offerings the wind picked up and rain began to fall. Sheltered in the cramped dusky earthy uterus we circled knee to knee and energetically heart to heart in the central chamber.

Hugh was as good as his word. He sat in silence as the witness to the story. It is powerful to share in front of a witness, the songs the stories the silence all expanded reverberating within and without shifting in a manner that is richer and deeper, changing all of the participants in ways beyond measure. When Hugh left us, and we all crawled out into streaming sunshine, he carried a new piece of the world in his bosom, grateful smiles and hearts connected at a soul level. I often wonder how his version of the story is told or mayhap he is still sitting with it and stirring it for himself in his own cauldron. On returning home I looked up the meaning of the name Hugh, which means 'mind heart or spirit' how about that for yet more evidence that magic is tangible and dripping through the story that we have named time. If you choose to wander this way please remember to honor the gatekeepers of this phenomenal vista, the Visitor Center provides an excellent lunch or afternoon tea, and you can never drink too much tea in Ireland!

As the land holds parts of its story through its many names, so we grow in our life experience and our story through trying on many different names. Our birth name, nicknames, medicine names, and we may possibly discover our original name.

I have facilitated an exercise called 'What's in a name?' For two minutes I ask people to share the story of their name. Its meaning, the ancestry, who they are named after, middle names, the spelling, nicknames, and any other pertinent information.

In sharing, as with all aspects of life it is important to only impart information that you wish the other person to know. Some of you may have read *Lord of the Flies*, where a chubby boy in glasses confides to a would be friend, that at his old school, everyone called him Piggy, which he hated. So what does his confident do with this new information, he tells everyone that the stout bespectacled youth is known as Piggy. A classic example of how quickly people give their power away.

What's in my name? I was born Andrew Steed. Andrew is the patron Saint of Scotland. My mother is a Scot and I am very proud of my Scottish ancestry. I have met many people in the USA who tell me they're Scotch, my nana rolls in her grave at this one. In bonnie Scotland, Scotch is broth or whisky, not a name for the people. Through my Grandparents lineage, I am part of the Davidson Clan, which means son of the beloved, and the Innes Clan, which means Island or One Choice. Andrew means strong, Steed is one who tends horses I believe I have the power and energy of the horse running right through me. Do I have a middle name? No, I was nearly given the name of Steven, I am thankful my mum and dad changed their minds. What's wrong with the name Steven, nothing, but my initials would have been ass!

As far as nicknames go, my most endearing one has to be Harry. Harry was born on a stormy night in Thetford forest, Norfolk, the same county as Swaffham, home to the Iceni. I had gone camping with my best friend Mark, and a bunch of mates, about seven of us in total. We had planned to run through the woods all night, but the heavy rain dampened our spirits. Inside the cramped tent all eyes fell on me. I was the one who was the 'games master' unbeknownst to myself at that time I was the Bard, the playful soul, the keeper of stories, who always had a trick or two up his sleeve. So I introduced them all to 'Hey Harry".

It's a simple word game, which consists of a set pattern of words that are passed on in a circle. It goes "Hey Harry?" "Yes Harry", "Tell Harry", "Hey Harry?" "Yes Harry", "Tell Harry". This continues uninterrupted until someone pauses, stutters or makes a mistake with the wording. At that point a weird and wonderful name is chosen by the person who lost the thread of the rhythm, for example, Mark makes a mistake and calls himself 'The wicked soul man. Now the person who addresses Mark says, "Hey Wicked Soul Man?", whereby Mark replies, "Yes Harry", and then he is told "Tell Harry". After playing for a good hour, all my friends had gone through a number of fabulous names, and I was still Harry.

I worked hard for my nickname of Harry, and I have thoroughly enjoyed owning it! In my research of this name I have found three meanings, adventurer, leader in battle and home ruler, the latter I have always considered to be in part the King, and therefore as Harry I may choose to be an authentic Sovereign or a Tyrant, when I forget I can so easily be a tyrant, and when I remember, I live and breathe in sovereignty.

I remember hearing a story years ago of a woman named Nora who didn't like her name. A gentleman remarked on what a pretty name it was. She looked at him as if he were half crazy uttering, "I hate it".

He inquired who had given her that name, and if she knew why they had called her Nora. Nora sighed "My mother chose it for me, after her best friend who was named Nora".

The man smiled and gleefully shared "You were clearly named after someone your mother loved. That's glorious, you were named out of love."

Nora pondered for a moment before exclaiming "I'd never thought of it quite like that before. Maybe Nora's not such a bad name after all." If she had looked up the meaning she would have found that her name is from Elanora, meaning light, and woman of honor.

My daughters name is Aylish, (often spelt Eilish) it means God is satisfied, or oath of God. She is named after one of my heroes, Liz McColgan, a Scottish marathon runner, who chose the same name for her daughter. She gave birth to her child in late November 1990 and by March 1991 she was fit enough and strong enough to compete at the World Cross Country Championships in Antwerp, and the gutsy runner finished third. Three again, it's the Celtic way!

My daughter's middle name is Rose, which is the flower, and in the Celtic world this flower represents healing and the gift of sight. She also carries her mother's name Colbert, which means renowned, bright and famous. So her full title is; God is satisfied with the healer, who has the gift of sight, renowned, bright, and famous, who tends horses!

My son is named Christy meaning Christ Bearing, also from Christopher the patron Saint of travel. He is also named after one of my heroes, Christy Moore. Moore is an Irish folk singer with a whole lot of class, and magical talent. I have seen some great live singers in my life, Bob Marley, Police, The Clash, Sarah McLachlan, well I like them, but my favorite amongst them all, is Christy Moore. I'll never forget the day in Finsbury Park, London. I was at a Fleadh, an Irish festival. I'd seen Mary Black, Mary Coughlan, Nanci Griffith, all were phenomenal, and then on strolled Christy Moore. He walked on stage with his acoustic guitar. He wore an old sweater and jeans. His portly figure, aging years, and semi balding head, didn't exactly scream 'American Idol' or 'Pop star'. All the other singers had backing bands. Christy had himself. It was two o'clock in the afternoon, every one was sitting down, some had eaten too much, some were probably wasted, the fact of the matter was no one was ready to get their groove on. That was all about to change. Christy's deep melodic sound and quick fire stirring lyrics had us all on our feet. By the end of his show, we were bellowing for more. There was one rule of the festival. No encores. It was the only way to get through all of the talented bands lined up for the day. Now the producers had a problem. This crowd was demanding an encore. When the yelling and shrieking reached its crescendo, Christy Moore walked back on stage, minus the guitar. He then proceeded to sing acappela to the multitude, who in respect, stood in absolute silence, goosebumps flittering across the skin in tingling admiration. I swear you could have heard a pin drop on that warm summers afternoon. I've never forgotten it. There are not many people who can stir an audience like Christy Moore, he's a master artist, and my son proudly carries his name. Make sure you pass on the stories of the names in your family. It is deeply empowering.

A wonderful feminine who I met whilst studying with Brooke medicine Eagle introduced herself to me as Rivertree, we had the opportunity to commune in nature whilst questing in the Black Hills of Montana. I remember watching her carve a stick in her spare time. Every day she would whittle away at it, and on the thirteenth day she presented it to another classmate who has Multiple Sclerosis, the stick looked like a flowing river carved from the branch of a tree. I went to Rivertree and told her "You really own your name."

It was a few years later, after Rivertree had traveled to Scotland with me that I received a call to say she had passed into spirit. Her life partner asked me to sing her home, to help her transition, and so I did, and in doing so I heard her call through the ethers, "I am Rivertree, I am Donna Faye Keith." I was struck by the use of her birth name, and so I looked up the meaning, Donna is mother, Faye is of faerie, and Keith is Warrior, She was and is a Woman Faerie Warrior. Both names are so resplendently appropriate.

I invite you to consider what's the meaning of your name? If you do not know it's meaning then invest in the research time and find out. Local bookstores, the internet, the library, any of these will help you with your search.

Do you have a medicine name?

Are you desperately yearning one?

Are you waiting for an indigenous elder to call you 'Squats like a toad' before you are complete? Medicine names come from spirit, and we all carry our original name, a name that is deep within us, that expresses the highest aspect of who we are. So if you wish to find the name that is in your heart go there and listen to the quiet voice of Spirit.

The Celtic tradition of entering a cave or sleeping on a faerie mound, wrapping oneself in cow hide, to receive a vision, was, and still is a common practice. It is said that it was this way that the Tain Bo Cuailnge, the Cattle-raid of Quelgny (Cooley) was brought to the Irish people. Sanchen Torpest, Ireland's Chief Bard was ridiculed by the High King for not knowing Ireland's epic and greatest story. Making it is his business to recover this treasure he sends his sons to find Fergus Mac Roy's grave and ask Fergus for the story, to sleep on the grave and connect with spirit. There are also tales of St. Columba wrapping himself in cow hide and communing with spirit entities at sacred mounds. With this knowledge simmering in my cauldrons I inadvertently followed in my ancestors footsteps to receive my own vision.

I knew that Boleigh Fogou, a ceremonial iron age Celtic cave, was situated close to the head of Lamorna Cove deep in the shadows and whispering woods of faerie close to the most south westerly point of enchanting Cornwall. My instincts told me that I could reach out and touch it from the Merry Maiden stone circle and the piper stones near Boleigh farm and even though there is so much public right of way in the Isles I did not fancy leading a group of pilgrims in search of the fogou unless I'd been there first myself and had permission of the land owner to sit and sing in the mouth of this venerable womb. So for five years I twirled a mazy jig with the Maidens and ignored the calling of Old Bet to dance to a different tune.

Chapter 3

THE BETWIXT AND THE BETWEEN

In 2004 I prepared to return to see Penny Lally at Rose Farm in Chyanhal and experience one of the greatest Cornish Breakfasts on this planet. Penny is a talented artist, poet and a lover of the land and all of its life forms. She runs a pet cemetery, which supports the running of a sanctuary for beloved animals. The occupants, sheep, cattle, horses, pigs, geese, chickens and wild fowl are show animals, they live their lives among the lush green grass of rolling Cornish countryside. This is their home until they die. They all have names and the freedom of the farm reminds one of the spirit of Animal Farm, at the beginning of George Orwell's book, when the animals chase Mr. Jones off Manor Farm and a glimpse of equality washes through the stream and saturates the land. There truly is a feeling of equality in the bones of the earth at Penny's place. Her love of space was echoed firmly in her refusal to turn her barn room into three apartments to make more money. She told the architect in no uncertain words where he could stick that idea. Instead a weary traveler can rent this spacious abode that is furnished with antiques and a four-poster 17th century bed which is fit for Royalty!

On all my visits I drum and dance on her top field where the sheep nod their heads to the beat, and her one Scottish Highland Cow named Willy would witness the pilgrims song and creep ever the closer as we connected with the spirit of this energy charged nemeton. Recently Willy passed into Spirit and in May 2008 I sat upon his grazing grounds under the lengthening shadows of Bert and Mabel, the two Neolithic standing stones on her top field, remembering and celebrating the life of this shaggy beast.

Penny is a Celt, offering hospitality to all, her farm is aptly named, Rose, which as already mentioned, means healing and the gift of sight, Penny offers these gifts in abundance, living true to the meaning of her name, which is Weaver, and what spells and magic she interlaces on the loom of life.

As I packed my case and got all of my paperwork together I stumbled upon the story of Duffy and the Devil where Old Bet plays an important role in the beat of her drum.

Duffy and the Devil

The sweet promise of Lughnasadh hung fervently in the air with the smell of the fruits of the underworld, apples, it was cider pressing time. Squire Lovell was known for the strength and quality of some of the best lip smacking, brain whirling scrumpy to be found in these parts. As he rode his dashing white horse past red dappled trees he heard a screeching and screaming that upset the apple cart and put a dampener on his delicious juicy day.

"You're a good for nothing lazy trollop," shrieked the shrill tones of his chief apple picker, a daunting looking woman in her late forties with biceps the size of cooking apples.

"I'm not lazy," spat a tearful young woman. "I'll have you know that I make the finest pies in all of Cornwall and if you'd let me cut up the apples my way I'd prove it."

Squire Lovell raced to intervene just in the nick of time as the young woman's braids were being tugged fiercely and a well aimed boot was about to kick her behind. A cloud of dust from his horses hooves clouded the scene for just a second and then out of the mist walked the tear stained exotic dark skinned face and beautiful form of a young goddess, Duffy. The radiant features of Duffy made Squire Lovell's knees go weak and there was a surging in his loins. His normally composed voice flipped up an octave and he squeaked,

"Can you spin and knit?" Clearing his throat with his most manly cough he croaked "You seem dreadfully unhappy here. How would you like to come and work at my manor house?"

"Good sir, my name is Duffy, and I make exceedingly good pies and I would love to come work for you at the big house if you'll have me."

"Grab your things young Duffy you are now my housekeeper."

"Well good riddance," hissed the chief apple picker quietly but viciously so Squire Lovell didn't hear, but Duffy just flashed her the widest grin, and she skipped off behind the Master of the Manor to work at the finest house on the outskirts of Newlyn.

The exuberance of spirit soured like milk left in the baking hot sun as she stepped across the threshold of her new world. Thick dust carpeted the floors, clutter spewed forth from every crevice and the worst of it lay on the large attic floor. The winding staircase soared to the top turrets where a filthy old spinning wheel sat covered in cobwebs, and unspun fleece was piled high to the ceiling.

"Hop to it Duffy my dear. I need socks first, my toes are poking through all but one of my pairs, and I need a hunting jacket, oh and trousers to match."

Duffy's belly felt like it was lodged in her throat. Thick bile and apple vomit threatened to explode from her nauseated frame. Gritting her teeth into a wide grin she managed to murmur, "I'll see to it first thing in the morning sir."

In the betwixt and between of the morning mist, Squire Lovell went hunting and Duffy sat overwhelmed in the mess of the mansion. Finally she went to her safe haven, the kitchen and before long the mouth-watering smell of freshly baked pies wafted through the air. Squire Lovell was so taken with the scrumptious meal set upon the table that he forgot about his need for new socks. It was only as Duffy went to blow out the parlor candles that he remembered.

"I hope your knitting and spinning are as good as your pies Duffy."

"I'm sorry sir but I didn't get to the attic today, mayhap tomorrow."

"Be sure you do young Duffy my feet need warm socks."

The next night Squire Lovell was treated to a mighty fine feast and again the spinning had been neglected.

"Duffy there is no doubt about it, your pies are the best, but tomorrow less stirring and more spinning."

Duffy trudged reluctantly to the attic and gaped at the magnitude of her task. Where to begin she had absolutely no idea. Spinning was as foreign to her as the Emmets and sawzneck's were from merry old England. (An Emmet is the Cornish word for ant, which is used to describe tourists and sawzneck is a variation of Sassenach, which derives from the Germanic name of the Saxon settlers who invaded the Celtic lands). She kicked wildly at the piles of fleece, stamped her foot and cried, " Oh the devil can spin and knit for this messy old Squire for all I care."

A rasping laugh quivered and nibbled through the shimmering fleece. Duffy gripped the spinning wheel her knuckles whitening as she gawked in aghast at the spindly impish features of a grotesque little man who emerged cackling from the heap of sheep's clothing scattered across the floor.

"Duffy my dear," squealed the high pitch grate of the leering little man. "I will gladly do all of your spinning and knitting you care to wish for. But at the end of three years on the stroke of the Samhain dawn you will be mine. You must come with me at my behest unless," he slavered twirling his wiry tail, "you can guess my name? And for good measure you can have as many guesses as your little heart desires."

"I'm in heaven," chuckled Duffy, "You have a deal. I will find out your name within three years and Squire Lovell will be the finest dressed, best fed man from here to blooming London." So with a spit and a shake the agreement was bound fast.

To her delight, the next morning Duffy found a fine pair of woolen socks waiting for her in the attic. The Squire was tickled pink and hurried off to church with his trouser legs rolled up to his knees to show off her dazzling handiwork.

"And you should taste her pies" he bragged to the whole congregation.

The garments flew freely from the old spinning wheel, britches, shirts, coats, blankets the finest woven most intricately spun designs you ever laid eyes on, the mischievous imp held nothing back. Such talents and such beauty soon won Duffy a stream of admirers. The flowers and chocolates reigned in on the manor and it was not uncommon to see a dozen plus men vying for the right to woo and court the bewitching Duffy. She flirted and giggled at the mounting attention, but she never lost sight of her goal. She had been born into poverty and her elders and 'so called' betters had looked to ingrain on her that her place was at the bottom of the heap, yet Duffy was destined for greatness. Her prize was to be the Lady of the Manor. She worked all the angles to get the Squires attention and basked in the evidence of his growing jealousy. Finally when a strappingly handsome young lad had gained access to his kitchen and was sampling one of Duffy's tasty meat pies, the Squire exploded. His face turned beetroot and he blurted out the question she had so neatly manipulated, "Duffy will you please marry me?"

"I will," beamed Duffy as the young man who had come a'courting choked and coughed on the piping hot pie.

If Duffy thought the title of Lady Lovell would elevate her status in the Manor House she was sadly disappointed. The Squire seemed only interested in two things, meat pies and warm socks. Her existence in her shell of success was lonely and unfulfilling.

As Bridget dipped her hands releasing the waters of spring, Duffy took to wandering down to the gristmill where she watched in awe of the women who gathered on the green. They danced and sang, as the flour was ground. Old Bet, the Miller's wife, kept the beat drumming wildly on the hide of a sheep stretched across a giant sieve.

"Jump in and join the dance Duffy," crooned the rich silky voice of the old hag Bet. Her twinkling eyes never missed a beat, and she had fathomed Duffy's secret skill of weaving, guessing that the little Imp had tethered the Squire's new bride in the sticky strands of his web and would eventually make her dance to his tune. Old Bet was indeed a witch, a wise one, with the patience of the rising moon and she encouraged Duffy to dance, watching to see if she was willing to dance through her fears and into her dreams, to fully hear her own unique music. For three years she watched Duffy's dance spiraling chaotically, desperately seeking the freedom from the jaws of the mouth that feeds her, and it was not at all surprising to her when Duffy hammered on the mill door in floods of tears one late October morn.

"Old Bet," she pleaded, "please help me, I am at my wits end. I struck a bargain with the darkest soul that has ever lived and unless I guess his name by Samhain dawn, I will be his slave forever and a day.

Old Bet's shrewd eyes soaked up the scene and in a clear concise voice she blew words of wisdom into Duffy's heart. "When you can name your fear lass, it no longer holds power over you. I will help you be free of this Imp if you will make an oath never to make a bargain with the likes of him again."

"I swear, never, never, never, shall I make a deal with such a devil"

"Good, then here is what you need to do," grinned Old Bet. "Tonight, Samhain Eve, is a full moon, a blue moon. Bring a flagon of the Squire's strongest scrumpy and meet me before sunset at the Boleigh Fogou. Every sprite, hobgoblin and Imp will be there, watching the witches dancing in the cavern.

So as the shadows darkened the day Duffy's strides lengthened and she made her way to the faerie dell in Rosemerryn wood. A large clay jug was filled to the brim but not a single drop was spilt onto the earth until Old Bet's hands seized the handle. Carefully she offered a drink to the land and heaving her drum into the yawning mouth of the cave she left Duffy hiding behind a brambling hawthorn tree. "Keep your eyes and your ears open young Duffy and by the time the first sun rays welcome in a bright new year you will be free."

Duffy watched in awe as Old Bet trudged bravely into the chambers gaping black jaws, swallowed up by the magic murkiness of the dense dark cave. The brilliance of the pregnant moon illuminated an unusual assortment of mortals and otherworldly folk who flocked and flew and danced and sang to the beat of Old Bet's drum. Whirling around faster and faster, skipping through the mud, shimmering and shaking, trancing and prancing. There in the thick of the mêlée leapt the Imp, a manic grin carved deep in his hideously misshapen face. Duffy had been to many a Golowan Festival for midsummer in Penzance, and though she had twirled through the eye of the needle and jigged in the shadows of the 'obby 'oss, never had she seen the likes of the Samhain Ball. Each time the little imp swung his gangling body and swished his spindly tail past the booming drum that echoed the tribal beats of Old Bet's wild magic he was treated to a huge swig of the Squire's prized applejack. When he had drained the last drop his gleeful song slurred tipsily off his tongue and rolled into the coolness of the night into grateful ears of an expectant Duffy:

"Duffy my lady it is you I'll claim.

Duffy my pretty you'll never guess my name.

I'll take you away and I'll never stop

I'm terrible, I terrify, I'm TERRYTOP"

Duffy's heart leaped to her throat. She gazed in wide eyed merriment and whispered the most delicious sound to grace her new year, her new life 'Terrytop."

Suddenly as she scampered through the brush to make her way home, Duffy heard a commotion to light up the night. Thundering hooves, baying hounds and the panicked cry of a frightened horse. Peeking through tangled vines, Duffy spotted the bucking horse of Squire Lovell. He was desperately hanging onto the reins as his horse and dogs danced crazily towards the dawn. He had chased a hare to the brink of the cave and stumbled right into the blue flame of the Witches lair. Spooked dogs and a terrified Squire ran hell for leather as the ghouls and goblins, fey folk and Witchy women flew after their prey and Squire Lovell was chased this way and that, in circles, over hedges, around the craggy coast and he barely got home with his breath.

He burst in the front door and bolted it behind him. Duffy sat casually sipping a hot mug of steaming tea having taken a direct route home. Old Bet's Wild Hunt had allowed the stricken Squire no such luxury. Huffing and spluttering having been chased to the brink of daybreak he wheezed. "Duffy my dear you will not believe what befell me this haunting eve. I have raced the hounds of hell, their tepid breath still sticky on my neck. A Coven of Witches, an army of sprites, pixies and hobgoblins, chased after me. They tried to scratch, bite, claw and mayhap their intention was to kill me. They were the hunters I was the prey. I felt like the hare that I had hounded over the heath. Duffy my dogs are still out there I hear them howling. What should I do?"

"Strange things can happen when you stir up the goblins." Duffy murmured softly, stirring the Squire's superstitions. "Fly quickly through the shadows and save the dogs. The sun will soon pierce through this dark night and all will be well. As fierce as the manic hunters charge was my dear Squire, the storm has passed, they have long gone, listen, it is only the cries of your hounds searching for their masters voice. Go round them up quickly and I will heat up a broth for you and bake you a pie."

"Good Duffy I will be back to feast as soon as I can." Gingerly Squire Lovell scampered back into the night. As swift as a sparrow, Duffy flew to the attic. Sitting in the rickety old chair laughing wickedly was the imp.

"Duffy oh Duffy it's you I'll claim.

Duffy you'll never guess my name!

Three more times you may try,

Then Duffy my dear with me you'll fly."

Duffy trembled, for effect her lip quivered and she asked pleadingly "Is your name Lucifer?"

"No that's my uncle" he spat tartly.

"Beelzebub then?" She croaked barely audible above his menacing chuckle.

"No, no, no He's a cousin. Soon you'll be mine, mine, mine, mine," he jeered keenly. "One more guess, make it good make it count"

"If I am right don't you dare deny it Terrytop."

The little imp fell out of the chair staring aghast at Duffy's wide grinned face.

"What did you call me?" blurted the exasperated imp. "How did you know?" he raged. He staggered to his feet kicked over the spinning wheel and screeched, "You'll not keep a piece of my magic" and promptly disappeared in a puff of sulfur and smoke.

All of the fine clothes that he had spun and knit over the past three years turned to ash where they lay.

It was a bitterly cold November cock crow and the Squire was tired, frustrated and shivering in the morning mist. He had just located the last of his hounds when his socks vanished, then his shirt, followed by his coat, his pants and in a flash his woolen underwear disappeared.

When the back door to the Lovell Manor was pushed open Duffy looked in wide eye surprise at her naked husband, frozen blue as ice with only his leather waistcoat and his riding boots on. Through his chattering teeth he exclaimed, "Duffy the strangest thing has happened."

"So I see." marveled Duffy trying to hide the smile from lighting up her face. "The very same thing has happened here. All of my hard work, every bit of spinning and weaving that I have sweat and toiled over has vanished in a puff of smoke. Some dark magic is at work I fear my dear, you disturbed the goblin dance and this is their revenge.

"Duffy I believe you are right," stammered the Squire as he bent over the hearth seeking the comforting warmth of the rekindled Samhain fire. "They were livid, nasty screeching biting sprites. Well there is only one thing for it. You will need to get spinning and make me some warm woolen clothes." He barked.

Duffy had been expecting this response and was ready to lure him in and spit him out. "I'll get right too it my dear, I just hope that the mischief at hand is not a spell cast on any clothes I make for you. Imagine if you were bowing before the Lords and Ladies at court and poof! All your fine woolens disappeared, or if you were attending a family gathering and your aunt Muriel was to see, well enough said, I'll be getting to it. I'll have a new pair of underpants to you in a jiffy."

"Stop, don't you dare touch the spinning wheel Duffy, not now, not ever. I will get the village weavers to make my clothes and you my dear Duffy do what you love to do best, bake pies."

So Duffy spent her mornings dancing with Old Bet at the Mill, her afternoons baking pies, and her evenings cuddled up with Squire Lovell as they learned to love each other dearly.

Treasure of the Tale

This is variation of the Rumpelstiltskin tale that offers the reader more than a morsel to chew on. Knowing the meaning of names adds spice and dimension to the insights. Duffy whose name means Dark Skinned, an absolute beauty who takes her light into the depth of her darkness so she can live authentically in her own skin. Where are we like Duffy in our own lives? Have we recognized our authentic beauty? Do we acknowledge our beauty from our heart each day? What is beauty to us? When do we look at ourselves through ego eyes and when do we see ourselves as an expression of the divine? What dark recesses within us are we currently shining our light into? What dark caverns are we avoiding and hiding from? Are we comfortable living in our own skin?

Terrytop means the Highest Harvester who looks to harvest Duffy's soul, who seduces her with an illusion of greatness. So often people want the glory and are not prepared to do the work. There is a 'give it to me now' mentality that has many people grasping to be at the top with the power without the substance of growing through the process to support the fullness of that power. What are we harvesting in our life right now? What seeds have we planted? What seeds are we watering and which ones are dying from neglect?

As a Master Firewalk instructor leading people to dance across the hot coals I have experienced people walking the fire for the first time wanting to lead a firewalk the following week in their own backyard. The person who attends their first sweatlodge and proclaims that they are going to build a lodge and start pouring water. The person who decides they are going to lead a pilgrimage to sacred sites without first going to these sites and connecting and grounding the work in the land, without studying the stories of place, without making relationship with the ancestors and with faerie. Magic is so very tangible. Leadership and power can be incredibly seductive and some people want the fast track degree to that power. The internet and cyberspace is a festering ground for the 'in a jiffy', lightning labels that people can buy without being centered in the work. Purchase the title of druid, or ordained minister within a week or within a year. A druid's training took over 18 years of constant study. In my experience it is not that medicine people are trying to be exclusive they are guarding the secrets so that the whole community can prosper. Being a medicine person is certainly an honour and with that goes a lot of hard work, what the group sees is the juicy flow of spirit and not the preparation, travel, study, and physical labour, carrying the tools, chopping the wood etc.

Are you prepared to travel to the other side of the world, to the 'edge of the world' to sit, listen, absorb, work diligently at being the container and then be humble so that Spirit can do the work through you? Stirring your own cauldron for sometimes years at a time?

I spent 10 years studying to pour water for lodge, and I am still learning. Once we have connected to the fullness of the wisdom, the immense depth of the vibration of energy and the ability to discern and move the flow through us and around us, and are able to protect ourselves, others and the worlds between the worlds then we are ready to share it with the people.

Squire Lovell's name means wolf. Here is an amusing twist to the saying 'a wolf in sheep's clothing'. He looks to 'save' Duffy at the beginning of the story and then tries to mold her into what he needs rather than accepting her for her gifts. She tells him straight "I make exceedingly good pies". Who are we rushing around trying to save? How do we try and mold people into being that which they are not? Where are people trying to mold us? Are we putting on our own cloak or are we picking up and putting on someone else's? If we are wearing someone else's cloak where, when and why are we doing this? Where are we celebrating people in acceptance of their gifts? Duffy knows what she does best and she loves doing it, baking pies! What are we good at, what are our gifts? What is it that we love to do? When do we give ourselves permission to do what we love to do?

Old Bet is the wise one whose name means God's Promise and she asks Duffy to think carefully how she gives her oath in the future biding her to a promise never to make a bargain with the likes of the imp again. Our words carry such magic, are we clear in the oaths that we make? As Don Miguel Ruiz phrases it in his book the Four Agreements 'Are we impeccable with our word?'

Old Bet feeds the Imp Applejack Scrumpy, apples are the fruit of the underworld and Jack has a rugged earthy aura and means one who supplants. Bet gives the Imp cider in a bizarre trade for Duffy. His consequent intoxication supplants his vision. Including giving his power away by sharing his medicine name. Where are we seduced and intoxicated in our lives? Where does our ego lead us to give our power away? I have a tattoo on my back that carries me, it is medicine, it is what I believe in, an artistic expression of symbols and treasures that reflect the Celtic story woven deliciously in colorful ink upon my back. Recently I whipped off my shirt to show a group of people my tattoo, why? It was ego driven, look what I've got, in that moment I desecrated my medicine, in understanding it I reclaimed the power, my tattoo has my back, it is not something I will show again through ego! Where are we so absorbed in our intoxications that we miss living through our spirit?

The disappearing clothes have many layers! In looking at Squire Lovell I am led to ponder; What are we chasing that will take the shirt of our back? In the case of Duffy; Where are we claiming the rewards for something we did not do? Ultimately if we do not stir the cauldron we do not have a rich creamy broth, Duffy did not spin the yarn so the garments fell apart, what is falling apart in our lives that either needs stirring or emptying so fresh ingredients can be added?

Old Bet also invokes us to walk into the wisdom of our own power by naming our fears. She croons "When you can name your fear lass, it no longer holds power over you." So it begs us to examine our own fears and be brave enough to put them on the wind. So I invite you to pause and reflect on the magnitude of these questions and be real with yourself. Once you have found threads of remembrance let this stir in your heart and as we journey into the winding knot work path of this book may we all have the courage to peel off the layers and examine the root our fears and the importance of speaking our own impeccable word, our tynged, our geas, our oath.

The reference to Golowan is from the seasonal celebration in Penzance for the coming of Midsummer, they were banned in the 1890's for fear of fires spreading as the locals lit tarred barrels and set off copious amounts of fireworks, however the traditions flame has been rekindled as crowds throng the streets mid June and the Morris dancers, 'obby 'oss and Mock Mayor parade through the streets in a wild container of archaic revelry, mixing Cornish tradition with contemporary imagery and ritual. In 2000 I was fortunate enough to join the Serpent dance and jump through the eye of the needle, jumping through the flames for protection is an ancient rite. This modern day celebration of St. John's feast, John means God is Gracious', is a phenomenal testament to the people of Penzance and the strong Cultural & Community Arts Organization.

The Tale and the Land

So as I prepared for my journey to Cornwall by soaking up the succulent morsels of Duffy's tale, a small still voice called "Boleigh Fogou", it was Old Bet beckoning me to her lair. I found myself on the internet and googling information on the ceremonial cave. To my delight I found a phone number to Rosemerryn Wood and a quick phone call introduced me to the gracious and hospitable guardians of the land, Rob Donaldson and Laura Shaw. Two finer people you will not meet. I was invited to bring the group to spend the day on the land and in so doing we all fell in love with the bluebell woods, the huge Rhododendron trees, and the moss filled frolics of faerie scattered in abundance over every nook and cranny. Rob invited me in for tea and nestled by the open hearth I basked in the tranquil energy of the blossoming retreat center that is fed by the ancestral workings ingrained in the land.

My first steps into the Boleigh Fogou were sticky, squelchy and musical. A sucking gurgling symphony accompanied my every footstep, gooey wet mud squidged over my boots and grumblings spewed forth from the mouths of some of the bewildered pilgrims flustered by the fresh sludge caking to their boots. Unperturbed I forged on into the depth of the long chamber passing a small side chamber to stand in the heart of the iron age cave. The fussing of the pilgrims echoed through the cavern as some of them gingerly trudged through the heavy molasses while others hung back at the entrance with their noses wrinkled and their brows all a furrow. It was then words reminiscent of Old Bet were channeled through Tessy, a twinkling eyed jolly soul who was on her third adventure with me, Tessy has an heir of timeless age upon her, she is like every ones granny, a farmhouse mothering figure with a beaming face and a fay spirit, "For goodness sake, it's the Mother's Blood let it slop all over you". Those profound words stuck more permanently than the surface mud, I infused the essence of the rich soil into my veins and I rejoice in slopping the blood of the mother over my face and my body and sharing Tessy's insight with any squeamish traveler.

So it was with great delight that I returned with eight pilgrims in May 2006 and on the third night of heavy rain I followed in the footsteps of two of the pilgrims who had slept in the fogou the previous two nights and the ancestors of old, who had conjured magic within the granite walls, who had prayed, sweated their visions, who had hidden in times of war and smuggling and who had stumbled into this den of iniquity this sanctuary of soulfulness this mysterious mound that holds answers for those willing to listen and be patient amongst the trickling waters, sopping mud, shifting shadows and stunning stillness. I made an offering to faerie on the threshold, black liquid seeped into the soil as I poured draft Guinness onto the ground calling on protective spirits, honoring the ancestors and the sidhe, as I scattered copious crumbs from a juicy fruit cake, I called on the grandmothers and grandfathers, the shining ones, all those seen and unseen and gave thanks for my life on this good day.

I ducked my head and crawled into the small side chamber where I had laid down a sleeping mat and my sleeping bag earlier that evening. Now in the betwixt and between I squeezed my body into the already damp wrappings of the sleeping bag, my modern day cow hide, and I lay my head on the wet earth and surrendered to the visions of the night. The intense sound of the darkness welcomed my visitation inviting me to sink into sweet surrender or flee into desperate despair.

The Celts challenge us to journey through the darkest night to find the dawn of a new day. In the claustrophobic confines of this chambered womb, wrapped in the bindings of a fabric hide I breathed in the purpose of the night, and I trusted that all would unfold in an authentic and prophetic birth. The constant drip, drip, drip of rainwater permeating the crevices of the cavern soon soaked my covering skins. Every so often a droplet would fall onto my face and as the night spun its web so my birthing waters encased me in a moist covering akin to the dew, lush sperm sparkling in the orgasm of the mothers womb. I cannot say I slept at all that night and I can also not say that I was awake, I was on the edge all night long, I drifted in the betwixt and between and I came face to face with faerie. I remember the dance, and the high ceremony where I was gifted a faerie name. The words sang through my body, expanding my core, a name offered in two tongues, in the sounds and syllables of the shining ones and a translation into English. The moment that the name was fully rooted in my body I awoke, if in fact I was ever asleep, and regardless I remembered clearly my given name I knew my quest was complete and I struggled out of the slippery drenched sack and crawled through the mother's blood to the threshold of the womb. As I tottered with my first steps, I was made welcome by the first shafts of light, a burgeoning new dawn. I poured fresh Guinness onto the land and with a sprightly skip in my step I danced the essence of my new name. A name that to this day has never been shared with anyone, a name that I will probably never share with anyone, a medicine name.

One major piece to sit with when working with a medicine name is who needs to know it. Names carry power. How often in life do we give our power away? How often in life do we miss the spark of greatness within us, and the phenomenal opportunities that are right in front of our nose? How often are we so obsessed with everyone knowing our greatness that instead of the strength being spirit reflecting it is ego driven?

Chapter 4

ON THE EDGE

In the heart of the lodge of Boleigh Fogou I had spent the night on the 'edge of the world' and the next day we went to the edge of Cornwall, through the picturesque village of St. Just out onto the cliffs where an ancient cairn can be found at Bollowal Barrow that dates between 2500 – 1500 B.C. This unusual shaped chamber lay undisturbed in recent times. Cornish antiquarian W.C. Borlase discovered it under mining soil in 1878. A striking structure 35 feet across with walls up to 10 feet tall and a passage six feet wide all the way around. There is an entrance grave and the central oval structure is a tranquil space to honor the continual saga of life death rebirth.

Within a hop skip and a jump you are on the precipice of a 300ft drop. Thin trails wind through the lush vegetation meandering south towards Lands End and North towards Cape Cornwall. On a clear day the Scilley Isles appear some 30 miles off shore on the edge of the horizon giving a glimpse of the possibility of the Lost Lands of Lyonesse, this Cornish sunken city has links to the Irish Tri na nog the Scottish Isle of Eternal Youth, where it is said Manannan Mac Lir hosts his royal court in the land beneath the waves.

Just as Bollawal Barrow lay hidden, so do other burial chambers, wells and ancient mysteries, mayhap under the surging tide, just like Lyonesse waiting for the arrival of a new age of chivalry and adventure.

Under splashings of sunshine that brought out the shimmering blues and greens of Manannan's hair, our intrepid band of travelers sat with dangling legs over massive rocks snuggled in the spongy grasses of the cliffs delight. So the Sea God Mannanan Mac Lir inhabits the courts of the Lions Hall in Lyonesse. Wait, he lives off Wales courting Rhiannon doesn't he? Hang on he lives off Ireland married to Fand, yes? As I explained to the bemusement of a woman at a holistic faire a few years ago, "We are going to Tintagel in Cornwall the birth place of Arthur."

Not possible," She protested. "Arthur was born in Wales."

"Yes he was," I agreed.

"But you just said you are going to King Arthur's birthplace in Cornwall."

"Yes I am," I giggled. You see in the Celtic world duality is a given, it is all yes and yes, and it is all a part of the mystery, so just as Arthur was born in Cornwall and Wales so is Manannan Mac Lir found living in the Sea off Wales, Ireland and Cornwall. This marveling at the mystery is a portal to weaving the magical tapestry of life. It is at the core of the extremities of the saying 'Believing is seeing', those of us that hang on to 'Seeing is Believing' are challenged to connect with the deeper layers of magic that swirl around us and within us in each and every moment. Let me ask you, do you believe in the Loch Ness Monster? Yes, no, maybe? Some people want to prove that Nessie does not exist, you can run every test known to us two leggeds and it would mean nothing to my Celtic spirit. My answer is simple, Nessie was not where you were looking, she was hiding behind the veil. The opposite is also irrelevant to my Celtic nature, those people who need to prove her existence with photographs etc. I need no recorded documentation to unequivocally believe in her. When we accept that the great mystery is part and parcel to this ride called life, we can unwrap the gifts and celebrate them with abandon. As we feasted on our picnic to the gentle lapping of the waves I beguiled the group with the telling of 'The Man Who Had No Luck.'

The Man Who had No Luck

A young man lived in a comfy house with stunning views of a babbling brook, an apple orchard and a field of summer corn. He had a great job, with definite prospects working with people he liked and a flexible schedule. Yet he was always looking at others and thinking 'How come they're so lucky?' 'Why don't I have as much luck as them?'

One June morning as the summer solstice hung on the breeze he sauntered into the village and sought out the services of the old hag, the wise one. The man entered a room full of hanging herbs, bottles with all colored liquids were crammed onto shelves with worn books and a selection of cauldrons big and small. A craggy face with piercing intelligent eyes looked up at him and the wizened one smiled a crooked grin and cackled "So you're here to ask me why you have no luck?"

"How did you know that?" stammered the young man.

"The same way I knows where to find your luck," was the shrill reply.

"Where?" Gawked the young man.

"Where it's always been that's where, but no good me a telling you. What you need to do is go and ask the Queen of the Faeries who lives at the edge of the world she'll let you know where your luck is. So the young man set out on his quest and he walked for a day, a week, a month, a year, a year and a day until he came upon a pack of wolves. He noticed how their fur shone and their coats were full and glossy. He carefully crept around them giving them a wide berth so that he would not be heard, seen, or smelled. He held his breath as he tiptoed towards the path he sought and let out a huge squeal as he came face to face with a lone wolf. "Ah! You made me jump" He spluttered as his eyes took in a scrawny old wolf with shabby hair and a sickly gait.

"Where are you going?" Growled the wolf.

"I am off to see the Queen of the Faeries at the edge of the world to find out why I have no luck."

"Hmm. If you find her, will you ask her why I am not like my brothers and sisters, why I am so thin, why I have such a lack luster coat?" Pined the weak old wolf.

"I will indeed," declared the man and off he went on his way. He walked for a day, a week, a month, a year, a year and a day until he came upon a forest. Tall pine trees towered above his head causing streams of filtered sunlight to illuminate his trail. As he wove his way through the web like strands on the forest path he noticed one squatty little pine tree with weak limbs and a sickly hue.

"Where are you going?" Squeaked the little pine tree.

"I am off to see the Queen of the Faeries at the edge of the world to find out why I have no luck."

"If you find her will you ask her why I am so tiny, why I am not tall and strong like my sisters and brothers?' the shrill shaky voice yelped.

"I will indeed." declared the man and off he went on his way. He walked for a day, a week, a month, a year, a year and a day until he came upon a cozy thatched cottage with a higgledy piggledy twisted fence, blooming roses with creeping ivy and bursts of colorful fragrant flowers shooting sunlit smiles amongst lush green grass. He approached the large brass knocker gleaming brightly on the weathered oak door and hammered three times. Faint footsteps echoed more clearly and the large latch clunked as the heavy door whined as it slowly swung open. Standing in a ray of sparkling sunlight stood the most beautiful woman the man had ever seen. A voice of liquid lavender caressed the air plucking and stroking his heartstrings stirring memories of a time before time.

"Would you like to join me for tea and scones? The jam is home made and the clotted cream is to die for." The green eye goddess spoke with a lilting laughter and a welcoming smile. The man stumbled into the inviting warmth of sumptuous hospitality. "Where are you going?" She crooned.

"I am off to see the Queen of the Faeries at the edge of the world to find out why I have no luck," Stammered the gawking man.

"If you find her will you ask her why I am so lonely?' the gentle voice shimmered.

"I will indeed" declared the man, "I'll go ask right now" and off he went with the sweet taste of summer strawberries smeared across his lips and lingering on his tongue. He walked for a day, a week, a month, a year, a year and a day until he came to the edge of the world. He stood perched on the craggy cliff staring at a thick wall of mist. He could hear the rolling waves crashing on the jagged rocks beneath him and he knew one more step would take him free falling to his death. He was about to holler into the impenetrable vapor when the luminous figure of the Queen of the Faeries floated through the haze and hovered ominously before him. His lips twitched, his tongue stiffened, his throat scratchy and parched, he reached desperately through his swirling mind to find the fragments of his questions to no avail. Rooted to the spot as the hare looks into the dazzling eye of the eagle, the magical mists engulfed him. The hot breath of the Fata Morgana licked his mind clean and the empty cavern roared with the shrill laughter of mocking madness. Gripped in the talons of the temptress the man was whisked into his own lair of luck.

"Look carefully," she rasped, "for luck is within all that you seek, did you listen? Do you understand the truth of the question? Go find it, find it, find it." A cacophony showered and splintered through his aching brain. Just before the dizzy spin of release flung him to his knees, a faint jagged whisper pierced into his churning mind and three droplets of illuminated wisdom washed down his spine. As his brain thawed to release a tidal wave of thoughts his heart tickled with the answers for the three friends he had met on his journey. The mists had cleared, the Queen was gone, and the man gingerly got to his feet with a purpose to find his luck. He walked for a day, a week, a month, a year, a year and a day until he came upon a cozy thatched cottage with a higgledy piggledy twisted fence, blooming roses with creeping ivy and bursts of colorful fragrant flowers shooting sunlit smiles amongst lush green grass. He approached the large brass knocker gleaming brightly on the weathered oak door and hammered three times. The dainty footsteps of the stunningly gorgeous green eye goddess danced toward the bolted door and with radiant joy she swung it open and fell into the arms of the waiting man. Tones of honeycomb kissed the air as she sighed softly into his ear, "It is so good to see you, come in, tell me did you find the Queen of the Faeries? Did you find your luck? Did you happen to ask her why I'm so lonely? So much to discuss, so much to listen to, come in, come in, the kettle is on."

"I have good news," beamed the man. "The Queen of the Faeries said you're so lonely because you're lacking company. She suggested you try finding a partner, mayhap get married if the occasion suited."

"Brilliant," Sparkled the lonely woman. "Are you married?"

"No, I'm single," Sputtered the man.

"Then what are you hanging around on the threshold for, come on in and let's dine on love." Invited the alluring green eyes of the red headed goddess.

"I'd love to come in but I have to find my luck, no time to dally. I'll send the first single man I meet to come a calling. Best of luck, I'm off to find mine." He swung his torso around to meet the gate and strolled purposefully toward the horizon leaving the stunned gapping face of the beautiful goddess behind.

He walked for a day, a week, a month, a year, a year and a day until he came upon a forest. Tall pine trees towered above his head causing streams of filtered sunlight to illuminate his trail.

As he wove his way through the web like strands on the forest path he noticed the squatty little pine tree with weak limbs and a sickly hue.

"Oh hello again?" Squeaked the little pine tree. "Did you find the Queen of the Faeries and find your luck? Did you ask her why I am so tiny, why I am not tall and strong like my sisters and brothers?'

"That I did," declared the man. "Its simple. You have a huge treasure chest packed with gems and gold buried right underneath you. This bag of booty is stopping your roots from getting the nourishment and nutrients that they need for you to grow strong. All you need to do is dig up the sack of loot and you will grow strong and tall."

"Brilliant," piped the thin voice of the little pine tree. "Look over there, two workers left a shovel and pick leaning up against my strong sister. Go grab it and dig up the gold will you?"

"I'd love to, but I have to find my luck, no time to dally. I'll send the first person I meet to come and dig it out for you. Best of luck, I'm off to find mine."

So he walked for a day, a week, a month, a year, a year and a day until he came upon a lone wolf, scrawny with shabby hair and a sickly gait.

"Hello old friend" Growled the wolf. "Did you find the Queen of the Faeries and find out why you have no luck? Did you ask her why I am not like my brothers and sisters, why I am so thin, why I have such a lack luster coat?" Pined the weak old wolf.

"It's simple," avowed the man with a twinkle in his eye. "Your coat is so drab, and you are so blooming thin because you are lacking in nourishment, what you need to do is eat the first dumb animal to cross your path."

"What a delicious idea." salivated the wolf, and he got straight to it and chewed up the first dumb animal, the juicy lucky man, that had so fortuitously crossed his path!!!

Treasure of the Tale

Even if you knew how this story was going to end I bet it still held your attention until its 'dying' words!!! Let's begin with the man who is not given a name, without one he universally becomes all people. He obviously is living in the world of the grass is always greener on the other side, coveting what others have, not celebrating what is in front of him in the present moment. So how are we akin to the man with no luck? Who, what, where and how are we coveting? Where are we seeing the sweet riches of life for others and not ourselves? The young man goes to ask others where is his luck. Where are we looking outside for the answers that we know lie within? The man is gifted with ways to help others and in so doing he will witness his luck but in his haste to find it he misses the opportunity to be in the present moment and hear, see, experience the fullness of the adventure. Had he celebrated a relationship with the garden goddess, relieved the pine trees roots of riches his wisdom would have kept the wolves at bay. Where are we missing an opportunity to serve? When are we so far ahead of ourselves that we miss an opportunity to celebrate ourselves in the present moment? Where are we doing the same thing the same way and expecting a different result? This is where we are the dumb animal being eaten by the wolf! And how about going to the edge of the world? How are we dancing on our own edge? Are we afraid to step near our edge? Do we ever or always throw ourselves off the edge? Whether it is the edge of my chaos or the edge of my stillness, I want to live on that edge and understand myself because of it, to stay away from my own chaos would hold me hostage in fear of the constant changes in my life, to be consumed by my chaos would be to be whipped and flipped into creating huge dramas. To be on the edge is to surrender to the storm, I choose the edge, when I am conscious, fully present, I choose to surrender and shapeshift,. I choose to be a wise oak bending and swaying with deep roots witnessing the gale and dancing through the eye of the storm, the fire, into the gentle stillness of bright new birth.

The Tale and the Land

On the conclusion of such a wonderful punch line amidst a fair share of chuckles the group dispersed to wander and contemplate the vast beauty within and without and examine our own 'luck' and the gift of the present moment. We were all gathered at the edge of the world on a sparkling sunny day, with only a hint of a breeze after three straight nights and days of rain. As I stopped and stood at the lip of the cliff marveling at the sunlight sparkling on the Celtic Sea, the face an old woman approached from behind me. She joined in the merriment of my laughter with her own husky giggle. I remember feeling the strangeness of her emergence wash over me. Hadn't I just skipped down the winding track passing no-one, where did she spring up from, had I missed her in my glee, before my brain could catch up with my fleeting thoughts, the old woman leaned in toward me and mischievously chuckled

"Are you at the edge of the world?" My jaw must have slammed into the rocks below, I must have looked like the gawping man as I gaped blankly struggling with what I thought I had heard her say. "There's a group down here at the edge of the world, are you with them?" She mysteriously sniggered.

"I am staying a Rosemerryn, near the Boleigh Fogou" I stammered.

"That's nice." She muttered and she sauntered off down the old beaten path with her shawl fluttering in the breeze and her basket dangling by her side. I stared at her leisurely gait for some time, my mouth still hanging unabashedly open and my mind racing. I remember turning towards the circled women to ask them if they had seen where the old lady had come from and when I gazed back down the coastal path she had disappeared. Maybe she went behind a ridge line, and mayhap she skipped through the veil. I am sure that some would explain away the moment of magic and of course all things are possible, so with this possibility I leap into the wonder of the mystery and thank the faerie woman for her visit and the remembrance of being a man with a feast of luck who is dancing more and more on the edge of the world!

Just as Wales and Cornwall claim Arthur's birth so the might of Merlin graces the nooks and crannies of the Blessed Isle of the Dead. One of my favorite Merlin haunts is his cave at Tintagel. I gave up the need to go exploring the high bluff with the crumbling walls that is said to have been Arthur's home, where Uther Pendragon disguised as Gorlois the rightful Lord of Cornwall and owner of Tintagel Castle, climbed the spiral staircase to the bedchamber of Igraine, Gorlois' wife, and unbeknownst to her she committed adultery with him and Uther's seed was planted, swelling her belly with the boy who would be king.

Tintagel castle is an enigma and a mystery. A vivid imagination is needed to paint the picture of a castle, you will need to feel it rather than see it as so little remains of the once glorious riddle. What was Tintagel defending? The castle is built in a place where attack by sea would be nigh on impossible and breaching by land a sheer folly. When you see the entrance to the old castle you will understand. A thin track leading up a steep hill that could fit two people abreast at most would be death by suicide! Hence Merlin's magical intervention. Uther was magically transformed in the guise of Gorlois, which totally fooled the guards gaining him entrance as the Master with full access to his castle and the bedchamber of the lovely Igraine. The castle is also the setting for the ill fated boon, the Cornish equivalent of a the Irish Geas or Welsh Tynged, the fate that must be followed upon honor of death, that Tristan grants to King Mark in the legendary Tristan and Iseult saga, a boon that prevents Tristan following his heart and marrying the love of his life Igraine, instead bringing her from Ireland to marry his Uncle Mark the King of Cornwall. As a side thought the Tintagel story throws up a couple of obvious questions. I think of us homo sapiens are quite an enigma very much like Tintagel we are our own castles, so what are we defending? Where do we agree to do something before fully understanding what it is which then compromises what we feel in our heart? In every tale there are a multitude of questions to invite the stirring of our soul.

If it is your first time visiting this area and you have the legs and lungs for it, the castle is a spectacular feast and a windswept romp. I remember lying on the outer rocky crop that houses a vast portion of the old ruins including the cookhouse cave. With my belly hugging the wispy grass, my face buried into the smell of the sun scorched wind kissed earth with tumultuous winds and pounding waves seemingly awakening a hidden dragon inside the rock itself. A dragon that stretches yawns and shimmers as you lay clinging to its weathered back.

As a frequent visitor to this enchanted coastline, my blood boils for an excursion into the underworld. Several exquisite caves are burrowed beneath and around this derelict fortress. My favorite is the window cave commonly known to be Merlin's lair.

My first visit to the beach at the foot of Tintagel Castle was as a boy and it sewed an intrigue, a desire to explore beyond the guard rails and roped off paths in life. My flexible joints and youthful limbs had no difficulty sliding and scrambling down the steep rock face beyond the signs that read "Passing this point is at your own risk', On each occasion of my early years we reached Tintagel at full tide which meant that my yearning to wander the gaping caverns of Merlin's Cave churned and spiraled inside my heart guaranteeing my return. Merlin's Cave is a tidal cave only accessible when Mannanan Mac Lir has withdrawn his seed and plunged into the ocean deep, during which time there is a window of opportunity to stand before the waterfall spray that plunges from the stream above and meander into the mouth of the magicians den. There is always an intense excitement that swirls like the tide with the knowledge that twice a day the cave is kissed clean by the salty splashes and a pumping thrusting current that drives forcefully into the inner recess' of this mystical slippery womb. Being first on the beach offers a virgin cave to an eager lover, but tarry too long and the wrath of a scorned lover be upon you as the God of the Sea gallops on the crested mane of his frothy steed and explodes in orgasmic pleasure into the mothers dark enclosure. Anyone ever getting cut off by the surging tide faces a costly and embarrassing helicopter rescue.

Returning to this rocky descent with a group of pilgrims came with the warning that is wise to heed. "We are all responsible for our own story. Go onto the beach at your own risk, go in the cave if your heart sings and listen and watch the tide!" I always chuckle when we need to head out of the bed and breakfast early to catch low tide, for as King Knut, one of the great fools of the British Isles found, the tide waits, and stops for no-one, so it is climb aboard or be left behind. In most part the pilgrimages have no time constrictions and that is one of the glories of being a witness and not a tourist, however when nature offers a glimpse of greatness we all jump over the moon!

I have constantly been amazed at the determination and dexterity of the human spirit. In my trim and supple forty six year old body I can still scamper up and down the rocks with the assuredness of a mountain goat, but to watch, support and/or encourage pilgrims of all ages, and as old as their seventies, of unique body proportions and some with deep fears of failing, with difficulties of asking for and receiving help, of deep rooted fears of heights, who are willing to grapple and grunt their way to the waters edge is remarkably rewarding.

One of my favorite recollections in May 2004 was seeing a full compliment of pilgrims waiting for me by the minibus after an early breakfast, I have to say that I have not ever left anyone behind, my warning of tidal constrictions does wonders for the prompt appearance of sluggish travelers. On that trip we had one delightful and sincere woman who was always late, even she had heard and heeded my warning that the minibus was pulling out at 8:00 am come what may. Our arrival in the small village of Tintagel was greeted by bright sunshine and a healthy and hearty walk down the steep road, that twists and turns toward the sea. By 9:00 am the landrovers are running and for a small token of thanks, a quid or so, you can be ferried up and down the sloping path.

A quick stop off at the bathrooms adjacent to the English Heritage shop dispersed the group and as the guide I pointed the way to our precipitous plunge to the underworld below. As I waited for the stragglers to begin their descent the Pixie in me came out to play. "Do you have your blue ticket please?" I asked earnestly.

A stricken face of an anxious traveler exclaimed nervously "What blue ticket?" "The blue ticket I sent everyone with your packet of information, you need your blue ticket you can't get in the cave without it."

By now another pilgrim had meandered up to us. " I know I have mine somewhere" she exclaimed.

"You do?" cried the first traveler. "Yes I'm sure its here somewhere" declared the new arrival.

"I don't remember ever receiving a blue ticket" the shell shocked pilgrim whispered.

"Everyone was sent one" I affirmed.

"Yes, I know I got mine" the second traveler confirmed as she desperately rummaged through her belongings searching for the elusive blue stub.

"My husband must have mine" insisted the first pilgrim. She frantically searched the horizon for her mate and with fraught eyes she spied him already sauntering on the beach below. "John" she bellowed, "Do you have my blue ticket?" It was all too much for me, my mouth cracked into a huge grin and whispered giggles shifted to rumbling laughter.

My twinkling merriment was infectious and soon all three of us were chuckling whether in relief or in magical mischievousness or a combination of the both. We skipped in glee and slipped and slid our way to join our companions. You can imagine the look of sheer incomprehension that spread thickly and quickly across my thin features as my eyes fell upon a group of strangers heading towards the mouth of Merlin's Cave. The beach had been empty when we arrived so where on earth had these explorers been conjured from? Had Merlin spat them out of his craggy lair? What magic was afoot?

"Look there's a staircase leading from the castle entrance to the beach" yelled one of the pilgrims that I had been ribbing about the blue ticket. Sure enough, English Heritage had built a strong secure safe route making the beach easy access for all. I had been in this spot barely a year before and watched the disappointed face of one traveler who decided her health could not risk the climb. My jaw must have still been wobbling and dragging in the sand at the sight of the new portal to Merlin's mysteries when my Pixie nature was jabbed in the ribs by a faerie dart. The woman who had fallen first hook line and sinker over the blue ticket looked through her remarkably faerie features and with gleaming eyes she sputtered "So that's what the blue ticket is for, you can use the stairs rather than roll down the rocks". A huge guffaw rippled through us as we bounced across the sand. This faerie spirit has become a life long friend of mine Mary Cameron and her husband John have traveled on three pilgrimages and are planning their fourth to the Isle of Skye, it has been a blessed journey to have built a friendship with these two beautiful people who host firewalks, shamanic classes and energy work at their intimate holistic healing center at Walkingwinds in Palm PA. The deepest part of this budding friendship is the journey of ancestral healing that has taken place between us. My clan the Davidson's and John's clan and Mary's adopted clan the Cameron's were mortal enemies with most of the Davidson line perishing at the Cameron's hands in the battle of Invernahaven in 1370. We have reweaved some of the fabric in this lifetime uniting our tartans in the building foundations of their newly built healing center.

Merlin's cave is full of darkness and light and the interplay between them creates shafts of shimmering light, faces mesh and merge in the dancing rock, dank and wet, dry and craggy. To step into this nemeton and follow the overwhelming music in the stark silence is a rare treat and phenomenal gift. About forty feet in the pools of water grow deeper and I always kick off my boots and wade, knee deep at times, toward the large rocks that lift you up to the cathedral window that opens majestically offering views into the crystal clear sea at the end of Merlin's haunt.

On my first couple of visits I missed the magic behind the magic. It was on my third pilgrimage in the September of 2001 after the pilgrims had left the cold sanctuary of the cave to warm their bones in the harvest sun that I noticed an off shoot chamber a dark crevice beckoned to me. The water was deeper and icy cold and after I heaved myself over a massive boulder I left the safety of the light and plunged my way into the sheer darkness of the beyond. My heart raced with the exhilaration of the unknown. Each step led to a darker shade of blackness, I was stepping into the void, I remember the distinct thought of entering a separate space, a different universe where there might not be any way back. I consciously left my torch stuffed in my pocket and I surrendered fully to the dark calling of each deliberate step. That first journey seemed to go on indefinitely and it was almost with surprise that my hands touched the roof and the concave rough jagged structure that marked the ending of the cave wall. I sank slowly to my knees my breathing heavy and fast and I curled up on the clammy gritty floor and marveled at the overwhelming sense of safety that penetrated my being in this isolated tendril of the mother's womb. I lay for a moment, for an eternity, they seemed to be the same in that space, that breath. The onward charge of Mannanan Mac Lir leaping and lashing on the rugged rocks just beyond this craggy refuge, dark place of spirit brought to my attention the gushing flow of the incoming tide. My head told me it was time to crawl, scramble, walk and wend my way into streaming sunlight and my heart gently stirred the music of the moment into the magic of my cauldrons and coaxed me to add my song to the story of this sacred site. Lifting my voice I sang in thankfulness, in joy, in reverence, in beauty. I sang between the worlds, I sang from the depths, in the depths beyond the depths. In the courage to step forward not knowing if I could go back I had discovered there was no going back, my return was an authentic rebirth, as every cave experience offers when we are fully present, in total acceptance, we can shed layers. In wide eyed wonder I stumbled into a piercing shard of light, the salt water kissing my legs and feet and Merlin gently guiding me across the sand to the old path, the steep climb up the rocks that was then the only safe route, now rarely taken because of the newly built wooden stairwell that rises out of the sea.

I have since shared the sanctity of Merlin's hidden chamber with a number of pilgrims, each time we walk into the darkness, each time it is a thrill, yet there is something so tantalizingly special about my first encounter when I stealthily strode into the virgin cave in 2001. I think that was part of the rush, I will always cherish losing my virginity, being so naked and raw.

Seven years later in May 2008 I ventured into that holy place for the second time that month. Four of us pilgrims were drawn to the sanctity of silence burrowed into the ocean stone and we picked our way through the rock pools to the gaping window on the other side of Merlin's cave, a stranger came following until he tripped and his foot slipped into an icy pool of water soaking his shoes so there was some relief when he headed for the sunshine for I knew somehow that the stillness of the cave would be left undisturbed. The four of us carried ourselves peacefully clambering into the darkest recess where we sat listening to the melody of Merlin. After an age of tranquility the gifted voice of one of our party graced the onyx shadows honoring the divine feminine with a song to the Bone Mother, her hauntingly powerful delivery sent shivers of harmonic love tingling down my spine. As the vibrations of energy washed over us the two other pilgrims began a lingering interplay between their wooden flutes. The music flipped and fell spiraled and whispered compellingly calling ancestral songs and a faerie frolic in the veiled alcoves of a world within, between and beyond this world. Suddenly one of the players was on her feet moving in disharmony against the rhythm, which accentuated the flavor of the moment with an unusual aroma that was both palatable and satisfying. It was after she had sat down and the waves of energy seeped deeply into my pores that I was compelled to add my voice to the stillness of time. I have sung on every trip into this magical nook and on this occasion there was a vast difference. I was not singing, the song was not only singing me, the power of each word each note reverberated through me, around me, beyond me. Everything was a tone richer, deeper, I felt myself surrender and shift to an even greater flow of spirit a oneness that transcends any word, thought or explanation, it simply IS and I was part of it. The juice of the song that I learnt many moons before on a ranch in Montana working with Brooke Medicine Eagle spilled into the crevices, nestled in the cracks, and infused each granule of sand with a knowing, a wisdom of the ages.

I live in my heart cave, fire burns in me,
welcome to Great Spirit, welcome home in me,
welcome to my heart cave, welcome to my fire,
welcome home Great Spirit, warming my desire.

As the last notes diffused in the silence and a hush of awakened understanding flooded through me, I began to crawl, this was another pivotal rebirth, one that stirred and roused the essence of my being. As I slipped over the large boulder into the salty sea and teetered and tottered through the caves vein to the Cathedral window, I was seeing through new eyes, the window was the window of my soul, I am the sea, I am the cave, I am a pebble, I am a limpet that clings to the rock, I am a dropping from a seagull, I am the crest of a wave, I am the Merlin, and the Merlin is Taliesin and I am Taliesin and Taliesin is the Merlin and I am Merlin and I am the magic of a single grain of sand.

The Birth of Taliesin is told eloquently in the Mabinogian and I have taken its essence to spin the tale from my heart, remembering how I first heard it and how it shifted and changed me and after drinking deeply from the well of this epic I have stirred the pot and found its elixir to share in the following way:

The Birth of Taliesin

Before the eagle married the owl, their lived a wise woman of immense power, her name was Cerridwen. She had a daughter Creirwy who was as beautiful and radiant as the stars, it was said that flowers sprouted as her feet graced the ground, and she knew that this radiant maiden would fair well wherever she happened to go, it was her son Afagddu (avagthee) which she fretted upon. His very name was disconcerting, Afagddu means dim witted, one who wanders in utter darkness and he caused Cerridwen much concern. Afagddu was going to need serious help.

Cerridwen consulted with the wisdom of ages, and was guided to prepare a cauldron of inspiration, a magical mixture of enlightenment. So by the light of the full moon, she gathered herbs and roots, which she carried into a birthing chamber, a moist fertile cave, the mothers very womb, and here the ingredients were placed in a virgin cauldron to be stirred for a year and a day.

Cerridwen hired the services of an old blind man by the name of Morda, who in turn, gave a young boy, Gwion Bach, the task of keeping the liquid on the boil. Gwion Bach dutifully stirred the pot. Slowly and surely he stuck to his task, and as the year passed, and the brew neared completion, a drop of the steaming liquid splashed onto Gwion's hand. He immediately tried to cool the scalding flesh, lifting it to his mouth and desperately trying to soothe his blistered hand. In that moment, so it came to pass, Gwion swallowed the wisdom meant for Afagddu, he knew everything past, everything present and everything future. Which meant that he knew that Cerridwen knew that he had swallowed the inspiration meant for Afagddu, and she was out to kill him. With an ear splintering crash the cauldron cracked and the remaining black slimy gunk oozed and sludged onto the floor. As Gwion jumped out of the way of the bubbling mess, he was well aware that the liquid seeping into the earth was useless, and he knew he had to flee the sanctuary of the womb.

Using his new found knowledge Gwion shapeshifted into a hare and bounded down the mountain. Cerridwen changed herself into a hunting hound and she charged after him closing the gap with each racing stride. Gwion spotted a river and hurled himself in turning himself into a blue salmon, Cerridwen shape shifted into an otter and swam effortlessly after him. Gwion leapt from the waters as a salmon and sprouted feathered wings soaring high, high, high into the sky, a dove, gliding gracefully to freedom. Cerridwen transformed into a hawk, and with talons ready to strike, she dropped on her prey. Gwion, seeing a cornfield below, exerted all of his remaining energy and shifted into a single kernel of corn. There he buried himself into the safety of the soil. Cerridwen scratched at the rich fertile earth and transformed herself into a red crested black hen. She pecked and pecked at that corn, until she found that single grain, and she swallowed it up.

Some say this was the end of Gwion Bach, but nine months later Cerridwen gave birth to a baby boy. She knew immediately that it was Gwion. She did not have the heart to kill him, so she wrapped him in leather and cast him out onto the sea.

Some say he drifted for days, some weeks, some say it was even years. The babe aged not one day, as one is accustomed to in the realm of faerie, where a day is equivalent to a year and a day in the world of mortals. It was on a May eve that Elffin, King Gwyddno's son, who had been granted the salmon rights that year, pulled up his nets, revealing the unusual looking prize. Now Elffin was a known wastrel, a spendthrift, who was eager to find anything of value to pay off his gambling debts, so he waded in and dragged the leather casket from the water. Whether he thought it was gold, or ale, it's hard to tell. What can be for sure is that he jumped back in amazement when a small boy pushed himself out of the leather folds, and bravely faced him. The babe spoke words of wisdom, and a light emanated from his brow. Elffin stuttered "Taliesin", which means 'shining brow', by which the babe uttered back "Yes, I am Taliesin". With this they went back to King Gwyddno's court.

When Gwyddno saw the babe he scoffed "What is this?" Elffin ushered Taliesin forward exclaiming "Father I have found a poet."

"A poet, what use is a poet?" roared Gwyddno. It was then that Taliesin stepped forward and sang these words.

"I am Taliesin, I sing perfect meter which will last until the world's end. I know why an echo returns. Why a cool breeze blows, why silver always shines. I know why milk is white, blood red, ale bitter, ocean brine. I know how many spears will make a confrontation, how many drops makes a shower of rain. I know why there are scales on a fish, why snakes shed their skin, why black feet are on a white swan. I have been a blue salmon, a hare, a boar, a deer rutting, a branch, a spade, a blade in the hand, a hound, a bull, a stallion. Upon a hillside grown as grain, reaped and into the fire thrown, from out of that roasting I fell to the ground, pecked up and swallowed by the black hen. In her crop nine nights lain, I have been dead, I have been alive, I am Taliesin.

The Treasure of the Tale

Celtic druids were poet-priests. According to Celtic belief, poets understood the power of language so deeply that a carefully crafted poem could change the world. Poetry was not to be taken lightly, for its purpose was to enchant. So Taliesin's magic seeps into the fabric of our lives today. All of us must stir the cauldron. If we persist with the courage and tenacity to keep stirring, we will transform knowledge into wisdom. Affagddu did not do the work, if we sit in the darkness waiting for someone to do it for us we will remain in an ignorant bliss, a desperate despair.

We need the courage to allow ourselves to live each day as if it is our last.

When I no longer fear death, I do not fear life, and I am then willing to truly live. Am I willing to allow myself to die on a daily basis? I embrace the Celtic cry, "This is a good day to die". Gwion does the work and through the transformation surrenders to his death and rebirth. Being cast out on to the sea to drift, it is interesting to note that when we expand we need time to contract, which is why we all need to be patient with the process. The pursuit of understanding myself, can take a single splash of a moment, several hours, days, weeks, or years, and it does! Gwion goes to the earth, the mother, and when I remember to listen to what the earth has to tell me, when I am willing to put my heart on hers, and to make love to her, then I move into a place of Sovereignty. It is in these times that I can be the 'Merlin' of my own story, the wise sage who draws from the source of all that is and connects with the origin of life, glimpsing, hearing, and understanding the melody of the singing strands of the Dagda's harp resonating in the belly of the Calliach's cauldron in the core of the earth.

In the story Taliesin discovers he has the ability to shift with the new found wisdom, he finds the power of his voice, and he discovers the truth of his original name. Deep within us all is that spark of creation, the sound, the symphony of who we are. What Frank MacEowen, in *The Mist-Filled Path,* eloquently describes as the Celtic Oran Mor:

For me, it is undeniably connected to specific Celtic essences that exist in an eclipsed state waiting to restore and fuel the soul of modern people in an age of dynamic soul loss. The low droning sound and the holy rhythm of the Great Song continue for me. It resonates within my heart, and I know it to be the song of the universe. It is the song of life It is the song of the shapers and the shapes...an ancient melody that one hears in the wind, in the waterfall, in the beautiful strains of sound in Celtic music, song, chanting. It is a healing song, and enlivening song heard in the giggles of a grandmother, the whispers of a lover, the questions of a child.

The Oran Mor is our ever unfolding creation story, every breath, every beat of our hearts, each crashing wave, each woven thread on a silken web, an all embracing melody, the Great

Song, the glowing embers of creation. It is poignant to note that in Scots Gaelic the word Creator means shaper and not maker.As Taliesin let go so must we. Let go and trust the higher power, whatever name you give it. Releasing all attachments to the outcome. As we are cast adrift, we align with Creators will, and not our own. Now we can sing the symphony, for we are the song of life. A tale of life death rebirth, a constant journey that we all undertake whether we are conscious of it or not.

When we actively stir our own cauldrons, the energy centers within our bodies we activate them and we can reach a state of An Sith, peace and harmony and we can stimulate ourselves to live our life's purpose, existing in our fullness, opening ourselves to the wisdom available past, present and future. The Celtic people recognized three energy centers within the body. The cauldron of warming that is our base, our root, situated in the belly and pelvis. This cauldron is always upright, and will be until we transform into spirit. It is where all of our food and water goes to be digested. In this cauldron I exist, I am. Gwion Bach is fully in the place of warming as he stirs Cerridwen's cauldron, being fully present with himself and the task. In tasting the three drops of inspiration, he shifts into the passion of purpose, he is a shapeshifter, a poet, and he is reborn into the strength of who he is. Here he takes action, he thinks, and he follows his calling, he is in alignment with his heart cauldron. In our heart center we find the cauldron of calling, if our cauldron of warming is I am, then this energy center is I act, when we are in synch with our life purpose the cauldron is upright, when we forget who we are, we slip into what in the 'Harry Potter' world is known as our *muggle state*, and we all have one! The cauldron flips over and we wallow in the shadows of unconsciousness. Our third cauldron is the fire in our head, the place of wisdom, where we know, more than we think we know, for thinking is an action and is in the heart. Here Gwion Bach takes ownership of his original name, Taliesin, and he shares his wisdom with the world. This continual journey of life, death, rebirth as an every day occurrence invites us to remember ourselves. As the great Bard Amergin says:

Am gaeth i m-muir

Am tond trethan

Am fuaim mara

Am dam secht ndirend

Am séig i n-aill

Am dér gréne

Am cain lubai

Am torc ar gail

Am he i l-lind

Am loch i m-maig

Am brí a ndai

Am bri i fodb fras feochtu

Am dé delbas do chind codnu

Coiche nod gleith clochur slébe

Cia on co tagair aesa éscai

Cia du i l-laig fuiniud gréne

Cia beir buar o thig tethrach

Cia buar tethrach tibi

Cia dám, cia dé delbas faebru a ndind ailsiu

Cáinte im gai, cainte gaithe

I am the wind on the sea

I am the stormy wave

I am the sound of the ocean

I am the bull with seven horns

I am the hawk on the cliff face

I am the sun's tear

I am the beautiful flower

I am the boar on the rampage

I am the salmon in the pool

I am the lake on the plain

I am the defiant word

I am the spear charging into battle

I am the god who put fire in your head

I made the trails through stone mountains

Who knows the age of the moon

Who knows where the setting sun rests

Who took the cattle from the house of the warcrow

Who pleases the warcrow's cattle

What bull, what god created the mountain skyline

The cutting word, the cold word

I recall the words of the 12th century German mystic Hildegard of Bingen that the heart is in the body, the body is in the soul and the soul journeys to the ends of the world and I remember Tom Cowan, an author and Celtic shamanic practitioner, laying out a compelling argument that only 10% of us is being who we are and the other 90% of us is yearning to be all the other aspects of ourselves, the wind, the sea, the mountain, the flower. This makes sense to me in my belief that all things are connected, we are a Celtic weave, a knot that goes on forever connected in the oneness of all, so as Amergin declares I am the sun's tear, so it is that I am also the sun's tear. How cool is that!!!

One of the greatest questions I have asked myself is 'Who am I?' It is a lifetime question. One to mull over to ponder to deepen the awareness of the authenticity of who I am. In 1998 I was intrigued by a question; 'If I was a symphony, what would I be?'

After sitting with this profound query, I scribed, or more accurately held the pen while the answer flowed out of me. These are those words, written in the classic Celtic style of the 'I am.'

I AM

I am the morning dew, the summer breeze

the rolling ocean, deep rooted trees.

I am one with the stars I am the light of the sun

dancing colors of rainbows I am one with the one.

I am the virgin snow, the first bloom of spring,

I am he who lives dreams, she who has wings.

I am the moonlight that shimmers on a waters edge,

the cascading hues in an emerald forest.

My flame rides the wind, traverses the sea,

rooted in earth I am the sacred oak tree.

I am brother to all I am their sister too, Mother, Father in me, is Mother, Father in you.

I am your mirror, reflection, an eternal ray of light,

I am a dewdrop in the morning, the stillness of the night.

I am the chorus, the soloist, the lyrics and the song,

Cruithear the conductor, in the flow, I am as one.

Cruithear is the Scottish Gaelic word for Creator, the shaper.!

Now it's your turn. Take some time, find a quiet space and ask yourself,

'If I were a symphony, what would I be?'

Chapter 5

SOVEREIGNTY WITH THE LAND

Pixy dust and grinning Spriggans lead a merry dance, where knockers and knackers will spin you through the underworld and the small people will gaily wave on a trail that leads to nowhere, and how do you know where you are if you are on a trail to no where? Breath for then you will know where you are for you are now here which strangely is nowhere! Confused yet? It's only when we think we are lost that we perceive ourselves to be not where we are, and so in fear, we run from ourselves and don't know where we are. Once we find ourselves, then we return to knowing and we know we are where we are, now here, nowhere! Get it? I love this spinning thread of a Celtic weave. I had a pilgrim travel with me in 2002 and she dreaded getting lost until I asked her if she was going to accompany herself wherever she went. Once she accepted that she was, she gave herself permission to head on a quest day, willing to lose herself so she could find herself anew. It is one of those delicious truths that haunts us when we our not present with ourselves. It is impossible to get lost if we are willing to be present.

I remember going camping in the Blue Ridge Mountains of Virginia. We had found a beautiful glade where the deer roamed free off of Scenic Drive. I worked quickly and concisely to erect the tent and set camp before nightfall. Kindling was plentiful but good logs needed to be scrounged from the forest floor. I set off into a thicket and traipsed gleefully through the dangling limbs and swaying shadows of the dancing grove. Deeper and deeper I fell under her calling trance, I swayed, I turned, I blazed my own trail under and over around and about until I was surrounded by dense walls of sharp needles as a darkening sky sought the light of a crescent moon. As I stood in the silence of my desperate screams, my heart skipped a beat and my stomach met my throat. I was lost. I have an actors voice and with my lungs full I screamed for help, my booming voice scattered in the loneliness of the expanding forest. The fear was pumping and my brain was conjuring imaginative horrors of a never-ending trail where no breadcrumbs would lead me home. It was then that I breathed. I laughed and breathed. I was lost and had nearly consumed myself with being lost. I had been so close to drowning in my own fear, in my own panic stricken flight, leaving my body temporarily frozen, numb, paralyzed and terrorized, a victim of my own illusion that was quiet simply thawed by my breath. I was set free by a deep inhalation and as the fear was exhaled, I breathed in the bridge connecting my heart to my feet, my feet to the earth, sinking way down into the Calliach's cauldron below, and that beautiful heart bridge connected everything below me to everything within me and bringing the light from above me I connected to all below me through the light within me which sparkled brightly in my connected heart, the center of my Universe.

With this deep understanding of oneness, the fear dissipated and I was present with myself. In finding my center I breathed and laughed once more and chose to walk where my heart called me to walk. I picked up several pieces of wood and after several minutes of moving confidently forward I came to a clearing and in the dying light of day I made out the silhouette of my tent. The power of now, of being here in this moment, the connection to the breath allows us to see the wood for the trees and we can navigate any of life's challenges for we are living, experiencing the fullness of the journey, the depth of the quest.

There is a pulsating fervor that heightens the awareness of colors and hues when one is fully present, in the moment, sauntering down a timeless trail on a virgin forage into the unknown. Going on an adventure and seeking long lost treasure with invisible sprites nibbling at your heels. That is what each copse on pilgrimage conjures. Cornwall has more than its share of magical nemetons. The faerie folk of Kernow are as playful and delightfully mischievous as their puddings and pies. If you didn't have a sweet tooth before you arrived you will be sorely tempted to delve into the fae fruits of clotted cream, sticky toffee pud and the delectable treacle. As I instruct new pilgrims, the golden treacle that sumptuously drips from the crest of the piping hot steamed sponge pudding, is locally mined by the Knockers and Knackers and the Piskey folk, who generously wheel out barrows full of the sticky sugary syrupy treat for our lip-smacking pleasure, and long may it continue. The barrows of fae treacle are as much source of amusement as looking for haggis on the hills of Scotland. The gleam in my eye sparks the faerie magic in my soul! As much fun as I have spinning a yarn, the wee folk enjoy yanking my chain and opening my eyes so I can see life from a different perspective.

In 2006 the pilgrims wandered off from Rosemerryn on a quest day, being on the land in love and trust, going off individually where their hearts called them to go, some fasting, and all in silence. On this occasion I decided to go further a field on an exploration to find the Alsia Well. I had checked with Rob and Laura the guardians at Rosemerryn, who knew of the Alsia Farm, but not the way to the well. Two other locals offered blank stares and furrowed brows, so armed with my map I pulled myself up into the drivers seat of the minibus and squeezed my way up the tousled and tangled lane that leads to the main road and the Merry Maiden stone circle. Several miles later and many a snaking track that greeted my wing mirrors on each side with tickling greenery, I came to Alsia Farm. My only reference point for the well was in a book that I had once read and long forgotten, except for the distinct landmarks that I had written down in my journal. I was seeking a barn with a corrugated tin roof and a style, a wooden post with steps to climb over, which would lead me to the well. With this flimsy clue I looked diligently for the signs to bring me closer to this gateway of the underworld. To my left and right, high hedgerows bordered the fields, the only breaks being the occasional fence for tractors and farm folk to access the land. As I drove down the twisting lane I noticed one such fence to my left. Under it, watching me as I chugged slowly by, was a large hare. I grinned to myself at seeing such an auspicious sign and continued on my way looking desperately for a tin roof and a style. Five miles later I reluctantly accepted that I must have missed it and I retraced my tracks pondering whether the barn was up at the farm and could only be seen traveling this way. I looked through the occasional breach in the hedgerow and was once again greeted by the hare, who had not budged and gazed at me as I drove slowly by. Again I chuckled, thinking about the significance of hares in the Celtic world.

According to Caesar, the hare was one of the beasts held in awe by the early Britons. Queen Boudicca would release a hare before setting out on a campaign, invoking the goddess Andraste and seeking an omen through divination of the hare by watching which way it would run so she could prognosticate the outcome of the ensuing foray. Celtic artwork also depicts the hunter's relationship with the hare. As Anne Ross in *Pagan Celtic Britain* shares, "the animal naturally figures regularly as a hunted beast in the toreutic and iconographic tradition, and the hunter gods are frequently portrayed as holding a hare in their hands. One such relief from Touget depicts a hunter deity holding a large hare across his breast and grasping it by its front and hind legs."

In folklore the hare holds the distinction of being both lucky and unlucky. I remember as a boy being given a rabbit's foot for luck. Samuel Pepys carried one to protect himself from colics. On the flip side pregnant women ran the risk of having a child with a hare lip if one crossed their path, and some would swear that it was a bad omen to meet one at the beginning of the day. Some say a witch can transform herself into a hare or the hare is her familiar. These speedy burrowing mammals are found throughout Celtic tales and worldwide stories weaving magic and transformation. The hare is a shapeshifter, a symbol of fertility and a phenomenal trickster. In the African American tradition Br'er Rabbit is always spinning a ruse and teaching lessons. The First People of North America have rabbit stories. The Creek tribe has a wonderful tale in which a rabbit outwits a wolf and rides on his back using wolf as his riding pony. Alice in Wonderland is guided to a shamanic adventure through the rabbit hole by chasing after a white rabbit, which I would warrant had red ears as all good fae animals are so well known for! Then there are the stories of the rabbit in the moon connecting this mysterious beast with the goddess and the night. In the Chinese Zodiac the rabbit represents hope and being born in 1963, the year of the rabbit, I have always felt an affinity towards these enchanting creatures that move between the worlds, even to the point of refusing to eat their flesh. My mother served rabbit when I was about 13 and told me it was minced lamb, I was having none of it and something inside me resisted the flesh of my kin. She eventually admitted it was rabbit and had wanted me to try something new. I eat a wide range of foods and to this day rabbit is not one of them! Cerridwen the old hag tries to eat Gwion Bach. She chases after him in the form of a hound, while Gwion Bach chooses the hare as his primary animal after drinking the three drops of inspiration. Squire Lovell chases a hare into the Boleigh Fogou to meet Old Bet's mischief. The white wizard hare in the Irish tale of the Shee an Gannon and the Gruagach Gaire, is a doubly powerful entity with associations to Druidry and magic that leads people to the castle of the Gruagach Gaire and messes up the table until it is caught by the Shee an Gannon and has its brains dashed out. Yuck you might say, but then

Celtic tales are full of gore, which on the surface appears unseemly and yet when you seep into the juices of the bubbling brew the word magic and imagery is transforming.

The Shee an Gannon

The Shee an Gannon was born in the morning, named at noon, and by the evening was visiting the King of Erin to ask for the hand of his daughter in marriage.

"Ah so another intrepid seeker comes into our midst" Cajoled the King, "and you shall have your heart's desire for the price of a quest. Bring me the reason for the Gruagach Gaire's silence. Why has he stopped laughing? The Gruagach Gaire would always laugh hard and strong, so loud was his booming merriment that the whole world heard his crow, find out where his laughter lies and you shall win my blessing. Be warned there are twelve iron spikes in the garden behind my castle, eleven of which are adorned by the severed heads of those that came before you, nobles, princes whose eyes have fed the ravens, the twelfth spike I fear will wear your head on your return, for if like these fellows you come to me without the information I desire and I still am at a loss to why the Gruagach Gaire no longer laughs,I will surely slice your head from your shoulders and raise it to meet the full glare of the midday sun."

The Shee an Gannon said not one word, he left the castle to decipher whether he could shed light onto the secret silence of the Gruagach's jollity. He stepped o'er a glen with a stride, a hill with a leap, and traveled all day until evening. In the twinkling twilight he came upon a house, the master of the house agreed to give him a bed for the night with the offer of work should he wish to stay.

"I am looking for a man to look after my cows I will pay you well with the best food you can eat in this world and a soft bed to lie upon." The Shee an Gannon accepted the post and tucked heartily into his supper and as he licked the drippings from the plate the master introduced himself as the Gruagach Gaire.

Before the cock crow of sunrise the Shee an Gannon stirred, slipping from the sheets of silk and stretching to greet the first glimmer of a radiant new day. After breaking his fast in the stern silence of the Gruagach's company he set off to do the bidding of his morbid master. He gaily drove the five golden cows and the bull without horns onto the pasture remembering his hosts words well,

"Let them feast on the lush grass of this land but do not let them stray onto the land of the giant." The Shee an Gannon looked at the high stone wall that marked the territory of the giant's land. He could see the fine orchards towering above the wall laden with delicious apples. If you had been passing you might have thought he was going to rest his back against that wall as the cows and bull grazed but the Shee an Gannon flexed his muscles and drove through the wall making a sufficient hole for the five golden cows and the bull without horns to step through the rubble and graze on the land of the giant. Then with a sprightly skip he pulled himself effortlessly into the boughs of a large apple tree and munched and crunched on the sweet juices of the rich red apples and he threw the sour ones down to the cattle of the Gruagach Gaire.

The serenity of his mid morning snack was shattered by the reverberating crash of splintering limbs and cracking timbers as old trees snapped and saplings were uprooted. Stomping through the orchard snarling and growling was the grotesque figure of a five headed fiend.

"You poor misguided creature" roared one of the mouths of the massive giant, "You must be fattening yourself up on my fruits and sweetening yourself too. Mmm you smell tasty, are you as tender as you look? You are too big for one bite and too small for two. Which of my mouths should I feed, let me rip you into pieces so all can have a taste."

"You'll be too busy feasting and choking on your own words stuffed down your throat to have a bite out of me," mocked the Shee an Gannon as he sprung to meet his marching match. The might of muscles slammed and thumped, rocking the world that shook and quaked, all eyes intently watching the crazed dance of the brutal combat. They fought into the descending sun of late afternoon and early evening, until finally the giant got the upper hand and the Shee an Gannon knew he was about to die. He began conjuring images of those he loved to take across the bridge of his death to ease his journey. A truth flickered in his heart and a knowing in his mind as he gazed on the faces of his mother and father he realized they would never see him again, and that they would not know where his body lay. As he pictured his sweetheart he understood that he would never taste those tender full lips of the daughter of the King of Erin. Armed with such potent truth, an irrefutable force coursed through his veins and pummeled through his fists. A ferocious blow sunk the giant to his knees. A second strike and he crumpled to his waist. A third tirade saw the five heads bashing together, whipping and smashing the skulls apart. With the giant flattened and the battle won the Shee an Gannon took out his knife and severed the five heads from the giant's body, removing each of the tongues from the five silent mouths, he slipped the meat of their words into his pocket and slung the heads over the wall.

When he returned to the house of the Gruagach Gaire the five golden cows gave more milk than there were vessels to hold it, and the Shee an Gannon said not one word. He retired to his bed of silk and the following morn he went farther a field and again put his back to the wall and made an even bigger hole in the wall.

The five golden cows and the bull without horns feasted on the lush pastures of the giant and the sour apples that the Shee an Gannon threw down from his perch in the twisted boughs of an ancient apple tree whilst he devoured the succulent flesh of the summerland fruit. It was at this exact moment that the King of Tisean's son, who had set off on the same errand to win the hand of the daughter of the King of Erin, came across the five decapitated heads from the Shee an Gannon's battle from the day before. Gathering the heads up in a sack the prince of Tisean returned to Erin and laid these trophies at the kings feet.

"You have done exceedingly well," exclaimed a jubilant king. " One third of my daughter's hand is in your keeping." During which time the Shee an Gannon was disturbed from his reverie by the reverberating crash of splintering limbs and cracking timbers as old trees snapped and saplings were uprooted. Clomping through the orchard roaring and raging was a larger more terrifying vision of the colossal giant that he had slain the day before.

"You pitiful excuse for a man," roared one of the mouths of the massive giant. "You must be fattening yourself up on my fruits and sweetening yourself too. Mmm, you smell tasty, are you as tender as you look? You are too big for one bite and too small for two. Which of my mouths…"

"Let me stop you there, I've heard this nonsense before, so be prepared to eat your words for by the strength in my arm, the truth in my heart and the promise on my lips you are going down" spat the Shee an Gannon as he launched himself to tackle his fuming foe. Locked in the dizzying dust of a death defying battle they fought into the lengthening shadows of the disappearing day until finally the giant got the upper hand and the Shee an Gannon knew he was about to die. Conjuring images of those he loved to take across the bridge of his death to ease his journey, a truth illuminated in his heart and a knowing in his mind. Gazing on the faces of his mother and father he realized they would never see him again, that they would not know where his body lay and as he pictured his sweetheart he understood that he would never taste those tender full lips or seek the soft warmth of the flickering tongue of the daughter of the King of Erin. Armed with such potent truth an irrefutable force coursed through his veins and pummeled through his fists. A ferocious blow sunk the giant to his knees a second strike he crumpled to his waist and a third tirade saw the five heads bashing together whipping and smashing the skulls apart. With the giant flattened and the battle won the Shee an Gannon took out his knife and severed the five heads from the giant's body, removing each of the tongues from the five silent mouths he slipped the meat of their words into his pocket and slung the heads over the wall.

After driving the cattle home the Gruagach struggled to catch all of the milk in the overflowing cauldrons that had been begged borrowed and bought. The Shee an Gannon ate in the somber presence of the master and said not one word and at his earliest opportunity he slipped off to bed and slithered into silken dreams.

The next day he drove the cattle even further and came to a stronger higher wall, which crumbled to his touch, and once again the five golden cows and the bull with no horns dined on a banquet of sour apples and lush green grass. As he dangled his legs from the highest bough of a grandfather apple tree the son of the king of Tisean discovered the rotting heads from the previous days battle and was rewarded with a prize of two thirds of his hearts desire by the king of Erin. Meanwhile the Shee an Gannon was greeted by the reverberating crash of splintering limbs and cracking timbers as old trees snapped and saplings were uprooted.

Stamping through the orchard bellowing and belching was the biggest bawdiest beast the Shee an Gannon had ever seen.

"You pathetic miscreant," bellowed one of the mouths of the titanic giant. "You must be fattening yourself up on my fruits and...."

"Woah woah, don't tell me, let me guess," giggled the Shee an Gannon. "sweetening myself too Mmm I smell tasty, am I as tender as I look? I am too big for one bite and too small for two. Which of your rotten foul smelling mouths should you feed first, why don't you rip me into pieces so all can have a taste?"

The perplexed expressions of the five gawking faces met the acquaintance of the Shee an Gannon's flying fists as he sprung to meet the befuddled lump. They fought into the dying embers of the descending sun until finally the giant got the upper hand and the Shee an Gannon knew he was about to die, conjuring images of those he loved to take across the bridge of his death to ease his journey illuminated a truth in his heart and a knowing in his mind, gazing on the faces of his mother and father he realized they would never see him again, that they would not know where his body lay and as he pictured his sweetheart he understood that he would never taste those tender full lips or seek the soft warmth of the flickering tongue or feel the moist juices of passionate desire of the daughter of the King of Erin. Armed with such potent truth, an irrefutable force coursed through his veins and pummeled through his fists. A ferocious blow sunk the giant to his knees. A second strike and he crumpled to his waist. A third tirade saw the five heads bashing together, whipping and smashing the skulls apart. With the giant flattened and the battle won, the Shee an Gannon took out his knife and severed the five heads from the giant's body, removing each of the tongues from the five silent mouths he slipped the meat of their words into his pocket and slung the heads over the wall. When he arrived back at the Gruagach's house the rich milk from the five golden cows flowed copiously over the cauldrons forming a stream across the floor.

While the Shee an Gannon said not one word, the son of the King of Tisean picked up the severed heads of the slain giant and arrogantly rode to seek favor from the King of Erin.

"You have won my daughter with your feats of courage young man and have kept your head in the bargain, however you will not lay with her until you can tell me why the Gruagach Gaire no longer rocks the world with his raucous laughter."

On the fourth morning that the Shee an Gannon broke his fast he looked into the deep sad eyes of the Gruagach and challenged him directly.

"Why do you no longer laugh so all the world hears your joy?"

"You were sent by the King of Erin" accused the Gruagach. "Be gone from here before I set the dogs on you."

"If you do not tell me willingly I will force the answer out of you," growled the Shee an Gannon. With a face like Cuchulain in the midst of battle, the Shee an Gannon leapt from his chair and tore savagely after the fleeing Gruagach. Stripping ropes of untanned sheepskin from the wall, the Shee an Gannon bound the Gruagach's hands and feet so his little toes were sticking in his ears.

Tethered and trapped the Gruagach hissed, "release me and I will share what you wish to know."

Free from the bondage the Gruagach spilled the story of his journey into sorrow. "I lived in this castle with my twelve strapping sons. We caroused together, belched and laughed like there were no tomorrows, we played cards on this very table when a wizard hare came bounding in, jumped on the table and despoiled it. Before we could react it scampered off. We were ready for him next time he scuttled and sullied our den, pursuing him to a distant glen we saw him dart into a large abode where a man dwelled with twelve daughters. The hare was tied to the side of the room close to where the young women stood. A steaming cauldron bubbled with the boiling broth of a great stork. The man beckoned me to go and sit at the end of the room with my boys where a bundle of rushes leaned against the wall. He disappeared from the room and on his return he carried two pikes, one of wood the other of iron and asked me which of the two I would choose. I took the iron one, my thinking was that if attacked I could defend myself. He then instructed me to take the first portion from the cauldron and I speared a small scrap of the stork and the man lanced the generous portion all that was left in the pot. We had to fast that night as the man and his twelve daughters feasted upon the stork and threw the gnawed bones into our chops. We were frozen to the spot on account of those stork bones brandished in our faces.

In the morning as we were gathering ourselves to leave the man came to me with twelve loops of iron and one of wood and invited me to decide whether I would rather put my head in the noose of wood or my twelve sons in the nooses of iron. I had no intention of putting my head in a wooden noose so instructed him to clasp my sons in iron. He looped the iron rings around the necks of my sons and placed the wooden one around his own he then snapped those loops taking off the heads of my boys and throwing their heads from his door, leaving his own unscathed. He then grabbed me and ripped the skin off my back and took a black sheepskin that had been adorning his wall for seven years and fixed it on my bloody back, every year since I shear myself and use every clipping to darn and sow the stockings I wear."

As his voice trailed off and salty tears flowed down his weathered face he pulled up his shirt to reveal the coarse black wool sprouting over his shoulders and trailing down his spine.

"I see why your laughter faded and it is no small wonder, but tell me does the hare still tear up your table?"

"He spoils it regularly, especially when I play cards" grumbled the Gruagach. "Then we need to play" grinned the Shee an Gannon and the deck was not fully shuffled before the white wizard hare dashed through the doorway and wreaked havoc escaping the grabbing hands of the two companions rushing wickedly on the wind of the fading night air. The Shee an Gannon ran in hot pursuit with the Gruagach closely following on his tail. As the hare went to enter the castle door where the twelve sons had lost their heads, the Sheen an Gannon grabbed it by its hind legs and dashed its brains out on the wall. Its severed skull rolled into the great hall resting at the master of the castle's feet.

"Who has dared interfere with my fighting hare?" roared the maddened man.

"It was I," challenges Shee an Gannon, "and had your pet had manners it might live yet."

The Gruagach joined the Shee an Gannon by the fire looking into the boiling carcass of a giant stork bubbling in a cast iron cauldron. The man with twelve daughters went into a room and returned with two pikes, one of iron and one of wood and proffered them to the Shee an Gannon who willingly accepted the wooden one.

"You may have the iron one for yourself," he remarked casually as he dipped the wooden pike into the cauldron spearing the fleshy carcass leaving the small bite for the master of the house. The Shee an Gannon and the Gruagach tucked in to a mighty feast which took the best part of the night and when morning shook off its dark coating and spread its light upon the world the master of the house presented the Shee an Gannon with twelve loops of iron and one loop of wood and invited him to select a noose to wear. "What use are twelve loops for the Gruagach and myself, I will take the wooden one and let your daughters wear the iron."

In a flash he tossed the nooses around the girls necks and snapped off their heads. Then turning to face the distraught master of the house the Shee an Gannon boomed, "Now I will do the same to your scrawny neck unless you bring back the Gruagach's sons full of life, strong, healthy and bounding with joy."

The man shuffled out of the castle and returned shortly with the strapping boys bounding in behind him. The castle walls shook and an earth tremor vibrated through the land as the Gruagach Gaire released a blissful roar of undulating laughter.

The Shee an Gannon shook his head dully and cried, "You have done me a disservice Gruagach for the world has heard your call and the daughter of the king of Erin will be wed by this time tomorrow."

"Then why are we standing here moping. We have miles to cover and a short time to do so, come lads we have a wedding to stop and a wedding to attend."

They had not traveled far when a woman's keening stopped them in their tracks. "Why do you cry so hard good mother?" inquired the Shee an Gannon.

"What do you care?" sniped the woman through her snuffles, "I have lost them and that is as much as I will say."

"Tell me your tale and I may be able to find them," coaxed the young cow herder. "You will find them in London, they have been dragged off by the King of the Sassenach for beating his three sons at hurley. They have played them many times and each time my sons were victorious and the spoils of their game were to render three wallops of their hurleys to the losing side. They beat the kings sons so often and so hard that the princes complained to their father, and now the king has decreed that they will swing from the end of rope in London this day."

"Then I will retrieve them henceforth."

"You have no time to dally here," cautioned the Gruagach.

"My friend do you smoke a pipe?" queried the Shee an Gannon.

"I do not" said he.

"Well I do and I swear I will return before you have filled the bowl."

The Shee an Gannon thrust the pipe into the Gruagach's hands and with the blink of an eye he had returned with the three boys safe and sound. Taking his pipe back he finished filling the bowl and struck a match and with a satisfied smile he invited the whole party to attend the wedding of the King of Erin. They made haste and when they were but three miles from the King's castle they joined the snaking line of a throng of people shuffling towards the crowded city.

"We must clear a path" cried the Shee an Gannon.

"That we must" agreed the Gruagach and tossing people aside they ploughed their way through. They reached the wedding ceremony as the daughter of the king of Erin and the son of the king of Tisean were on their knees preparing to speak their vows. The Shee an Gannon leapt and struck the bridegroom so hard that he spun around the room flying under a table on the other side of the Great Hall.

"What rogue threw that punch?" demanded the King of Erin.

"I did," spoke the Shee an Gannon stepping into view of the whole court.

"State your reasons clearly and carefully for striking the man who has brought laughter to the Gruagach Gaire and won my blessing to marry my daughter is an act of treachery and I have an iron spike waiting to be decorated with a severed head," hissed the king.

"Well I can oblige you there for you will have a head to add to your collection if you so desire," grinned the Shee an Gannon. "For I have traveled here with proof that it is I who will marry your daughter this day for bringing you the news of why the Gragach Gaire stopped laughing and why his thunderous roar will tickle these celebrations and ripple through the land, and if you doubt my word ask the Gruagach himself."

And without further ado the Gruagach Gaire stepped forward and shared his tale. He explained how the Shee an Gannon had looked after his five golden cows and his bull without horns, he told them how the fifteen heads rolled from the three giants shoulders, of the wizard hare's brains that were splattered on a wall, and how his twelve sons had been brought back to life" and in a confidential whisper that had all of the court leaning in, in enraptured silence he declared, "the Shee an Gannon is the only person who knows the intimate details of why I stopped laughing and the only one to see the woolen fleece I carry upon my back,"

When the fifteen tongues were produced that fitted the fifteen giant heads, the Shee an Gannon married the daughter of the king of Erin and the son of the king of Tisean spent the night in a cell and in the morning he was thrown onto a blazing fire until he was nothing but ash. The wedding celebrations lasted for nine nights and nine days and the last was said to be better than the first.

The Treasure of the Tale

This tale like so many Celtic tales is bursting at the seams with elixirs of healing. A description of the name Gruagach from James MacKillop's Dictionary of Celtic Mythology states 'gruagach, gruacach, grógach [OIr. grúacach, hairy, long-haired; goblin, wight, enchanter; wizard-like]. Solitary fairy of Irish and Scottish Gaelic traditions, sometimes seen as a giant or ogre. His characteristic long hair links the gruagach to the woodwose or wild man of the woods. In Scotland the term gruagach may sometimes also refer to a fairy woman dressed in green or to a slender, handsome man.' It is interesting to note that Gaire means small one, so the Gruagach Gaire is the small giant wild man of the woods while the only reference to Shee an that I could find is the old Irish name Sheehan meaning Descendant of the Peaceful One and Gannon is Fair Skinned. So this 'light of peace' sets out into the world to restore laughter and win the right to marry the daughter of the king of Erin, the name Erin means Ireland so this tale leads us to the light one that is descended from peace mating with the land, a story of being in Sovereignty. The Shee an Gannon is willing to die for his vision, he embodies the Celtic expression *this is a good day to die* by passionately following his dream knowing that the king of Erin has a pike waiting with his name on it. It begs the question of us, are we willing to follow the depth of our dream?

Remembering that we are always the characters in every story, we can sink into the meat of the bones and find which pieces are playing out in or lives right now. He is told not to go onto the land of the giants and yet he breaks down walls and flouts rules to find his answer and the courage to live his truth. Are we willing to break through the walls of our fears to move into our dreams? What are those walls? What do we fear? What are the colors of our dreams and are we picturing them in technicolor with us in the center?

The Shee an Gannon knew that it served not only his best interest but the best intending for the world, to return laughter to the land, he knew that the giants' desire to own the land was an expression of *dominion over* not *sovereignty with* so he broke the rules to serve the land. What rules do we follow that do not serve a higher purpose?

Do we possess the courage to leap into authorship of our own story and redefine our lives because of it?

Revising Our Story

I grew up celebrating Christmas. I love Christmas and I believe in Christ. The line from an Alpha Blondy reggae song comes to mind regarding Christ, "he was a long haired Rasta man," he was also a shamanic wizard, a rebel, an outcast, an amazingly courageous author of his own tale and a beacon of light for others to find the truth of their own stories, I am not a Christian, and yet I celebrated Christmas each and every year. It took me until I was 45 to work out that I would make the Winter Solstice the focus of my celebrations. I was thankful for a good friends insight into this who suggested that I make this move, the clarity of that suggestion brought the light of the rising sun flooding into my consciousness. By changing the date of my celebrations I also changed the meaning of my celebrations and reached a depth and understanding because of it. I still decorate the 'one tree,' now with an owl perched on top and faeries dotted on the branches, my family still exchange gifts but we took the roots of our celebrations to the first shaman and looked at the story of modern day 'Santa' through new 'old' eyes.

Evolution of a Story

Imagine living in a time where there was no electricity, the warmth of the fire a necessary lifeline in the harsh cold of winter. The Christian carol *In the Bleak Midwinter* has a verse that could have been spoken in pre-pagan times:

'In the bleak midwinter, frosty wind made moan,

Earth stood hard as iron, water like a stone;

 Snow had fallen, snow on snow, snow on snow,

In the bleak midwinter, long ago.'

As the days shortened and the dark, dark nights reached out their frosted frozen claws the tribe would have celebrated whole heartedly the return of the *Sun*, who in our patriarchal world today becomes the *Son*. Before temples like the Bru na Boinne were built to mark the rising sun at the winter solstice, the shamans were said to have climbed a tree to get the first glimpse of the sun's rays. These shaman would paint themselves in the colors of the underworld, red and white. They would wear the totem animal of the tribe and just as the Celts became a forest people and a deer people, so the indigenous people of the Isles would watch the shaman adorned in antlers climb the 'one tree' wearing bells to invoke spirit, and receiving the gift of sunlight. The shaman descended the tree to bring the gift to the people. The similarities are unmistakable. Red and white painted bodies became Santa's suit. The antlers are the flying reindeer with bells, and the one tree becomes the chimney and the presents are the gift of sunlight. So with this act of the shaman the tribe knew that lighter, warmer days were on the wind and life would continue. Is it any wonder that temples like Stonehenge were built in alignment with the seasons? The largest trilithons of Stonehenge mark the passage of the sun during the winter solstice, which leads me to the conclusion that this was the most important festival, the old year dies and a new one is born. Is it any wonder that the Christian calendar moved the birth of Christ to December 25th to echo the traditions of the ancestors and emphasize the symbolic beginning of new life? So with the agreement and support of my children I broke through years of conditioning and we remembered ourselves by honoring and focusing our celebrations authentically to the beat of our own drum, our heart, our truth.

So the Shee an Gannon breaks the rules and brings the five golden cows and the bull without horns to feast on the land. He also offers them apples. Cows in the Celtic world are representative of wealth and their milk is life force, poetry and abundance. They eat the sour apples thrown down to them while the Shee an Gannon eats the sweet apples. This is the fruit of the underworld whose limbs were used to make druidic wands and the sacred Isles of Avalon and Emain Ablach, the paradisiacal Isle off the coast of Alba, Scotland carry the root and seeds of the word apple within them as does the Cornish name for Samhain, All Hallows Tide which is Allantide and in Cornish oral tradition is the 'apple time', and to commemorate this we bob for apples! So as the sour apples hit the earth and the cows devour them they are transformed into the sweet nectar of abundant milk. What alchemy are we working in our own lives?

Looking at the bare basics we can ask ourselves how are we recycling?

And one that I love to address is how do we transform our own shit? Are we wallowing in it or are we fertilizing the land, our lives?

The Shee an Gannon then fights the three giants on consecutive days. He gets out there and does the work, he takes off their heads, gathering the wisdom, the head being the seat of the soul and the receptacle/cauldron of wisdom. He takes the tongues and puts them in his pocket, the meat of truth, the vessel of our word magic plucked from the cauldron of wisdom and placed in the cauldron of warming, he carries them by the cauldron that represents 'I exist, I am', in his pocket, right by his root chakra. So with these tongues he knows, cauldron of wisdom, who he is, cauldron of warming, and he is driven by the cauldron of calling to act, to do the work. Wow, are we willing to do the work each day, to become conscious of living our passions and having the courage to express our unique creativity?

Are we willing to transform the mundane and see the pilgrimage and greatness in each action so what was once a chore becomes an extension of our magical dance, cleaning the toilet bowl is an opportunity to sparkle the 'holy chalice' another opportunity for expression and transforming our shit! For we are doing it anyway!

The Shee an Gannon forces the Gruagach Gaire to own and speak his truth. Looking from the Gruagach's perspective, he knows the land, Erin, and its king are looking to find out where the wild rich gigantic laughter has gone yet he refuses to share this with the Shee an Gannon until he is bound in leather ties with his toes tickling his ears. As I pondered his reluctance to share I came to the conclusion that he was embarrassed. He had forsaken his sons to save his own neck, choosing to put his sons heads in the twelve iron loops.

He is also faced with having his skin ripped off his back and having a dark woolen sheepskin fixed in its place which brought to mind a bunch of phrases clanging to be heard, *he lost the shirt off his own back, he got fleeced, he wears his true colors, he is the black sheep* of the family. I mulled over this piece thinking about my own back. I wear a tattoo on my back that is a picture of what I believe in this world, it carries the symbols of the Celtic world that are true to my heart. It supports my vision by having my back. However my back faces all that is behind me, all of my past is wrapped up in my body and if I do not process and deal with my own shit and transform it into fertilizer then it will be stuck in me and I am swimming in my own sewage, which feels like carrying the weight of the world on ones shoulders. Isn't this what the Gruagach is doing? He is embarrassed about the past and will not face it or take responsibility for his part and only when he has hit his lowest point, i.e. he is trapped with nowhere to go, bound by the Shee an Gannon, is he able to release the burden that he has carried on his back! If and when we are the Gruagach in the story of our own lives, how are we releasing the burdens of our past?

Are we so stuck in the challenges of our childhood, our interactions and relationships from yesterday that we are missing the opportunity to receive and be the gift of the present moment?

Are we complaining that we are the black sheep of the family?

And in moaning about not being accepted are we failing to accept ourselves?

Are we in relationship with someone who continually fleeces us and we keep going back for more?

Who are we fleecing in this world?

Who are we trying to get back at?

The Gruagach Gaire is offered a wooden pike or an iron one and he chooses the iron one to stir the pot and stab a piece of the giant stork that is cooking. The stork is a transformational bird that is associated with birth and change. The Gruagach chooses the metal pike to protect himself, what is he afraid of that he needs protection?

Is it that he approaches this task in fearing change itself?

Does he approach the pot feeling unworthy, less than, that it would be disingenuous to take what he needs?

So when he goes to get a portion from the cauldron, which is a place of plenty, he pulls out a tiny scrap. I believe that in this great journey that we call life that there is enough for everyone. If we concentrate on lack we create a wasteland, if we focus on prosperity we create a thriving realm full of possibility. So where are we focused on lack?

When do we martyr ourselves and refuse to eat from the banquet table and instead fight for the scraps from the floor?

I pondered on the significance of the iron and wood and other than iron scratching the pan I found that wood is an unreactive material, which means it is unlikely to react with the ingredients in the mixture. I remember as a kid my mum would always tell me to stir with a wooden spoon. So I ask where in our lives are we spoiling the broth?

Are we failing to add our flavor to the dish or have we contaminated it by dominating other people's flavors?

To echo the theme of transformation there are 12 sons and the Gruagach which makes thirteen the number of transformation which is mirrored by the twelve daughters and the man. After restoring the Gruagach's sons to life the Shee an Gannon sets off to stop his love marrying an imposter. On the way he meets a keening woman whose sons have been imprisoned and were to be hung because they had beaten a more powerful adversary many times and then those that they had fairly defeated abused their position and had the victors quashed. Do we get jealous of other people's success?

Do we tear people down behind closed doors with word magic that poisons the brew?

Do we try and undermine others with our words and actions?

Are we willing to stand up and fight for those who are persecuted or do we walk on by? The Shee an Gannon, the light of peace, goes to London and returns with the keening woman's sons in the blink of an eye. He is willing to sacrifice, make sacred, his pilgrimage to meet the daughter of the king of Erin, to go to the king of Sassenach, the 'Saxons', the enemy, and face those who would oppress him and seek justice. When we all stand up in the light of peace and face the persecutors things can shift rapidly in the blink of an eye. When I was a kid the thought system prevailed that the Berlin Wall was a permanent fixture, in 1989 that thought process shifted as the wall came toppling down. The Shee an Gannon, the light of peace, put a shoulder on it on November 9th 1989! The son of the king of Tisean is exposed by the Shee an Gannon and the Gruagach Gaire, he had collected the giants heads and presented the wisdom as his own. impressing the king of Erin. He also laid claim to bringing the laughter of the Gruagach to the world. His fraudulent claims are laid bare to the bone for wisdom is gained through experience and when we deceitfully claim to be something we are not, our voice is rendered useless on the wind for we are not able to hold the vibration and the depth of knowing if we cannot speak the truth of it from our own tongues, the fifteen tongues that fit perfectly into the mouths of the giants heads from the Shee an Gannon's pocket testify to this. When are we like prince Tisean?

Do we try and impress others by pretending to be what we are not?

When do we speak falsehoods as absolute truth?

When do we try and take credit for someone else's idea?

I love that the celebrations were for nine days or three times the three levels of being and that the last was better than the first. This says so much, in the Western world where coming first, especially in the USA is the' be all and end all'. I love that the last is the best, this begs the question do we stop to smell the roses?

Are we being the witness and not the tourist in our own life?

This expression also calls to mind that we save the best until last and that we move into our elder years with strength and courage to meet the great adventure of death knowing we lived rather than crumbling into the frailty of old age.

Finally, let us address the hare in the story. The Shee an Gannon follows this universal transformative trickster after watching it mess up the table. The hare is thrown into the midst to provoke a reaction and gets the Shee an Gannon to chase after him for intuitive teachings. He gets caught on the threshold, the entrance to the rabbit hole, the castle, and the Shee an Gannon grabs the hind legs, the lucky rabbits foot and dashes out its brains, releasing the wisdom from the head of this magician hare's cauldron which rolls into the great hall announcing the arrival of new thought, new wisdom and the seeds to create new life. So the Shee an Gannon gains great victory by amongst other things watching the divination trail of a hare which connects with a thread to Queen Boudiicca, whose name we have established means victory, who called upon Andraste. whose name means invincible. while releasing a hare, whose name translated means to tease, excite or harry. An exciting invincible victory for the peace of the world where laughter reigns and ripples through all aspects of the world.

The Tale and the Land

So as I sought the Alsia Well. I was hoping for an invincible victory that was guaranteed to excite me, Andrew, who as you know has traveled with the nickname Harry!

I certainly felt assured that I would find the well. So I passed the hare still sitting in the same spot intently watching me from under the gateway in the breach of the hedgerow. I turned a corner and continued toward the Alsia Farm. Ahead of me was a man riding a white steed.

He was steering the mare toward the farm gate as I trundled toward him and leant out of the window.

"Excuse me," I called. "Do you know where the Alsia Well is?"

The man reined in and focused his electric blue eyes onto me and as his mouth twisted into a perplexing grimace he shook his head. "No sir, I can't say I do, there are many wells in Cornwall but I don't know that one."

It was then that the bright light of dawn came rushing in. It was as if Thumper was whacking its left hind foot right across my brow desperately trying to engage my cauldron of wisdom from its misty slumber.

"Thanks, I think I know where to look." I sputtered and swung the bus around to head to meet the hare. Sure enough my long eared friend was still waiting under the gate. I stopped the vehicle and looked deeply into its eyes. It held my gaze for a moment that could have been a second or an age, time stood still and a huge grin spread across my face, we were connecting the golden thread, the clew. Ariadne gave Theseus a ball of golden thread to find his way out of the labyrinth designed for the minotaur by Daedalus. In those days golden thread was called a *clew* which as we say and spell it today becomes clue. The hare seeing that I had understood the clew suddenly whipped around and raced across the field. I watched, as Boudiicca would, following its trail until it disappeared along a path on the other side of the field. The hare had been true to its name, it had teased me and harried this 'Harry' into seeing between the worlds.

I pulled the minibus off the road as far as I dared into the hedgerow and I jumped out to make sure any oncoming vehicle could skirt past. Once satisfied that I was not blocking anyone's passage I walked over to the gate and pushed it open. On the other side of the hedgerow I saw what was invisible from the road, tucked against the hedge was an old barn with a corrugated tin roof and to the left of me was a style. By now I was laughing out loud and I knew exactly which way to go, I followed the hare. Sure enough an overgrown trail housing a rickety iron gate to the right of the path guided me toward a clump of overhanging hawthorn bushes, faerie guardians protect the most precious of hidden wells. I stooped in the waters of Alsia, where pilgrims of old carried weak children on the first three Wednesdays of May to receive healing, and I knew that I would lead the group to this spot three days hence which would be the second Wednesday in May. I remember looking at the sunlight reflecting off the waters edge and nestling into the breath of the moment being present in a space where I was content to sit in that instance forever and a day. Gentleness, soft peace and eternal gratitude welled in my heart and rippled through my senses. Alsia Well is a wishing well, a place where divination has taken place across the ages. Sweethearts would drop pebbles or pins and watch whether they floated together or apart. Sinking close meant a life together, tumbling away from each other would mean a separation, the amount of bubbles and splashes represented the number of years before this event would occur. A wishing well, a lovers well and when brambles are placed to float on the water the spirit of the well can be consulted. My songs sung and offerings laid I felt soulful as I skipped toward the minibus to head to Rosemerryn and greet the returning pilgrims from quest. I had found the magical well, guided by the hare, by faerie, I was tickled pink and the image of the abundant prosperous symbol of good fortune came flooding into my mind once more. This icon of spiritual rebirth, of the immortality of the soul, had waited so patiently for me to get it. It was the Celtic way, three times we had met eye to eye and this messenger from the underworld had helped me know where to go. It was then that I glanced down at my t-shirt that I had pulled on that day, goose pimples drove the hairs of my arms to stand erect I was wearing one of Jen Delyth's designs, three hares woven into a Celtic knot. I love how Spirit works when we are open to the magic, it is always present for us, and what a great present, a truly remarkable gift when we are 'now here' to receive it, which didn't we establish earlier is where we are, for in the presents/presence of Spirit we all 'know-where' we are!

Chapter 6

THE WITNESS

The only way to discover the limits of the possible
is to go beyond them into the impossible.
Arthur C. Clarke.

Since that awe inspiring moment in 1998 when my eyes grew as big as flying saucers at the sound of an invitation that changed my life, "Will you be our guide?" crooned by the psychic who led groups to Greece and was, unbeknownst to her or me for that matter, nudging me onto a pathway of leading pilgrimages as part and parcel of my life. She was keen for a one off visit, and I soon found that I needed no middle person to generate interest in sacred travel. Whether I am leading a group to the South West of England, on an Arthurian tour in search of our own Holy Grail, walking the labyrinth of St.Columba's bay on the precious Isle of Iona, dancing in the heartland of Yns Mon the Great Mother or moseying down winding lanes in a horse drawn gypsy caravan in the enchanted Emerald Isle where faerie spirits roam free, I am forever thankful for the opportunity to do this challenging, but immensely rewarding work.

Each and every one of these journeys has been memorable, mystical, deeply satisfying to the very core of my soul. The magic in my life keeps growing and I am oh so thankful to witness the sparkles of understanding that shimmer and shake each of us pilgrims as we gently unfold.

In June 2000 I was in the quaint city of Wells, the smallest of England's cities. The ornate 13th Century Cathedral stands as a beacon for this thriving community. Picnic lunches on the green, school children in their droves playing football during recess, holidaymakers and locals alike walking through the heart of a city that has the qualities of both a sleepy village and a bustling town, for within its heartbeat the school children disappear on mass leaving serenity in their wake.

It was on a lazy summer's day, warm and bright, that the travelers who had accompanied me had a free day. A choice to revisit Glastonbury, delve in the nooks and crannies of Wells, or board the minibus to explore the charms of Bath.

The engine chugged in delight as three of our party climbed aboard to head to Bath, a young couple from Ohio, and Grace who was the dearest elder from Pennsylvania. A youthful sprightly 70 year young woman. A smile as broad as the river Avon spread across her wizened face. Her blue eyes twinkled. Her white hair blown in the breeze was now being hidden by a summer brimmed cloth hat. She leaned over towards the drivers seat, and I knew what she was going to say.

" When are we going to see a crop circle Andrew?" these words crooned out of her mouth every day, sometimes more than once. In my literature I had advertised castles, caves, long barrows, chapels, quoits, even the gateway to the Underworld on the misty Tor of Glastonbury, but nowhere had I written crop circles. I giggled at her request and gave my usual reply.

"I don't know Grace, maybe it will be today".

As we left Wells on the winding back road to Bath, my eyes caught the many wildflowers cascading out of the hedgerows.

"Yes, yes, oh look," Grace's voice had lifted an octave. In an instance this playful elder was allowing her inner child to transport her back to her childhood youth. Her skin glowed and she visibly bounced up and down on the seat. I glanced out of the window at an 'S' shaped crop circle in a distant farmers field. It was a fleeting flash, due to a sharp corner that required my attention. It may have only been a moment, but for Grace it was her whole tour. It took a second to decide what to do, and a couple of minutes to find a lay by so I could do it. I pulled in, and began to turn the bus around.

Grace was flushed, her eyes sparkled, and her breath was quick as she spluttered," What are you doing?"

"I'm turning around to get a better look Grace, to get you a photograph," I exclaimed joyfully.

"You'd do that for me? No-one has ever turned a bus around on a tour for me before."

"Well they have now and this is no tour, we are on pilgrimage," I chuckled. Separating us from the crop circle was a steep embankment leading to a ditch, an eight foot hedgerow, a 200 ft cow pasture, a barbed wire fence, and a dirt track. We were high enough for Grace to get the shots that would be a prized treasure in her photo album. I watched keenly with immense satisfaction. It was a perfect day. The suns rays danced on the horizon, lifting out the exquisite colors on mother natures canvas, the strong wind of early morning had been replaced by a gentle breeze, the sky was a deep royal blue and we had found a crop circle. Yet this was not enough, I wanted more for Grace. "Time to go people," I blurted out quickly, my excitement getting the better of me.

 "One more picture," pleaded Grace. "We are going to get you something better than a picture we are going to visit the circle."

"Bless you Andrew but I am in no shape to be climbing fences" Grace chided.

A broad smile beaming from ear to ear I giggled "I've a better idea Grace, hop aboard the minibus". There was a narrow road that ran parallel with the hedgerow. I was hoping it would lead us to the dirt track in the yonder distance, the track leading to the circle itself. There was no room to turn the bus around so I began to back her up. On each side of the road was vegetation, which quickly became an 8 ft wall of dense hedgerow. The mirrors on the vehicle were dragging themselves through tangled vines as I edged her down to the bottom of this dead end drive. There was barely room to squeeze out of the sliding door.

"Where are you going? Its all hedgerow, there's no way through." Grace's voice seemed tinged with disappointment. She was right. It certainly appeared to be a formidable barricade blocking our way to a hands-on experience.

"Who knows, maybe we are missing something," I replied, more in hope than anything. It is vital to carry hope in your heart. It is crucial to look at the big picture it is blooming brilliant when you are one with the magic of life, putting yourself on the canvas in blissful color. Some call it destiny, some call it luck, I know it as, by the grace of God, our perception is our reality so I was concentrating on a way in, of being included rather than left out. There, tucked out of view from the road, was a gap in the hedgerow. An overgrown path led right to the track, all the way to the crop circle. We skipped, we jumped, we floated and we marched. Grace had set a deep intention to see a crop circle, and we joined her in this coveted adventure.

We were like four kids sneaking into the cookie jar, we giggled, we danced, we feasted on anticipation, and we entered.

It was a huge snake, a massive S made of eleven separate circles that connected this artistic phenomenon. The circles at both ends of the S were smaller, about 20 ft across, the larger inner circles at least 50 ft across. The hairs on my arms were standing on end. No one spoke for awhile. We were all absorbed in the majesty of the moment. Elizabeth and Patrick, the young couple from Ohio, had moved deeper into the circle with dowsing rods. I was standing in the center of the first large circle of the serpent. Grace moved serenely towards me, her aged body carried in her namesake, she was gracefully at one with this precious moment, her smile radiant, she was the fat cat with the cream!

"What do you reckon Andrew, people made or aliens?"

"Great question Grace, let's go within and ask."

We both closed our eyes and allowed our roots to sink deeply within the earth. As I felt the warm sensation tingling my feet, I became aware of the breeze, and then I heard it.

"Pick me up."

It was a firm yell. I opened my eyes and scoured the circle.

"You there, yes you, pick me up... here."

The insistent voice was coming from the earth. I bent down and saw a small white stone about two inches long. I slowly pulled it into my hand. It lay there looking at me. I glanced at it, flipped it over weighed it in my palm. It was a quite unremarkable stone. I went to toss it back down, thinking it obviously wasn't this non-entity that had spoken to me.

"Why don't you use you eyes and look at me properly?" It screeched.

My heart skipped a beat. The stone that I was about to discard had bellowed at me. I froze momentarily. Then I revisited the stone, this time with intending. One side was flat, almost the shape of an arrow head, a few shallow indentations upon it, a second side looked like a foot, it was also smooth, the third and last side was a mini mountain range, with brownish coloring in the pocketed marks of the stone. It certainly seemed a more interesting stone on the second inspection, but still nothing special, no earth shattering revelation here.

"For goodness sake really look," the stone sighed incredulously.

It was as if it was hearing my thought process.

"What am I looking for," I whispered in my mind.

"Be the witness, be here, then you will see."

Nestled in one of the mountain folds of my vociferous stone, I saw the answer. It was so clear, only a fool could have missed it. Engraved unnaturally, as if it had been branded, was the perfect silhouette of an S, the snake. The exact shape of the serpent crop circle. The realization took my breath away.

"Well what do you think Andrew?" Grace's voice was right on cue.

I raised my head to meet her deep blue eyes.

"I know Grace, without a shadow of doubt I know. We are standing in a circle authentically made. I have my own proof right here".

I walked deliberately to her and shared my uncanny experience.

The two of us left that circle with deep satisfaction. It was the continuation of a profound relationship with the rock people. I had connected with stones before, but something had awakened inside of me, and I have found, especially in the undisturbed pockets of the Isles that the stones allow me in to the memories of their stories.

There are always magical signs flickering in the Universe. We have to be present enough to weave them into our walk and understand what is being offered, confirmed and remembered by them. I have met people who are determined to see faerie and they hunt hard for them. I say walk with soft eyes, if faerie wishes to reveal itself to us, it will and faerie encounters come in all shapes and sizes.

I have believed and worked with the Fae for many years. As a wee boy I found a portal in the form of a small wood. I was out on heath land exploring with a friend from school, we were both about 13 at the time and we stumbled out of Hardwick Heath, in Bury St. Edmunds, into the most magical copse that

led us to a huge cornfield. My friend's name was Peter Sibley, it is interesting for we never hung out at school, in fact we seldom got together, maybe seven or eight times over a course of one summer and when we did, we always went to the same place. We both recognized the magnitude of the place. There was a shift in how we felt. My heart beat faster, a sense that we were the only ones who walked here, the only mortals who knew this place existed. We even swore a pact to keep this magical discovery to ourselves. Keeping such a secret may seem an easy thing to do, but it wasn't. Our summers were spent on that heath land with a bunch of other kids always looking for adventure, but I never broke my oath.

I tried five years later to take a girlfriend to the moss strewn mushroom ring wonderland and it was no longer there. Had houses encroached through this space as the boundaries of the heath land were squeezed or was this amazing portal still waiting for innocent eyes and hearts to stumble across the veil? Another edge to the story of course is in the name of my friend. Peter means 'Rock', and Sibley has several interesting connotations, one is 'Brother', the other traces its roots to a title borne by various oracular priestesses, a name given to pagan prophets. So I traveled with my rock brother and priestess into the world of Fae!

Glastonbury Tor 1999 was the first time I saw tangible proof with my eyes into the faerie realm. I had chosen to ascend by the steeper path on the backside of the Tor. To the right of the path is a small copse, a ring of faerie trees that were calling to visit. I was with two other pilgrims and in honoring the teachings of the first people of North America we sat in a pipe ceremony. Part of this visionary ceremony is to be in silence and my face must have looked a real picture as I witnessed a small man about three foot tall jump out of a tree and run through the veil disappearing from view. My jaw felt like it was grazing the ground. This was my introduction to leading pilgrimages and I was initiated at the Gateway to Annwyn.

I was introduced to a new dimension of faerie. Glastonbury is the sacred Isle of Avalon and the Neolithic ancestors carved into the breast of the mother a dragon, using ox blades and red deer antlers to make the trail. This dragon serpentines the mound allowing a willing climber to ascend an octave as you scale the heights of this rough outcrop. It is a place of light and shade. I have climbed to immediately descend due to the chaotic vibration on the hill. I have slept in pure sunshine, swayed in the howling winds and on one memorable June afternoon I watched a dark storm approach from Cadbury Castle, legendary site of Camelot, and the heavens opened with a downpour fiercer than the monsoon season I experienced in India. That day I lay on the Tor to receive a healing from an ankle injury I had sustained working with Faerie at Carsaig Bay in Scotland. The person working their reiki magic on me was a pilgrim wearing a pair of pointed ears as was my 14 year old daughter who sat beside me as the rain lashed through us. In the downpour of the Tor I experienced a total cleansing, I lay in the midst of the storm as the water drops smacked into my skin causing pain and pleasure in the same instance. I opened my arms to embrace the squall, and surrounded by the faerie magic I walked differently. The following day I lay down the crutches and walked into the center circle at Stonehenge to celebrate the unfolding circle at sunset, the conclusion of the Cornwall and England pilgrimage and my healing, it was the thirteenth day since I had fallen at Carsaig, and the transformation in my physical body was complete, allowing me to drift into the spiritual and emotional aspects that were bubbling in my cauldron of inspiration.

I stayed in Glastonbury when I first went to walk the tour. I later chose to house people in the nearby city of Wells. I had ventured to the smallest city in England on my first pilgrimage to Somerset. Wells has more of a village feel that a town or city, though on a Friday and Saturday night it can get lively and there are often beggars under Penniless Porch that leads to Cathedral Green. One can even dine in the old jailhouse without fear of being locked up! Wednesday market is always a treat and in recent years they have taken to lighting up the Cathedral at night, which is a glorious sight.

One of my favorite places to stay is Canon Grange with Annette and Ken Sowden. Their 16th Century home is a comfortable dwelling bursting with antiques and charming Somerset hospitality. The house overlooks the Cathedral and though there are parking difficulties the central location to this quaint city makes it so worthwhile.

I have sat on what I call the 'village green' watching a full moon rise above the 13th century cathedral in the silent echo of a summers eve. For me Wells is a safe haven, less jagged than some of the disruptive energy that can swarm through Glastonbury's shadows and although I remind pilgrims that we are in a city and to be careful, for cities have a different demeanor than the sleepy villages we had been frequenting in Cornwall, there is a sense of safety and gentleness compared to the likes of London and even Cambridge or Salisbury. I love meandering by the moat surrounding the Bishop's Palace and heading through a gateway into a field that leads to more fields, in the center of the city you wander into rich fertile countryside.

I love making relationship with the landladies and landlords of the bed and breakfasts we stay in. I want people to go wow what a beautiful place, so I try to go back to the homes that offer the very best in Celtic hospitality. What is interesting is the demeanor of the folks in different counties and countries. There is a vast difference between the pace of life and the character traits of a Cornish Village to a Somerset City. You may still be able to get cream teas and scrumpy, but there is a marked change in the accents and the appearance of the welcome. On the whole my experience is that Cornish people are earthy with big hugs, wide grins, with stories to tell and a twinkle in the eye. Somerset natives tend to be more reserved, some might say stiff upper lip, but to me they are like a refined wine that when you first sip you sense a warmth and a comfortable glow and after a couple of glasses, the walls come down and the naughty natives come out to play. One of the bed and breakfasts owners that always provides top notch service is Dennis Gripper of Bekynton House. A few years back I had a group of seven pilgrims staying with him and one morning they sulkily boarded the minibus and complained about their accommodation. I was surprised for I have been working with Dennis for a number of years and his house is beautiful. The mumblings and rumblings were that Dennis did not appear to be very friendly. Later that day I went to see Dennis to see what was going on. Dennis must have been in his early 70's and yet his demeanor has always been sprightly. He invited me into his home with a smile and the kettle was on for tea. "These folk are a bit more reserved than the usual groups you bring." Dennis' statement brought a smile in my heart. Its amazing how two groups can perceive each other as being standoffish. What I needed was a bridge and Dennis willingly obliged by building it. Before I could say too much Dennis jumped into a story:

> *"It's been an interesting journey running a bed and breakfast, you get all sorts of people coming to your door. I remember years ago opening the door to a young couple, a girl from Germany and a young man from Italy, they asked if I had any rooms available and I did, the one that has the private bathroom. I showed them the room and left them to settle in. They stayed for three nights and then after their final breakfast the young man came to pay the bill and he only gave me half the money. I asked him if he was paying for his lady friend too and he looked me earnestly in the eye and said I don't know her, we only met when we both came to your door looking for a single room. You put us in together so we thought that must be what you do here."*

Dennis' deadpan delivery had me in stitches, how could anyone ever think of Dennis as reserved! Once I shared this tale with the pilgrims whatever was not

sparking in their relationship clicked in now as the ice was once and truly broken. Humor is a beautiful connector. May the power of tickling laughter be upon you! Finally if they had just known the meaning of Dennis' name they would have discovered some of the Celtic lilting laugh. Dennis means 'Follower of the Wine God' and Gripper is 'Foot First'! So they were stepping foot first into a precious concoction of the Gods!

Perspective is reality. When we flip the switch to embrace a bigger picture and put ourselves with passion into that picture new worlds open their doors and invite us in. I was working in a school once and I asked the students to describe Scrooge in one word. I have since asked the question to many audiences and the overwhelming response has been: "Miser," "Stingy," "bah humbug." What would your word be? My word is "Wonderful."

Audiences often have a knee jerk reaction, "What do you mean wonderful?"

"I say that he is the most free spirited giver, a keeper of the flame of the season." the audience have moved from puzzled faces to a gradual understanding and yet often someone will cry,

"Yeah but that's not until the end of the story." and I say, "Interesting so which part of the story are you stuck in?" Is our past holding us so tightly that we can not breath in the present moment and see the transformation within ourselves and others? It is in our willingness to release the old patterns of negativity to make room for a new weave, a space for brighter more luminous colors of every hue to flow in our life. Be gentle with the old frayed garments for they have served us well in getting us to who we are today, without those threads we would not be the person that stands inside of us. Let us dust, clean recycle and release for each of us there are closets in our past that need to be aired out. Whatever our past it is time to let go of being the victim and begin embracing the hero of our own life story.

Chapter 7

THE TALE, THE TELLER AND THE LAND OF TWO LAKES

KEVIN'S SONG

Where Kevin was the eagles came

Down from the highest mountain tame,

And sat amongst the other birds,

to hear the wisdom of his words.

The speckled trout would swiftly guide

To the reedy waters side

And there the mountain deer would stand

To eat the green moss from his hand.

The snarling wolf and savage boar

Lay down together at his door

And so defied all natural laws

About the cave where Kevin was.

The Story of Kevin

Nestled in the valley of two lakes, where three rivers the Avonbeg, the Avonmore and the Avoca surge together at the 'Meeting of the Waters' is one of this world's most beautiful and magical glens. The heart of the valley is named Glendalough after the upper and lower lakes, a modern variation of Gleann Da Locha which simply translated means the valley of the two lakes. Glendalough is where St. Kevin sank his roots in the 6th century through the granite of this glacial valley, way down into the fertile soil in this world and the underworld and he made love to the land.

There are many tales attached to Kevin's story, that Kevin was born of royal birth at the Fort of the White Fountain, he was fed on a tree of paradise, which in the Celtic world is a blessed cow, white with red ears, a faerie cow, Brighid's cow, and its said he supped on this never ending supply of milk, which to the Celt is more than just milk. This nutritious opaque fluid full of vitamins, protein, lactose and yummy fats is a rich source of poetry, and supposedly Kevin was weaned on this nourishing nectar for a year and a day.

Kevin's connections to the fay are a constant in his story. He was baptized and no less than 12 shining ones were said to have witnessed the naming ceremony. His mother Cavella called him Caveyin, Kevin, which means Beautiful Shining Birth.

I particularly like the legend of the three monks who challenge him to go into the woods and bring back fire by carrying it in his bosom. On his return he brings a bright flame and has no burns in his cloak. So is this literal or figurative? To the Celt it is most definitely yes and yes. As I have sat with this part of his tale I conjure images of an ancestral vision quest. Kevin goes to find that divine spark within him, the embers to light the passion in his own heart. When we seek guidance from spirit and are willing to sit and listen, as Kevin does deep within the woods, deep within his soul, we will open ourselves to magical visions. Kevin receives guidance from a shining one instructing him to go to Glendalough.

His many adventures are linked with his absorption into the natural world. Kevin is like the Ovates of old, the wild ones who seek the wisdom of the ages in solitude. He makes his home in what is now known as St. Kevin's bed, a small cave that at its widest is no more than four feet across and about three feet high. To visit this carved opening perched high on a perilous precipice is a dangerous trek today and not recommended for obvious safety reasons. For Kevin it was a tiny resting place for his weary head, it is also an entry point into the mother's womb, the underworld and a rebirthing chamber.

Writings claim that he would stand in the freezing waters of the lakes for hours upon end, inferring his desire to connect with the shining ones. These waters represent another entry point into the underworld. It is here that he befriends an otter that rescues his breviary from sinking into the depths of darkness in the icy waters of the upper lake. He befriends the otter and from that day forth the otter brings him a fish that they share for breakfast.

His connection to the animal world is legendary. A blackbird builds a nest in his outstretched hand as he sits in contemplation. He shares with pilgrims that all they need to learn is in his hand. I ponder my own willingness to approach each and every moment with the imagery of an open palm, so I might be open and receptive to all that comes across my path, that I may be a connector to offer the safe sanctuary of home in my handshake, my touch, that my reach may cross all boundaries with a sense of peace and well being, that the fragility of life has the opportunity to hatch from the egg and fly with great strength as the blackbirds did from Kevin's palm.

He continued to build relationships with creatures throughout his life, deer, wolves, boar, dogs and eventually humankind. His isolation from the world of two leggeds prepares him for his return, to bring the gifts of his learning to help the community prosper.

He established and built a monastery in the Valley of the Two Lakes in the 6th century, and when his body gave way and his heart stopped beating it is said that there were more forest animals and winged ones in attendance at his funeral than people, it was also reputed that shining ones flocked to his death as they had to his birth.

The Treasure of the Tale

The tumbled ruins of the monastery complete with a fine example of a 10th to 12th Century Round Tower are scattered on the landscape accessible 24 hours a day, 7 days a week.

My first visit to this spectacular nemeton was in 2002, and I stayed then and look always to stay in a cozy bed and breakfast with breath taking views looking over the lower lake. This sumptuous abode is the home of Penny and Pat Kelleher who are a delight to Ireland's glinting green. In Pat's words; 'We tend to conduct our B & B business here in Glendalough in a somewhat unorthodox fashion in so far as we are less interested in the commercial gain than the experience of being hosts to "nice" people. For that reason we are pleased to welcome you again Andrew as well as your friends. A real slice of Celtic hospitality!

It was from Penny and Pat's sumptuous abode that I met up with the small group of pilgrims who were off to spend their day in love and trust amongst the sun lit paths and creeping shadows of this treasure filled dell.

The previous evening the small group of travelers had gathered in the graveyard of crumbling monastery. Underneath the sheltered boughs of a maturing evergreen we discussed St. Kevin's love of all nature. You may recall that his name is infused with the shimmering sidhe, meaning beautiful shining birth. So for the pilgrims the following day would be a birthing for each and every one of them, as they followed in the footsteps of the ancestors and went on a quest on the land. Just like when Kevin sat so still that a blackbird nested in his outstretched hand, so the band of intrepid seekers would find the nooks and crannies that called and they too would silently witness the worlds around and within them. And as Kevin had been sent into the woods in his youth to bring back fire, to carry it in his bosom, so would the pilgrims seek their fire, the lightning bolt of passion in their hearts, to find the magic in their heartsong, to stir the cauldron of their hearts calling. Just as Kevin raised his consciousness of his life's mission as he followed his path to Glendalough. So the pilgrims would seek their vision with the courage to live their truth.

My experience of life is that many people are waiting to die, our fear of being who we truly are feeds the mediocrity of a stringent society that lures us with a mindless drivel of pettiness. So many people are wrapped up in the mall, the home depots of the world, the fancy cars and widescreen TV's. A society that readily recognizes a picture of Sponge Bob Square Pants and has no idea what the difference between a Rowan tree and a North American Mountain Ash, said tongue in cheek, they are the same tree! Or fail to distinguish the difference or even recognize a beech tree and a birch is a sad reflection of the boxes we have trapped ourselves in.

Have you realized that when we wake up in the morning we are in a box? We climb out of the bed, open the door to the box, move through other boxes until we reach the box called the kitchen, then many people will pour their breakfast from a box, and sit in the box eating out of the box. When its time to leave the box, we open the front door of the box and climb into a mechanical box, which we drive to a huge box that we call work. We go through thin boxes, long boxes, wide boxes, large boxes, and some people stuff themselves into fluorescently lit miniscule boxes that they know as cubicles. We spend the day hunched over in the boxes until it is time to get back into the mechanical box and drive to the box we call home. We go in the box and most people turn on the box and sit in the box watching the box! Whoa, I am sure you have heard of the saying 'think outside the box', well we don't have to go far, we need to breath, our ancestors knew to do this and by doing so lived in the moment. So take many moments and go outside and breath in the truth of this authentic ancestral activity.

Going outside and feeling our feet connected to the ancient mother and connecting to our breath was as commonplace a practice for the Celtic people as surfing the net is to today's generation.

So the pilgrims stood in the light misting drizzle and felt their feet getting heavy. When we allow our roots to go way down into the earth, we pull the energy from the Calliach's cauldron, the rich bubbling brew of life from the center of the earth, through the soles of our feet and we feel this energy seep up into our bones, our flesh, soaking us, feeding us, slowly flowing through the tendons, into each muscle, into the fiber of our being, swirling in the Cauldron of Warming, our belly where we exist, the place where all of our nourishment goes, and then we allow that juicy succulent life force to continue spiraling up, until it reaches the heart, our cauldron of Calling, our thinking center, where we act upon living our life's purpose, where we have the opportunity to listen and dance our own unique rhythm. Now we allow the energy of the heavens to drip a golden thread through the crown of our head, we feel it sliding, caressing, nurturing our Cauldron of Wisdom, the place where we know more than we think we know, activating our throat so we can speak our truth clearly and succinctly until it reaches its tendrils towards our heart, and now the bridge, from roots and wings, weaves a Celtic thread in our heart which glows inside of us, we then feel the energy vibrantly shining in us and allow that energy to flow in all directions, through the air, waters, earth, through the passion of our own fire to connect with all other beings seen and unseen in this world, the worlds between the worlds and beyond, and as a Celtic knot it returns to us allowing us to feel the connecting fabric of all that is and ever was.

It was from this grounded place that the pilgrims prepared to go on Quest in silence, listening, noticing, being the witness is a powerful gift. My birth mother's face looked far more tranquil in the light of the morn than it had the night before. My mother was about to set off on her first day of silence.

To give you a lead into her qualms of being in silence on the land, let me share with you a small part of her journey in reaching this tranquil glen. When my mother had first asked me about accompanying me on one of the pilgrimages I balked. I love my mum, and I was acutely aware that she was not cognizant of all that I do in my work and play. So I prayed on it and was shown clearly that my mother was a welcome addition to our motley crew of misfit seekers who confunded muggles and saw the blurred edge of worlds with soft eyes. My mother is articulate, sensitive, and has an abundance of energy, she is someone who is always on the go and is a mover and shaker. She had arrived in Ireland and thrown herself into the stories and wanderings with a gay abandon. However by our third day, coinciding with our arrival in Glendalough, she asked if she could travel with me to a neighboring town to go to the bank rather than have free time moseying around Laragh, the monastery and the hiking trails past the moss covered woodland copses, beside the gurgling river which would run fast and white on one side of the bridge, and inch its way slowly, dark and black on the other. I was puzzled why anyone on this trip would choose the money bank over the river bank, but I gladly accepted her request to join me. We had no sooner trundled past the local woolen mill than the tears flowed freely and rapidly down her cheeks.

"What's the matter?" I asked urgently.

"I feel useless," was her garbled reply. "I feel I should be helping someone in their garden, or cooking the breakfast. All these people are happy to sit and be. I don't know how to do that, I know how to do. I understand all this work you are doing with the ancestors, I get that piece, but come on now, you all believe in faeries! What is that about? I don't believe in faeries."

My reply was that she was exactly where she needed to be, I let her cry, and invited her to let everything unfold.

So later that day, I faced the pilgrims sitting by the worn gravestones in the cemetery of Glendalough. It was as if Kevin was reaching through the vines that clutched to stone and bark, and a blackbird perched on a nearby tree sat patiently watching us, listening to the preparations for the morning adventure, waiting for my mother to sing her truth. When she finally spoke her voice rang clearly and heavily with fear, determination and anticipation etched on her breath.

Gathered in the graveyard in the betwixt and between she once more affirmed, this time to the group, that she did not believe in faeries. She was not sure if she was going on quest, and was very uncertain of being quiet for the whole day. The pilgrims listened and added no judgments, no comments. I reiterated that the quest was a choice, to go in love in trust, to honor other pilgrim's silence and to follow where their hearts guided them. My mother found acceptance and permission to live in her truth. With this permission she was ready to walk into the wilderness of her own soul.

I asked that if anyone was fasting for the whole day to let Penny know so their breakfast was not wasted, and to let each other know if they were choosing to be in silence from the moment they awoke so as not to disturb each other with needless chatter. I gave them a meeting time to send them out onto the land, and a return time to gather at the upper lake to celebrate the journey and sing our thanks for the gifts bestowed.

The following morning we gathered in a natural alcove, where the river splashes down the forested mountainside, the moss glistens, and a huge rock shelters all that are within its presence. We smudged in juniper and sage, I offered everyone an animal card to support their quest and honor the nature spirits, the land, Kevin and the abundant wildlife in this National Park. I then shared the story that I always tell before sending people on day quests and Celtic three night vision quests. It is a story that echoes Rhiannon's tale, and is dedicated to my daughter Aylish. It is one of her favorites, and since I am often away on pilgrimage for her birthday, this tale of life, death, rebirth, keeps our connection across the Atlantic and deeply rooted through the veil. Her middle name is Rose and the main characters name is Rose, who is undoubtedly one of our heroes. Rose the gift of sight and healing.

May stillness be upon your thoughts and silence upon your tongue! For I tell you a tale that was told at the beginning... the one tale worth the telling.

The Tale of Rose

A beautiful callous Queen sat spinning in her castle watching the snowdrift across the distant meadows on a bleak mid-winters morn. The castle butcher had sacrificed a sow for the evenings feast and the warm blood was seeping into the stark white blanket covering the earth. Her gaze was affixed to the harbinger of death, the large raven hovering above the crimson stain, pecking at the rich offering of fresh blood.

The Queen stood and added an icy blast to the frigid wind, calling from her desperate heart. "I wish I had a daughter whose skin was as white as the snow, whose lips were as red as blood, and whose hair was as black as the Raven. I would swap my 12 sons to have such a daughter." This thought had swam around her head so often, but now she spat it onto the sudden storm that whipped a stinging wind and hammering snow from the heavens, and as all word magic it spun onto the air seeking to yield a rich harvest in the cycle of the seasons. The Queen's eyes were fixed hard on the Raven, an icy blue blast of frosted glare, and her chin jutted like brittle stone

"Your words are wicked, and they will come true." A rasping cackle brought an eerie chill that swept through the halls making the Queens hair stand on end. The high-pitched screech continued from the wrinkled mouth of a toothless, hairy chinned hag with blazing red eyes.

"You will indeed give birth to a daughter and in doing so you will never see your 12 sons again."

The Queen desperately sought the old crone partly to chastise her and partly to have her take back the words that echoed with a ring of authenticity twisting and stabbing at her hardened heart.

"No," shrieked the Queen as the hag vanished in the swirling blustery squall of driving snow.

"Guards seek out the old witch who disturbs my peace and threatens my sons". The guards searched avidly in the castle grounds and the deserted streets to no avail.

"I will not lose my sons even if I do have a daughter" schemed the Queen who ordered the 12 young men to be locked up in the tallest tower. The princes were not amused. The space was cramped, the arguments many, squabbles, fighting, testosterone flying, and the smell from the farting and belching left many a footman giddy.

From the Winter Solstice to the Autumn Equinox the tower door proved to be a more than adequate prison, but as the balance between the day and night birthed a thirteenth child, a daughter, an amazing transformation seized the princes in the tower, their necks stretched thin and long, their arms sprouted wings, their lips hardened into sun drenched orange beaks, their eyes blackened and their feet stretched flat and webbed. Where 12 men had stood, 12 swans now flew, gracefully and purposefully they soared out the open window, singing their songs of freedom, fleeing the stark jail that had imprisoned their restless spirits, and the beating of their wings carried them away from the castle and the Queen.

The exhausted mother found joy and sorrow in an instant, for as she looked into the bright blue pools of her newborn, smiling radiantly at the sound of the infants nightingale song, the screeching release of the fleeing swansong reverberated in her ear as a strangled chorus pecking sharply at her, for she knew they were her sons and she knew without a shadow of a doubt she would never see them again.

So it was that Rose grew up always feeling as if something was missing from her life, that something tangible was an arms length away, yet when she reached for it the veil revealed only an ache in her heart and more questions in her brain. The answers she received were vague and misleading, and no one uttered a word about her 12 missing brothers until she reached the transformation age. As she stepped into the bewitching hour of her birth 13 years from the fateful flight, the midwife that had birthed her and all the boys spilled the beans.

"Young Rose, what you seek is not within these walls, your siblings have flown the nest. Twelve sturdy boys cursed to fly as swans by day because of you Rose. You were the treasure that your mother bartered with for their souls. Find them and you will also find another piece of you. Do you have the courage to leave the sanctuary of the castle, the warmth of the hearth, the softness of your feathered bed? Will you fly Rose into the darkness and uncertainty of the wild wood? Go beyond the boundaries of the land you know with only your heart to guide you? If it be yes take bread and cheese and steal through the side gate before your mother gets wind of your plans and locks you in the tower and pawns you off for some dowry for the drooling love of a rich aging King."

Rose's jaw clenched and her resolve was set. She would not rest until she had tracked the whereabouts of her long lost kin. Rose's rich clothes and soft pale skin was soon weathered and worn by the savage storms, tangled thorns and burning sun. Travel stained and weary she sat at the edge of a stream and unwrapped the last vestiges of her victuals. Her spirits low, lost and forlorn.

"Spare a crust for a hungry old crone," squawked a toothless hag who stumbled hunchbacked toward her.

"I don't have much and you are welcome to half," beamed Rose, grateful for the company, the chance to talk to someone invigorated her, and she animatedly shared her quest to find her brothers. The old one listened intently sucking and chewing determinedly on the stale crust. Washing down the crumbs with the clean spring water she fixed her beady black eyes on Rose and squawked:

"Follow the stream until it reaches the sea. There you will find a long house with 12 long beds in it. By day wild swans soar through the sky, by night 12 men walk upon the earth. These are those you seek."

Before Rose could turn and thank the wizened shrew, she had disappeared deftly into the shadows of a dense thicket of brambles leading into the darkest recesses of the wood, the way Rose had come and was glad to leave behind.

With lightness to her step she flowed as water, tumbling her course toward the depth of the sea. As the sun glowed gold across the gentle waves and slowly descended in a rich splash of purples across the sky, 12 pairs of wings beat to the rhythm of the tide, and as the webbed feet gracefully glided over the waters edge 12 men walked from the crest of the wave onto the sandy shore where Rose waited to greet them.

Twelve god like silhouettes elegantly kissed white granules with dancing feet as they whispered their way towards the open arms of Rose. A moment etched in time, an echo of Rose's fractured past, surreal, a fresh moist painting absorbing into the canvas of her life, beautifully illustrated in the annuals of her mind. Every pore in her adolescent body radiated with surrendered joy so the splintered screech of corrupt anger that dislodged the scene into a murky madness, a torrent of rage, was an unexpected disturbance that split the night and shattered the essential portrait of hope into a blurred and muddy mess.

"Kill her!" Bellowed 12 contorted voices whose bodies distorted into monstrous muscle, clenched fists, taught manic grins, pulsating veins ripping through their wrathful throats as they converged on their prey.

"It was because of a woman that we are trapped in this state, and we vowed we would kill the first women we met, annihilate the slut!"

"Stop! You know not what you do," croaked a primordial hum that ricocheted through frenzied minds.

From out of the shadows crept the misshapen form of the ancient hag. Her eyes blistered through the thick darkness that hung so heavily on the air. "This is your sister Rose, and if you wish to be healed it will be through her not in spite of her. Now make your decision to hug her or hurt her, to nurture you or neglect you, for your fates are all intertwined in the connecting strands of the web of life"

With a rasping cackle the wise ones wisdom hung on the air and she drifted into the dusky twilight with a trace of remembrance seeping into the hearts of the reunited kin.

With hugs and laughter the 13 siblings became acquainted around the glowing embers of a dancing fire. As stories were told to call in the dawn light, a basket was woven from the harvested vines of a willing willow. As the first sunrays sparkled their song on the sea the brothers sprouted wings and luxurious white feathers replaced milky white skin. Rose knew the basket was for her comfort and hoisted herself inside. The swans clamped their beaks securely onto twigs and stem and heaved Rose into the air. Powerful wings surged on the wind and Rose was transported to a fruitful Island where honey seemed to drip from the trees.

A large cave called to young Rose, its mouth swallowed her and she lay on the cool damp rock and dreamtime enveloped her. Lying in the ancestral womb Rose journeyed to the heart of the cavern, to the center of a complex labyrinth where the Fata Morgana, Queen of the fay, Mother of the shining ones, shimmered in a luminous light, hovering in serene authority, awaiting her approach. Not a word was spoken and yet all thoughts were conveyed easily and effortlessly.

The silence was broken only once, by Rose, who screamed "Yes!" onto the wind. Affirming her agreement, accepting the quest offered by the Fata Morgana. If Rose wished to heal her brothers she must gather bundles of stinging nettles and intricately weave 12 shirts from this herbaceous plant. A task easier said than done for these harmless looking organisms emit a painful burn from the miniscule hairs that adorn both leaves and stem. An intense stinging pain followed by red and white blotchy blisters and severe skin irritation await an encounter with the pricking needles of the Urtica Dioca. The Queen of the Fay's demands was stringent. Not only was the acidic burning plant to be picked on new and full moons, the task was to be completed in silence. Not one word, not a single sound, whether in laughter or tears, could be uttered from Rose for the duration of the quest. A charge, if accepted, would consume Roses's teenage life. So her shrieked agreement was the last sound to pass through her lips for many a year.

Her brothers soon let Rose be. They had tried to make her laugh, included her in their conversations to no avail, watched woefully at the blisters that formed on the swelling wounds that evoked cries of anguish from the boys and a stoic silence from Rose, and this quiet stillness had a firm impact on them. They understood that her refusal to speak was connected profoundly to their healing. So on a Samhain dawn, 12 wild swans took to the skies leaving Rose surrounded by nettles and the weaving of one shirtsleeve.

Rose watched as the specks that were her brothers disappeared in the morning haze, she knew they would not return until her quest was done, her silence too painful for them. She sat at the entrance to her cave breaking her fast, both mourning the morning and celebrating the coming of a new year. She made an offering to the land before nibbling on a piece of cake and was about to reach for the fresh nettles when a strikingly handsome young man rode past on a gallant steed. Their eyes locked and in that moment they both saw their destiny, that each others lives were already tattooed on the stars and though Rose did not say it, she was thinking "What a fine piece of ass, I'd ride into the sunset with him, I'd ride into the sunset on him!" Such basic urges swept through her body bringing a stinging color to her cheeks, which had nothing to do with the blazing nettles.

Two hearts beating as one, aligned to the woven strands of the summer solstice sunlight, threaded on the dew, ripened in the soil and infused into the green nettles of the fading harvest by Aine of Knockaine, goddess of love and growth. How quickly their love took root, cultivating the finest blossom. He was none other than a prince and so Rose married into Royalty and all was well. Except for Rose's voluntary silence, her lost brothers and her love's mother, the reigning Queen, who took an instant dislike to Rose. She watched her daughter in law scythe and gather her crop on a burgeoning moon and malevolent seeds were planted and copiously watered in the Queen's devious mind. Ploughed, scattered, jealously tended until a spiteful plan grew like twisted thorns around an unsuspecting Rose.

For other seeds were at work, Rose's belly pushed forth with new life, and a child of the dark was born at Yule, the shortest day, where dark is dark indeed. All through the agonizing pain of childbirth Rose uttered no words, no screams of pain, no singing lullabies or cooing noises to welcome the gift of her son into the world.

As the mother and babe lay sleeping in Rose's bedchamber, the Queen stole through the night and seized the tot from Rose's arms, she tiptoed up the stairwell of the tallest tower and hurled the child off the battlements. The wailing infant plummeted to the rocky precipice below and was snapped up in the jaws of a waiting wolf.

The conniving Queen stalked in a ghostly silence into Rose's chamber and poured the blood of a dead dog from a frosted vial onto the bed sheets and Roses lily white hands, As the red liquid life force seeped into the crisp linens leaving a darkened stain of death the Queen cried "Murder, Rose has killed her baby!"

With accusations ringing off the castle walls, the court stirred rapidly as if ants were protecting their hill so courtiers appeared, as if crawling through the woodwork, until a swarm of curious onlookers jockeyed for position in the presence of a startled and frighteningly confused Rose.

"Rose is a murderer, she must die1" Shrieked the Queen.

"Kill her, hang her, burn her!" Screeched the bloodthirsty mob incited by the gory scene and the Queens indomitable accusation.

As the chilling words "murderer, " "baby," " killed," poked painfully through the cobwebs of Roses clouded mind an overwhelming grief seized her body, yet not one word, not a single sound of sorrow escaped from her lips.

"Take her to the dungeons," bellowed the victorious Queen.

"Stop," it was but a whisper that barked louder than the crash of thunder and was as fast as a lightning bolt in bringing the frenzied rabble to heel. All eyes focused on the face of the prince who strode purposefully into the room. His eyes met the innocent glazed stare of his beloved Rose and then swept to meet the combative glare of his deranged mother.

"Rose did not kill our son, she loves him as the oak tree loves water and sunlight, with the determination of the salmon to return to its home. I do not know what wicked sorcery transpired here tonight, but I do know that Rose would never harm our son."

As the prince keened savagely for the loss of his boy, Rose's shattered heart wept a silent storm that threatened to tear her body apart as her soul splintered into pieces.

In the settling gloom that racked at Rose's sanity, she found comfort in the sharp bite of the stinging nettle spikes and the raw blisters she willingly accepted from her dogged work on the seventh shirt. Her pace quickened as new life grew in her womb. The tempestuous sadness that hung thickly like a permanent fog on the misty moors were dazzlingly pierced by the bright rays of birth on a fresh Imbolc morn. Again Rose let no whimper or wail soil the air as a daughter, Brighid sucked in her first breath and was nuzzled to her breast.

The death of her son would never be forgotten and the life of her daughter was a celebration beyond the fertile rites of spring. Rose's unconditional love radiated from her heart speaking volumes in a language that went way beyond the capability of the spoken word. A peaceful rest upon mother and child as the rising of the Rowan moon was upon them. A deep peaceful sleep that was carefree and oblivious to the stirrings of cruel hatred that rustled through the drafty passageways leading to the sanctuary of soporific dreams.

The uncomfortable current of cool air blew threw the crevices of the castle wall and settled fiendishly by Rose's side. The Queen scooped up the sleeping child and skulked up the stairwell of the tallest tower and hurled the child off the battlements. The wailing infant plummeted to the rocky precipice below and was snapped up in the jaws of a waiting wolf.

The scheming Queen prowled in jubilant silence into Rose's chamber and poured the blood of a dead dog from a frosted vial onto the bed sheets. Smearing death on Roses lily white hands, delicately dabbing the stain of destruction onto her sparkling bright teeth, As the red liquid life force seeped into the pores, tarnishing skin and soiling enamel with the rich stain of death the Queen cried "Murder, Rose has killed her baby!"

With accusations buzzing off the castle walls, the court swarmed swiftly as if bees on honey, until a cluster of curious onlookers pressed and pushed for pole position in the presence of a startled and frighteningly confused Rose.

"Rose is a murderer, she must die, she has eaten her baby!" Shrieked the Queen.

"Kill her, hang her, burn her!" Screeched the horror-struck horde swayed by the gruesome scene and the Queens indomitable indictment.

As the unnerving sense of déjà vu rippled through the corridors of time and the gut wrenching accusations pierced through the hazy cloud of broken dreams, an overwhelming grief gripped Rose, freezing time and space in a perpetual nightmare, yet not one word, not a single sound of sorrow escaped from her lips.

"Take her to the dungeons no-one can save you this time sweet Rose," cackled the exultant Queen.

"Stop." It was but a murmur that stole the breath away and settled on the harried throng like a virgin snow. All eyes, all ears were alert to the anguished face of the prince who limped reluctantly into the crowded chamber. His eyes sought the grief stricken glare of his beloved Rose and then shifted to meet the disparaging glower of his disapproving mother.

"Rose, tell us you did not kill our daughter. Speak to me Rose. If you will not speak and clear your name who will? I can't save you this time. Please for the love of our children tell us all that you are not the monster that feasted on her young."

As the prince keened savagely for the loss of his daughter, Rose's splintered heart wept a silent reverie that threatened to rip her mind apart as her soul fractured into pieces. In a dumb trance she was dragged with her bags of nettles and flung into a reeking piss stained cell. There in the pitch black of fright, left with the inconceivable thought that she had gnawed and chewed upon the flesh of her own, she wailed within, a torrent of silent screams that slashed and tore brutally through the eternity of time. As her spirit broke, decimated beyond reprieve, her fingers worked instinctively threading and weaving, sewing and tying until her blistered hands were as raw as her heart.

The coming of dawn brought no light into Rose's world, she numbly hobbled past the jeering crowds and surrendered to her executioners demands as her hands were violently forced behind her back and tightly tied to a stake. She was vaguely aware of the bags of nettles heaped carelessly at her feet as a funeral pyre was built with Rose's thin blotched body the sacrifice, the wicker woman, the wanton witch. The crowing Queen stepped forth with a blazing torch and amid the surging and screaming of the jubilant throng of the townsfolk, she lit the dry brittle wood and watched in wonder as the flames swept toward the accepting Rose.

At first the Queen thought it was the drum roll of the executioners song, then she convinced herself that it was thunder and that the blaze must burn rapidly before the rains washed out the fire, and finally she succumbed to the truth that the loud steady beating came from the powerful wings of 12 wild swans.

The eager crowd directed their curious gazes to the sky as the swans swept toward the flames and working in unison they beat the savage inferno to a wisping trail of smoke. All was ravished except the delicate Rose and the stinging thorn shirts of dry nettles. As the swans pecked diligently at the binding ropes around Roses wrists the community looked on in awe. Life surged through Roses veins as she reached for shirt after shirt and flung them over the protecting bevy of swans. To the sheer amazement of the bemused onlookers, where webbed feet and flocks of singed feathers had fluttered on the breeze, 12 men now stood strong and true. Rose flung her arms around her beaming brothers and released her first words on the wind, "I am innocent I did not kill my babies!"

Rose's clear authoritative tone rang with authenticity and the gasping crowd bowed their heads with shame or looked accusingly at the Queen who was slinking into the shadows.

"Clear a path," wheezed a shrill piercing cackle. The toothless old hag wizened and wise shuffled her way firmly towards the transformed family and added two drops of pure sunshine to the already dazzling scene. For trotting alongside her was a shining bonnie boy and wrapped in a shawl of golden thread with the sweetest breath was a newborn babe, a wee enchanting lass.

"These are your children Rose, I shape shifted into the waiting wolf and I rescued them and raised them to be returned to you on this day of celebration, renewal, remembering and transformative power." Tears of joy swept unabashedly down Rose's cheeks as she embraced the delicious memory of moment, the unfolding of her grandest vision, without limitations, and all was well with the world and with the worlds between the worlds, for she had not finished one of the 12 shirts, a sleeve of unpicked nettles was left dangling on a vine, and one of her brothers stood beside her in the body of a man with one swan wing.

The Treasure of the Tale

From the very onset of this magical tale the threads of the colors of life death rebirth, of morning, night & the betwixt and between, of the upper, middle and lower worlds, the deep black of raven, the sparkling white of the snow and the gleaming red of blood weave intricately into the darkest depths of shadow, the brightest rays of light and the center of the heart beating authentically to the very core of courage, truth and love. How many of us throw harmful words on the wind neglecting to see and appreciate what we have? Do we secretly covet some fleeting fancy or perhaps worthy goal with a willingness to trade the precious pieces of our lives because we do not see them so? The Queen mutters "I would give up my 12 sons for a daughter: Ouch, the word magic returns with alarming speed to grant her request. So what words do we say to ourselves and to the Universe to manifest our dreams? Do we spend time trying to lock others into our vision as the Queen did, taking away the freedom of her sons so she can have it all? How are we holding other people hostage to our version of how life should be? Do we have the courage of Rose to leave the sanctity of safety to walk through the dark fears of the unknown? Are we willing to share what we have with a stranger or are we always complaining that our pockets are empty? In sharing her last crust willingly Rose finds the way to the edge of the world where her brothers reside. Their automatic response is to seek to kill her. Where are we striking out at someone who is trying to help us because of our past hurts entombing us in our story? Do we spend time truly listening to Spirit? Are we willing to go through the greatest challenge honoring our oaths and doing the work even when our critics would try to destroy us? Where are we looking to belittle or crush someone who does it differently than us? Are we deliberately looking to undermine someone in our life right now? Rose is branded a murderer thrown into the dungeons deep and instead of hosting her own pity party she continues weaving shirts in pitch darkness with a heart that is breaking, hands blistered and swollen with the appearance of losing everything. What do we believe in that generates such passion, determination and trust?

The Tale of the Land

With the silent bravery of Rose hanging magically on the mists the pilgrims followed their hearts and rambled their way upon their chosen path. I stood watching until the last figure slipped through the veil and out of sight.

My mother was one of the first to leave and one of the last to return and there was a new bounce to her step as she danced her way into the waiting circle as the day flickered towards the pursuing night. Under the boughs of the evergreen with a chirping Robin as our witness the pilgrims shared the adventures of their day. My mother spoke with the same rich quality as Rose's first words proclaiming her innocence. Her deep blue eyes held us all transfixed as she invited us to share the mystery of the essential secret of her day.

"Last night I had a dream," She crooned, "and in my dream I sat in this luminous grove where the water sparkled in pools of stillness and also surged vibrantly forward with its streaking white mane splashing carefree over rocks and tree limbs and all objects that stood in its path, a magnificent blend of the masculine and feminine, a pool to remember, a pool to sit and dwell upon the mysterious meaning of life. Well imagine my surprise and my absolute delight when on my wanderings, today on my quest, I stumbled upon the exact same pool of water. As I sat listening to the river's song I saw clearly that I am that fast paced white water, I am a mover and a shaker, I get things done, and then I looked into the sweet still eddy and I recognized that this is me too. I can sit and be, I can breath on purpose in the stillness of the moment, and I am a powerful being on this planet. As I giggled with a gleeful heart my eyes were drawn to something incomprehensible. Now this might not seem so strange to some of you." She challenged, "but it was blooming weird to me. In the stream was a stone the shape of a human heart and it was beating, it was moving. I have never seen a stone move like that before. On my children's life the stone was pounding to the rhythm of life. I sat there for some time in awe. I became pure stillness not wanting to interrupt the importance of this space. My heart connected to the stone heart and we merged together, we melted and were soft and permeable, with a firmness and strength of rock. When I felt it was time to leave this sacred space I walked in wonder leaving grateful footprints on the earth where St. Kevin had once trod. After I had strolled about fifty feet along the path I heard a voice tell me to head back and sit for a while longer by the wise waters of the magical pool. I turned to trace my steps to this peaceful nemeton and it was not there. It vanished into thin air. It was completely and utterly gone." She gazed at us all incredulously and I let out a full belly laugh.

"Well Mum, that's what you get when you come to Ireland on pilgrimage with a bunch of folk who work with nature spirits and you say you don't believe in faeries!" It was my mum's first faerie encounter and she has had many more since.

The land speaks volumes in the valley of the two lakes, St. Kevin never fails to offer an open hearted pilgrim 'a beautiful shining birth', feral goats and deer abound and the majesty of nature sings as blissfully now as it did before the Sons of Mil settled on this land. The shining ones hop leap and skip glowingly in this dell and just like the shimmering green moss, which in the Celtic world means abundance, they are peeking from every tree, stone, flower, and bush. Rose's story is full of mythical meanings and shamanic pathways for us all to explore and my mum's innocent cry gave her the gift of sight and allowed healing to vibrate in the worlds between the worlds. Power of the gift of sight on you, power of healing on you, power of the courage of Rose on you, power of a beautiful shining birth on you, power of innocence and magical belief on you, power of Glendalough on you.

Chapter 8

INTO THE BOGLAND OF IRELAND

A triple death sacrifice occurred when a member of the clan was selected to be offered in a macabre death ritual containing three mortal blows, like that of the Lindow Man, whom we will tell tale of shortly. This may have been more of a challenge for the Celtic tribes living on the Burren. Whereas much of Ireland is famous for its bogs where peat preserves wood for thousands of years, the Burren is a desolate moonscape with no trees to hang a sacrifice, not enough water for a drowning and so many thick rocks that burying someone would be a pile driving strenuous pickaxe and drilling extravaganza into the underworld. You may have heard of the 'bog people' whose preserved bodies have been discovered all across Europe. These peat wetlands provide cold acidic oxygen free conditions which prevent decay and as a result the flesh rather than the bone becomes mummified. Until recently the most famous bog body that I was aware of was the Lindow Man who was found in Cheshire near Manchester in 1984. It was during August and I was on my summer holidays from College. The discovery was a huge deal. What caught my attention in the news was not so much the gory details of how he was struck violently on the head, garroted with his throat slit from ear to ear, but the aspects of the preparation for the ritual. His body had been painted green, he was naked except for a fox fur armband and his last meal of burnt grain was laced with particles of mistletoe, a poisonous plant that has found its way into modern day Christmas celebrations where people kiss, now for life and love yet also used as the kiss of death. This custom has its roots in the Greek Festival Saturnalia and also in Nordic mythology.

Loki the trickster god of chaos has a hand in destroying Baldur the god of peace, light and the summer sun with an arrow carved from mistletoe, the only substance on earth that was able to harm him. It is a plant that grew not on the earth or under it, but grew instead clinging to the trunks of the apple and occasionally the oak tree, sinking its roots into the bark and sucking out the nutrients. This parasite with its small white toxic berries was a popular plant amongst indigenous people especially the Druids whose reverence for the oak was amplified by the discovery of the mistletoe feeding off the venerated oak, its unusual ability of remaining green and thriving during the winter whilst not rooted in soil is a testament to its otherworldly quality. This hemiparasite that is neither herb nor plant was viewed as a gateway to the other worlds with its in between qualities like the dawn and the dusk and the sea and the land. So how did we get to the kissing part? It is said the goddess Frigga 's tears for her son Balder turned into the pearly white berries of the mistletoe as she celebrated his eventual resurrection. Frigga ordered that the plant responsible for his death would now sing the song of her heart, the earnest reverberations of love, and that when two people met underneath it they would kiss. The climbing vines intertwine other qualities such as peace, the custom in Scandinavia was if two enemies met underneath a tree bough sprawling with mistletoe they would lay down their weapons and maintain a truce until the following day. Mistletoe was used widely as an aphrodisiac and was revered for both its healing and deadly qualities, a source of fertility and an abortifacient , a protection for the home causing beautiful dreams in the lengthened shadow of winter, the druids became quickly acquainted with the effects of altered states of consciousness, the toxic berries also induce epileptic fits and convulsions hence it quickly became the antidote for these convulsions, as well as delirium, hysteria, heart conditions and poison. Perhaps the druids who performed the ritualistic sacrifice of the Lindow man offered him mistletoe, the antidote for all poisons, to help him on his journey into the underworld, helping put him into an altered state to surrender to the savage blows that were about to come.

Were the Lindow man and other bog deaths through willing participation, divination, an accepted consequence for breaking ancient codes of honor, or the sacrifice of wellborn prisoners? Speculation is rife with theories of Wicker Man style ceremonies to appease the gods, to a sacrificial king in a mysterious fertility cult ritual. The discovery of so many similarly executed bog people across Europe hints at a commonly practiced ritualistic ceremony.

I find the burnt grain inside his stomach intriguing, we still hold onto a form of this ritual of the burnt bannock during the Yule and Christmas celebrations in the Isles. My mother would hide a sixpence in tin foil inside the Christmas Pudding and unlike earlier customs of a death sacrifice or the ritual fool for the day wearing a clown's crown we all now pull Christmas Crackers and wear the paper hats through the meal and into the night, a ritualistic gathering of the fools, and the finder of the sixpence is considered lucky, I wonder if this is a reversal of the custom or whether it truly was a feeling of being the chosen one or lucky to pick the burnt offering and make sacred your life through the sacrificial death.

The two peat cutters who discovered the Lindow Man had unearthed a human skull in Lindow Moss and initially forensics deduced it to be a middle age woman's and in all the uproar of the discovery a man came forward convinced that his macabre killing of his wife had been exposed and he pleaded guilty to the dismemberment, rape and murder amongst the swirling shadows of the sinister swampy bog only to find out that subsequent investigation revealed it was actually a mans skull close to 2,000 years old. I wonder if the Celtic ancestors were lingering here and involved in a bit of trickery!

As I stood on the expansive Burren from the Irish word Boireann meaning 'Great Rock' I was about to embark on a friendship with a dead man that would propel me into the bogs of the heartland of Ireland, life death rebirth, a trickster, Celtic oaths and transformation. It was on my first visit to Ireland that I had the good fortune to trundle down the winding roads across County Clare's treasured karst landscape which lay under a tropical ocean over 360 million years ago resulting in a limestone layer. Tectonic movement raised sections of the sea bed into a great plateau. The ice age carved wide river valleys and deposited boulder clay. With the clearing of the forests 6,000 years ago soil erosion set in. Now fissured limestone pavements with crisscrossing cracks known as grikes and solitary rocks known as clints have inadvertently become protective giant borders to an array of foliage and wildflowers where arctic, Mediterranean and alpine plants flourish side by side. The fractured crevices plunge into the earth flirting with entrances into the underworld where cave systems abound. I had the wonderful hefty task of helping an elderly farmer rebuild part of Leamaneh castle wall that had tumbled after a storm. I had stopped for directions near Kilfenora and was invited to make myself useful and pick up some of the strewn rocks of the O'Brien stronghold. Again I am floored by the meaning of names for Leamaneh is from the gaelic leim an eich which translated into English reads 'the horses leap' and O'Brien means 'high noble' so this 'Steed' leapt into the Burren via meeting the High noble one at the gateway of the Great Rock and in my introduction to this harsh beautiful, barren, fertile oxymoron landscape was to handle and lay stones in an ancestral wall.

One of the most well known landmarks of the Burren and of Ireland is the Poulnabrone Dolmen, the hole of the sorrows, a place that stands alone on a desolate bluff that may be swarming with tourists who click and whiz across Ireland's landscape on a mad dash to capture its soul in a flash of whirring film. It also may stand alone waiting for the next onslaught of visitors. When I pulled to the kerb side she called to me undisturbed by scurrying feet. For an instant I had her alone to lay in the clutches of her exposed bones. Now a rope is tethered to prevent the masses from entering the portal and in 2002 I was able to nap in her rugged jaws until the chit and chat of the swarming crowds awoke me from my slumber. What I love about this area is the wide expanse that swallows up the temporary invasion, by stepping beyond the dolmen, the cracks and fissures lead to pools of water, craggy hollows teaming with wild flowers and each step takes you into a reverent peace. It was in the stark serenity of the fading light that I felt his presence. As much as he called me into the sheer expanse of the sprawling boulders snaking their way across the land I heard the murmuring echoes resounding in my head nibbling into my consciousness of securing a comfy cozy nest before darkness claimed the day. My friend who was traveling with me was entranced and reached her hand out to waltz in her vastness to take the hand of the mysterious man whose presence had been felt by both of us.

My gentle hands steered my companion towards the hedgerow and our waiting car. "Did you feel him?" she asked gingerly. The man in question was the focus of a booklet that I had picked up on Jacko McGann who I refer affectionately to as 'the man of the Burren'. John 'Jacko' McGann discovered the Aillwee caves on his stomping grounds, the mysterious desolate region of rock land near Ballyvaughan, the thickets and fields close to Aillwee Hill. At seven he gave himself to the Burren when he fell asleep behind a boulder while tending his family's goats, waking up in the dark and then wandering into a hazel thicket and getting lost. It was several hours before he was found. This sense of adventure and exploration grew inside him and as he grew older he ventured further. Working as a herder, a road builder and in construction, Jacko took to investigating the numerous ruins scattered across this intriguing landscape. In 1944 he clambered into one of the many cave openings and walking into the dense blackness he lit a pathway that now invites thousands of visitors to trek below the surface to take in the stalactites and stalagmites and an underground waterfall.

It was while sitting at the table in our bed and breakfast sipping a welcome cup of tea that I noticed a painting on the wall that looked like the photo of Jacko in my book. It was with much amusement that I found myself sitting in Jacko's sons house.

Looking over a Turlough, a unique lake that appears and disappears in limestone regions of Ireland, Jacko's daughter in law shared with me Jacko's relationship with faerie. His grand daughter now runs a phenomenal five star B & B in Ballyvaughan where Jacko used to communicate with the fae behind a garden wall. It was in honor of Jacko that I went to the Aillwee caves. I am generally not one for purchasing a ticket and lining up with others for a tourist trip in any location but this was important for Jacko's presence had made itself known to us.

The cave is well worth the price of admission, yet I struggled with bringing pilgrims to a place so directly on the tourist route. Jacko had nudged me for a reason and there had to be a way to accept his invitation to know the Burren more fully. So I phoned the Aillwee Caves on my return to the USA and asked if we could visit them before they opened in the morning. To wander the cave network with one of their well informed guides in absolute silence. To go to the Bear's lair, to have the lights turned off so we could stand in the damp darkness, to stand before the waterfall and listen to its twinkling rushing symphony as our eyes feasted on the single drops splashing, trickling, merging and flowing across the smooth shapes shimmering in the lights guiding us through the belly of the Mother. It was an exhilarating feeling to be told yes which was heightened by the subsequent visits.

In September 2005 we moved ceremoniously into the silent darkness. We sang in the final chamber which has a natural altar that brings us all to the same place of awed peace if we are willing to open up to the Universal song. Our voices bounced off the walls in a harmonious reflection of love. As we exited the long tunnels two bats swooped in front of me and as I came to a T- junction one flew right into the depth of the womb, the other flew left toward the exit. As I followed the lone bat it flew directly at me so it could feel my breath on its cheek as it came so close to grazing my face, time and time again it arched towards the exit and flew again up my body over my heart over my throat over my cauldron of wisdom. I was washed in Bat medicine.

The bat represents initiation, rebirth, and extra sensory hearing. It was time for me to take a good look at how I moved through my darkness to open into the light of new meaning. Within nine months of this extraordinary encounter I found the courage to release myself from an unhappy marriage of 17 years. I had been waiting for my children to graduate from school before untangling the strings of a marriage in which I had felt imprisoned. I had fallen out of love very early but when the children arrived, my love for them kept me in the marital home. Life is too fragile to live a lie, to imprison oneself into settling into a second hand version of a wasted life, both my ex wife and I are worthy of finding love that makes the stars sing and the Universe shimmer with delight. As challenging as it was to leave the marital home, the rewards of being in my truth have been liberating. I ask myself, am I willing to dare to dream, to dream to dare to live my life on purpose and the resounding answer is YES!

Ireland is the home of laughter. Trickery is afoot in the hedgerows, amongst the stones, in the people and in the land. I loved one morning when a Landlady waltzed into the breakfast room where I was staying independent of the group and asked me if I wanted red or white ketchup! She meant red or brown and was quite flustered by her words, the Underworld was playfully teasing, for I had been working with the pilgrims on those very pieces and it had somehow channeled its way into her, whispers of the fae perhaps.

Leaving Ballyvaughan, the land seduced me into her nooks and crannies through the beautiful heart of Galway into Mayo and up to Westport when I was setting the route for the Irish tour in 2002. Croagh Patrick dominates the horizon standing 764 meters tall, my problem was that I had read it as 764 feet, a big difference only by 1800 odd feet, and talking feet I could see some pilgrims looking at me on the last day of the pilgrimage thinking what the fecking (good Irish word) heck were you thinking? The interesting thing was my gut was telling me to veer away from Patrick's mountain and I was not listening!

As beautiful as it had been driving through the crooked pass of the mountains all day, it was with a deep breath that my friend and I once more took to the road. We both retired into our thoughts as we traveled the long road east towards Dublin. We were both quite antsy in the cramped confines of the rental car, both itching to get out and taste the land again, as the anticipation of sinking our roots into the bloodline of our ancestors on some ancient mound shimmered towards its fever pitch, we saw a ring fort covered in soil with thick grass shooting from its bank and cows grazing on its glorious top. Most people sail pass the lay by that sits beside the lumps of earth jutting out the landscape west of Tulsk. We had come to the Cruachan, the 'Plain of Mounds' the Royal House of the legendary Queen Mebh, (Maeve) and later the inauguration site for the crowning of the Kings of Connaught, the O'Connors. It was with rich delight that my friend and I climbed the steep embankment on land where Kings were made, where Kings were buried in the heartland of Ireland, a place that was one of the three famous festivals of Ireland, a gathering place now deserted and brushed by the wind. On the top of the mound in the fading light of day I stood on ground of my friend's ancestors. She is an O'Conner and spirit had guided her home and invited me to begin a love affair with Maeve the intoxicating Queen of the South where we dance and sing the musical poetry of our own story.

It was the next day that I first met Davy Patton and his beautiful family, the gatekeepers to the Owenygat Cave, the Cave of the Morrighan. I had knocked on Davy's door having been given his name at the aptly named Cruachan Ai Heritage Center. From the moment I met Davy I liked him. First he showed me the way to the dark mouth protruding from under wild tangles of a spreading hawthorn tree. The faerie guardian creeps over the lintel that spreads across the vaginal wall of this delicious descent into the Mother. Having made introductions he left me to enter the chamber and invited me to stop by afterwards for a cuppa.

After sliding into the muddy damp entrance, the low wide opening thins out and allows you to stand in preparation for the clamber down. A careful scrambling descent across the wet, jagged, mud stained rocks, with hands pressed to the cold wall lining the trail that winds its way leisurely down into the Mother's juicy womb, squelching mud welcoming pilgrims boots, inviting all to stand or crouch in the thick, sloppy, darkness of this profound birthing chamber. My mother wept in awe the year she slid down the rabbit hole or more appropriately the cats cave named so for a Great female warrior who killed a giant cat who lived in the cave. Others would say it is more fittingly known for the cattle or raven with strands rooted deeply in the story of the Morrigan who drove her cattle through the Underworld. This battle Queen is the sum of her three parts, a triple Goddess: the Great Queen, the Phantom Queen, the Otherworld Queen, she is Macha, Badhbh and some have named the third sister Nemhain some Fea some Ana, whichever name is given, this formidable culmination of Goddesses that are of the land merge into a powerful single entity of life, death and rebirth. A Goddess of War, wild frenzied, a creator of violent panic in the splattering of battle and the glory of death. It is upon her fearsome face of destruction that her reputation seems to ride and yet this shapshifter who appears as the scavenging crow or ragged dark raven has a softer healing side. She is after all an aspect of Sovereignty, much maligned and misunderstood. As the land she has been severely raped by those who have parceled her up, divided her and claimed her as their own. She was ridiculed and abused as the horse goddess and protector of the people when forced to race while bursting with pregnancy, commanded to prove her speed against the King of Ulster's finest horses. It was on the finish line directly after her painful victory in a race that should never have been run that she delivered a still born child and threw a curse on the men of Ulster, a curse to render them weak when Ulster needed their strength, a curse that would take them to their knees and make them writhe around in agony as if in childbirth. She was spurned by Cuchulain in the epic Tain who wounds her when she is in shifted form an indication of the Patriarchal story of competition raising its head over the cooperation of the Matriarchal Queen of fertility and prosperity. She is a force to be respected and when her dark womb is entered with humble appreciation she offers sacred cleansing, Her methods of alchemy are not always comfortable as the leaf mold rots and is decomposed into the earth so the Morrighan picks the dead flesh away from the bone, consuming and purifying all. She is the harbinger of death, of life, and of rebirth. Her name is the sum of many parts and calls of the Great Bright Circle of Birth. When we are rooted in fear of death, in fear of the dark spaces, we project those fears and our perception becomes our reality, she becomes the terrifying dark entity to fear and dread. When we open up to her as the protector of the people, as the guardian of Sovereignty, then we fly with vision of raven, strength of horse, magic of poetry with healing of cow, into purification and transmutation of a bright new birth.

The Oweynagat Cave has spread her thighs many times over the years, swallowing me, rebirthing me, and inviting countless pilgrims into the sanctuary of her still fertile womb. On one occasion a man in his late 60's demonstrated strength and courage that impacted all in his presence. He had traveled to Erin's skirt folds with his wife and daughter, He was someone who normally stayed home on rainy days and had already stretched himself outside of his comfort zone on quest day as the heavens opened and bathed the group in a refreshing downpour that would have had some running for cover. The impression he left within us from our encounter with the Morrigan in her mushy fruitful loins was his dedication to go deep into the Underworld to remember himself. He has only one leg and his prosthetic leg was the old fashioned kind that did not bend, so he went both in and out using the power of his arms to propel him up and down the steep muddy narrow birthing channel. Tears spilled freely as we all went to our personal place of courage to explore living our essence trusting Spirit to guide us.

It was on my second visit to meet the Morrigan that Lugh called to me from the hearth place of Davy's fire. From my first encounter with this talented Irishman a trip to the cave is incomplete without a cup of tea with Mr. Patton, whose name translates to Beloved Skull, the vessel of wisdom in the Celtic world. As well as head or skull Patton also means Warrior of the town. So the guardian to the Great Queen is the Beloved Head Wise Warrior of this Community! Davy is an accomplished wood carver whose replica harps are avidly sought by musicians and museums. The intricate whittling and attention to detail in fashioning replica harps of Gaelic heritage from the 15th - 18th Century are a testimony to his respect for the master crafters of old. I met Davy before he ventured into the carving and decorating of the Bardic instrument of yesteryear. He is also a carver of the story of the Emerald Isle. Slurping through the bog lands, he pulls pieces of wood and finds the spirit living within. Pieces of wood that have been preserved for thousands of years get to share their story through him and his deep connection with Spirit. Above his fireplace hung a stunning length of bog yew, the tree of life death rebirth, with the figure of Lugh the Sun God etched from its flesh, pulsing with life. I knew that it was coming home with me and on that day I did not have the money in my pocket to make the purchase.

It was two years later that I ventured down the thin lane that led to the Morrigan, to Davy, and to Lugh. The pilgrims were all excited at the prospect of their descent into the Underworld and at meeting Davy. They all knew that I was hoping to carry Lugh with me that day and when we went into Davy's home they eagerly sought the wall above the hearth that now stood empty. Lugh was not there. I had not truly expected it to be there and yet a gnawing at my bones suggested that Lugh was meant to travel with me. Lugh the God of vision, the light of the fire and the Oath King who I was keen to work with through Davy's carving. This transformational board was to serve the community by helping myself and others step through our fears into the depth of our visions.

I had come into contact with a Fijian ritual through the deep transformation work offered by Peggy Dylan at Sundoor that shouted of Celtic threads ready to be woven into a gleaming tapestry of dreams. It was two years previous at the Winter Solstice that I had first put an arrow at my throat near Tara Hill and releasing what no longer served me I called in the new. With a power word ringing in my ears I placed the fletch end of the arrow on to a board and then moving my arms up and down three times as if the wings of a raven, I breathed and walked through the arrow, breaking it in half with my throat chakra. The same night I walked the fire for the first time and knew I was destined to seek the teachings of these ways and bring them to the people. Thanks to the wonderful work of Peggy Dylan and Sundoor I now work as a Master Firewalk Practitioner and lead arrow breaks with people of all ages. This process takes us immediately to the root of fear. It is an arrow for goodness sake digging in to the place where a tracheotomy takes place. Our beautiful voice box, the place where we are called to have the courage to speak our truth in this world. This dauntingly real ritual that has been brought to the world by Peggy's desire to bring healing tools to the people, demands of us to be impeccable with our word, to make a public declaration of how we are willing to walk through our fear into the brightness of the light, of Lugh, of our oath. Thanks to professional training with Sundoor I have guided arrow breaks on standing stones, oak trees, cave walls and even on my own heart. Please note that this work is of the highest integrity and if you are called to teach these ways go to the heart core and work through the teachings of Sundoor. Now as I stood in Davy's kitchen it was important for me to ask him to make me a similar carving of Lugh to have a representation of the Celtic Sun God, the visionary ray of hope. Davy beamed an impish grin when I mentioned Lugh and gravely shook his head at the thought that he might still be holding a piece two years later.

"They come and go quickly Andrew I rarely keep such a big piece for so long and as life would have it I do still have Lugh." My heart leapt and beat faster still as Davy's smooth voice added fae honey to the tale. "He's in prison, he's been there since you left two years ago. I teach wood carving at the IRA prison and I took Lugh in to inspire the inmates. As you know Lugh is the God of Vision and his fire has been illuminating creativity within those walls, apparently waiting for you to come and collect him. I'll go get him while you lead your group down the cave." The cherry on top was still to be delivered as both Davy and I made the connection to Lugh's auspicious choice of timing. When Davy placed the board in my hands later that morning he breathed deeply and his voice took on a richer lilting quality as he shared the fact that the IRA laid down their weapons that very week. They made a choice to walk in peace as Lugh walked from behind the bars. He is a Celtic key to releasing the light. Placed in my hands with goose pimples on my skin and shivers reverberating down my spine I carried the physical board and a spiritual knowing in my heart flames of the light and the dark, the masculine and the feminine, Lugh and the Morrigan, the phoenix and the raven. The Sun and the Earth, the Goddess and the God.

I had an opportunity at the airport to practice ancient Scottish Highland magic that is sewn into folklore, a spell known as the fith-fath. In his research Alexander Carmichael uncovered this invisibility spell one that was used by Lugh's father Kian when trying to out run the sons of Tuirenn, used primarily to shape shift into an animal it can be applied to a person or objects to render them invisible. Sometimes called the fee – faw or faw – fee, I had learnt it and use it on rare occasions. Now I needed to sugar coat and cloak big time. I was traveling with a hand carved staff five and a half feet tall, the piece of bog wood that measures close to four feet tall, a bodhran, the Irish drum, plus a carry on pack full of medicine tools, rattle, sage, pipe as well as chocolate goodies and Irish treats. All of these I considered hand luggage and was not prepared to put them below where cases are tossed into each other with reckless abandon.

So conjuring the mists of a magic cloud as Manannan would as Fionn did with his fae love, as St. Patrick did in the Feth-Faidha, more commonly known as St. Patrick's Breastplate, as he guised from King Laoghaire when he lit the fire on the Hill of Slane:

I arise today
Through the strength of heaven,
Light of sun,
Radiance of moon,
Splendour of fire,
Speed of lightening,
Swiftness of wind,
Depth of sea,
Stability of earth,
Firmness of rock.

So I whispered the breath of mist over my belongings, the staff being too tall for the overhead bins was going to have to sit on my lap for the whole journey, an absolute no no. So with these words I whispered with purpose and gentle feeling;

Faw Fee I put on me
power of invisibility
I carry magic tools that carry me
onto the plane and home safely
If anyone should chance to see
They will let me pass and let me be.

Did it work? Absolutely. The staff was tucked in the crook of my arm stretching from the headrest on a slant towards my feet. Did anyone see any of the artifacts, yes they did, one person even said, "you won't be able to board with all of those."

And melted when I retorted "Yes I will, these are medicine pieces, they do not belong below." This was after 9/11 with airport security high and I believe that the power of faerie assisted my intending of a pure heart to carry these tools to help all my relations heal!

Chapter 9

THE LANGUAGE OF POETRY

In September 2008 I carried to the shores of Ireland the language of the ancestors. Sharynne Macleod NicMhacha, a wise and learned Celtic scholar, shaman priestess and Celtic bard had agreed to translate poetry that I wrote so I could honor the stories through the oral song of distant tribes, the language spoken and absorbed by the trees, the rocks, the green shining land of Eire.

In choosing which piece/peace to speak first I went to the Celtic story and to the East to Imbolc and as easy a choice as Brighid would be my guidance led me to Boann. She who brings poetry to the people, the milk being the source of poetry and Boann's name meaning Sacred White Cow, both Brighid and Boann become the Buffalo Calf Pipe Woman of the Celtic clans, Boann's body snakes from its humble origins to kiss her son's forehead at the Palace of Love, the Bru na Boinne, Newgrange in County Meath as she flows purposefully on the path forged by her determined spirit.

Boann's Story

A well, an ancient well, a timeless well, well beyond the written word, well older than the spoken word, well of healing, well of wisdom, a magic well. A pool of sparkling water encased in shards of smoked crystal covered in the carved topping of sacred hazel hidden deep in the heart of the tangled forest. A well that was once of the people for the people now lay hidden in the clutches of a greedy few. Oh for certain it was not meant to be that way. In fact the guardians were duly chosen by the Druid's who had drawn a veil of secrecy an impenetrable wall of transparent mist masking the whereabouts of this precious life force. For after such misuse by gluttonous kings and ravenous warlords who insisted on charging a tithe for its use quiet gentle citizens gnashed their teeth and picked up their arms. A revolt quenched quickly by the Druids who gave safekeeping of the waters to a family whose honour was beyond reproach. It was agreed that the curative liquid would only be procured in the event of famine as the waters of the well were slowly running dry.

As seasons changed on the spindle wheel of life so the fate of the well's upkeep was put into the hearts of the sole survivors of the Clan Nechtan. Four hearty strong brothers who knew the shifting shadows that shaped the way to the well. For generations the well was left undisturbed as the waters swelled vibrantly and even the most resolute seekers failed to find the liquid fruits of the sidhe.

The only footsteps to grace the fleshy earth at the Well's glistening edge were those of the brothers Nechtan and the secret lay firmly on their tongue.

A forced political marriage by the eldest Nechtan to a willful independent youth whom Nechtan found haughty, whose flowing dark hair glistened with a purple sheen offering an exotic flow over sultry astute eyes, set in an attractive thinly sculpted yet stalwart frame, bore no blossom for the hapless couple. Boann was a mere 16 when she was bedded as the wife of the aging grizzled Chieftain. The conversation was stark, the mutual attraction limp the only intriguing factor from Boann's view was the hidden location of the Well of Wisdom. She had heard countless stories of its magical properties and now she was of Clan Nechtan and the secrets would be revealed to her.

She bided her time watching the mother's belly swell as the moon reached its full glare in the night sky. That day Nechtan had bathed in the stream that meandered by their spacious fort. He dressed himself in spotless linen removing his torc, his decorative brooch, even his dirk was set aside as he prepared to take the secret route through the darkening forest to the ancient Sidhe well accompanied by his three younger brothers Flesc, Lam and Luam .

Boann's eyes followed her husband's bulking frame like a hawk circling an unaware hare hopping casually through the meadow. "Will the pathway to the well open up for Clan Nechtan tonight?" She probed.

"Never you mind your young head about Clan business, I will return at dawn" Nechtan muttered dismissively.

"I am Clan Nechtan now husband and I am aware that it is our kin that guard the secrets of the healing well. I would join you and make an offering at this sacred gateway".

"You are Clan only in name woman. You are not blood, bear me a child and they will be granted access, that is as close as you will ever get to the healing well"

"You put too much importance on yourself husband, I hear the old well is failing, its powers diminished."

"Then you hear wrong, listening to tittle tattle is about your level, well feast on this bone, the well is at the height of its power. We guardians have kept the waters stirred in the well of Segais, drinking only enough for our well being. The salmon swim and suck the knowledge from the nuts of the nine hazels, we are the caretakers of this knowledge which will not be shared with the likes of you." A smirking grimace crossed Nechtan's ruddy face as he disappeared into the cooling twilight.

As quick as a flash and as silent as the as the wolf stalking its prey, Boann was on Nechtan's tail. She lingered far enough back so the party of four would not see or hear her as they traipsed their way through familiar paths of the dense dark wood. Boann felt a song lingering on the edge of her lips, a howling yelp of merriment, tonight she would strip naked and dance around the nine hazels and in that instant the glow of satisfaction drained from her eager heart into puzzlement and thickening disbelief. The brothers vanished, they took a step beyond an impenetrable veil, the narrow path ahead lay deserted and thick undergrowth barred passage. Any attempt to forge it would be a foolhardy plunge into the unknown where spirits tempt the unwary, luring them to their doom. Forlorn and despondent the chill air gripped her bones. She had dashed so precariously from the warm hearth of their home without plucking a scarf or shawl to keep the cold at bay, now that the excitement of the chase and discovery of the well had eluded her, the full force of the dark dank night nipped at her skin and tangled in her heart.

When the cycle of the moon had swelled to its heavy fullness in the bleak winter sky, once again Nechtan cleansed his body purging his jewelry and adorning himself in fresh sweet smelling robes. As the shadows thickened and night swallowed day, Nechtan braced the tepid breath of Winter's drool and stepped into the drizzling rain spitting steadily soaking the ancient trail. Grabbing her shawl Boann slunk steadfastly after him, her beady eyes fixed firmly on her quarry.

This time she would not let him slip from her grasp. She had plied him with all kinds of questions, short of begging she had used all her manipulative skills to extract the way to the well. Her probing had yielded little except scorn from Nechtan whose estimation of Boann seemed to be confirmed in her persistent questioning. The words immature, forbidden, petulance and greedy tyke were the ones that pierced through Boann's armor needling at her heart. The one small kernel she held onto was his slip that the properties floating from hazelnuts to Salmon in the rich pure water contained the elixir of eternal life and she was determined to taste it.

The four brothers made no effort to hide their trail, they walked freely and their voices lit up the night in a haunting song welcoming the driving rain and the onslaught of the coming cold. So Boann stood mystified when the voices and the hulking frames of the lumbering men vanished without a trace. She swore she could hear the echoes of the tune ringing from tangled branches and exposed roots in the thicket of the brush, glimmering lights flickered behind the barrier of thorns and protruding limbs inviting her to stumble and crash into the abyss of the dark wood. Her first step off the path harvested a gashing tear in her shawl and in fear of having an eye gouged out or being lanced by snarling twisted razor sharp splinters she stepped back and trudged dejectedly home.

As the Calliach's strength hardened the earth and the darkness engulfed the light of day, Boann changed tact. Gone was the arrogance of the ice maiden as a loving soft considerate young woman emerged. Nechtan put the shift down to her finally knowing her place. The acquiescent Boann might make for a suitable wife after all.

By the burgeoning belly of the full blue moon Nechtan washed and stripped the decorative metals from his body and took to the frosty eve with his trusted companions. Harmonious tones reverberated through the gathering twilight as the brothers forged their way through familiar paths. Boann kept stride to the rhythm of the song feeling the melody wash over her and through her. An ancient note, that opened a locked doorway in her heart, gave fresh bounce to her step. When the Nechtan men deviated from the path Boann saw clearly the gap, the slit that cut a clear opening through the wild wood. Slipping easily into the welcoming veil, Boann cautiously placed her footsteps into those of the Clan. When the brother's strides increased so did Boann's thus avoiding the spiked traps and hidden pits that guarded the secret way.

Tucked cozily in the arms of the moss strewn grove, affording her an unobstructed view of the well, Boann watched in awe. Sixteen sentinel stones, standing tall and strong perfectly circled the crystal wall of the faerie well. Nechtan stepped forward and lifted a cup to the moon and gracefully dipped it into the waiting waters. Stooping carefully he made an offering to the land and then in unison the brothers danced three times sunwise around the well. Their movements belied their stalwart frames, an intoxicating flow of memories remembered. Boann's eyes entranced by the delicate intricacies of her grizzled husband's footwork, the gentle sway of the bulking brothers who flew with the grace of swan on wings of dove until the circle was complete. Nechtan passed the cup until it was thoroughly drained and then as the covering was placed, capping the well, moonlight bathed them all in a lingering light that glistened with an edge of otherworldly wonder.

It was well into midnight when Boann awoke from her reverie and stumbled naked from her hiding place. The brother's song was now a distant echo as they reached the familiar path on the other side of the protected veil. Boann approached the well cautiously her heart heaving in her chest, the crystals breathing in the light of the moon. Her slender arms lifted the heavy capstone and gingerly she sought the cup. With water brimming at the edge she poured a drink onto the mother before whirling and twirling in the freedom of the dance. Fleet of foot with ecstatic light shooting and pulsing through her blood and bones she surrendered to the dizzying flow. Three times she circled the well traveling Tuatha, against the illusionary movement of the sun and as her footsteps mirrored her husbands she weaved a new pathway to the waters delight.

The well so long guarded, hidden from the people and long ago neglected in its use for the community, stirred and bubbled. Boann lifted the cup high into the air honoring the shining moon, liquid gold nectar for the gods and goddesses rained down her throat as she savored the fresh waters of life, draining the cup of its very last drop. Stimulated with the thrill of life force surging through her being she let out a primal howl. The sixteen guardians appeared to raise their stony heads and the crystals shards protecting the well's boundary throbbed and sparkled in expectation. In the blink of an eye the waters rose towering over the stunned expression fixed on Boann's mouth. For an eternity that made a mockery of this illusive measurement known as time, the water hung suspended in space waiting for the moon to dance it to the sea. Then in blissful rapture the frozen moment was over. Wave upon wave of purest water crashed down Boann's jaws, splashing, soaking, splattering and consuming. The unsuspecting girl was seized by the thrusting rawness of power exploding from the well, tossing her, lifting her, carrying her as its wild haired leader across the land. Breaking free of the bonds of captivity, the poetic waters of healing thrashed and snaked their way through Irish green to the taste of the sea. Nechtain heard the howl, the ensuing roar and when he looked upon the roaring torrent that swept by his door he recognized the glint of her eye, the toss of her mane and perhaps it was he who first called the river Boann or as we know it today the Boyne.

I have read comparisons of the Adam and Eve story and I have heard some people say 'here we go again, another tale about a woman doing it wrong!" Yet it is always in the perspective and the roots of the story. Boann is young and impetuous, Nechtan old and grizzly, set in his ways. A forced marriage between Boann whose name means both sacred white cow and in Sanskrit star, if we take the sum of two parts, Bo means treasured or precious and Ann means gracious and Nechtan whose name means pure water and is connected to Nuada which means to catch, take hold or acquire. So the Treasured Gracious Star meets the Pure Catcher who acquires his bride.

What intrigues me in this tale is the interplay of the feminine and masculine. The way our society today has an expectation on the woman to carry the man's name when a betrothal takes place, yet in the case of Boann and Nechtan this does not make her part of the Clan's intimate secrets. She can share a title, share a bed and the only part of her that is fully accepted would be the fertilized seed of her offspring. We have a classic motif of 'You can't do that,' which makes us more thirsty to participate in what is denied us. Boann follows Nechtan three times and twice she is denied. On the third attempt she surrenders in love, she no longer forces the issue and the path is revealed luminously before her. When we introduce the names of Nechtan's brothers we receive a new twist. Luam means peaceful, Lam is the forest and Flesc is a maker of flasks or bottles and add to that the meaning of the Well of Segais, which translates as poetry, the nuts and bolts of knowledge an interesting pattern appears.

By putting all of this together we get a peaceful calm forest where the pure waters are caught, bottled in the source of poetic knowledge. Boann unbinds the well by moving Tuatha, against the sun on the night of the 13th moon the Blue Moon, this transforms the waters releasing them from this bottled state and erupting, swallowing Boann and carrying her to the sea, her body stretching out graciously across Ireland bringing the precious treasure, the poetry of knowledge to all of the people. The sacred white cow offers her milk, the poetic source, for all to drink deeply.

The significance of the placement of the Bru na Boinne, the temple of the god Oengus known today as Newgrange, which is in sight of the Boyne, erected at the bend of her long gracious neck, is a testament to the ancestors who recognized that she speaks the truth of her milky source. She is a reflection of the Milky Way. She is a path of enlightenment. It is said that eating Salmon from the Boyne or drinking her waters on the night of a full moon releases that poetic wisdom into our bodies. Is it any wonder that the ancestors erected their temple Newgrange, to mark the return of light at the Winter Solstice by the rich track of the sacred white cow? Here beside their sun house in the twisting current of Boann's flowing life force, the salmon would return to their birthplace to breed, to die, so it is a place of life, death, rebirth. The salmon like the shaman is the traveler in search of its origin, its destiny. Here stands a testimony to magic. A temple that brings the golden thread of the sun into the dark womb so all life will grow again. A remarkable achievement to builders who imported stones from miles away in the Wicklow Mountains, from what would later become St. Kevin's home in the area around Glendalough. It was a collective community who worked diligently digging with red deer antlers and the backbone of an ox. Again those who began the work never saw its completion.

Boann plays the role of shaman, she goes on a journey in search of poetic knowledge in the depths of the Otherworld bringing the gifts of the divine with her and on her return she releases the treasure with sovereignty into our realm.

One other aspect of note is the numbers. Sixteen stones plus four men and Boann add up to 21 and two plus one is three, which indicates it's the Celtic way! I also liked the discovery of the Four men representing the four directions adding Boann to the mix as Sovereignty and when in the role of Sovereignty the well is no longer under dominion of its guardians as it is shared with the community.

So drink in the story and ask; where am I aligning myself with people/places for political gain against the true nature of my soul? Where am I entering into relationship out of duty rather than love? How do I find the love if I am entrenched in a loveless relationship and how do I release it? Am I willing to go into the darkness, to face the cold harshness of the world to find the essential secret the treasure of my life? Am I willing to make sacred, to sacrifice everything for my hearts desire? Will my hearts desire feed only me or will it provide a space and place for the community? Do I accept the opposite sex as my equal? Do I give my name away? Do I expect someone to give their name away and if they do am I willing to embrace them with the same rights as others hold who carry that name? What kernels of wisdom are we hiding from the community? What gifts of healing are we not sharing with the world? Stop, breath, have you found answers to these questions or have you brushed them aside in your race to get to the end? Our lives are worth too much to miss the opportunity to discover our pieces to this exquisite puzzle, our unique story.

To speak in the ancient tongue of the bards who carried this story into a new language a new time brings immense joy to my heart. I was anxious to greet Boann and call out the invocation that honors her story. I was not to be disappointed.

In September 2008 the River Boyne burst her banks. Heavy rainfall swelled the powerful flow of her body until she pushed free of those carved boundaries and sprawled out over the fields making her wider and deeper than I have ever seen. She knew I was coming and she swelled in wild joy as I spoke the Old Irish of these translated English words:

Ah Boann

Sacred White Cow

Whose power and strength of the Divine feminine

Released the waters so that we can all freely bathe in them

We can all drink deeply from the pool of wisdom

We remember you

We honor you

We remember

We speak in truth

A year later I found myself wandering in the Wicklow Mountains acquainting myself with the land as I prepared for another dazzling adventure, 'Find the Gypsy in Your Soul,' a horse drawn gypsy caravan pilgrimage through the Wicklow mountains to the Irish Sea. Once the route was set in my heart I had a few days for further exploration and I set off to locate the source of the Boyne. Now named the Trinity Well, the flowing source of milk is located near Carbury in county Kildaire. Boann's connection to Bridghid of Kildaire goes on! In the spirit of Sovereignty, I ended up asking five local people for directions to the well. The first two had never heard of it, the next sent me on a wild goose chase to the left of the well, the fourth person sent me far right of the well. It was the fifth whose door was closed with their house keys left dangling from the lock who came to share the way that took me past a derelict cottage and crumbling wall onto the property of a wealthy land owner whose long thin driveway leads to a stately looking home. The road was just wide enough for my vehicle and either side was the boggy wet pasture for a roaming cowherd. Concerned that my car would get stuck in the muddy meadow I left my car smack in the middle of the drive and picked my way through the soft grassland to the ornate origins of the Trinity Well, Boann's beginning, the life force of milky prosperity, the source of knowledge. With tears in my eyes I made an offering pouring milk onto the land and I circled her boundaries three times Tuatha to release the waters of wisdom in me. Retracing my steps in a place of pure gratitude I climbed into my car and headed towards the large house, I was uncomfortable trying to turn around in the field as I was unsure of whether the landowners would appreciate an intruder asking to be towed out of a muddy trench. Backing out of the long driveway was not an option as the driveway is on a blind corner of a busy road, and getting out, going forward was challenge enough.

As I came closer to the house and my turn around point a white cow stepped into the drive blocking my path. It stared at me eye to eye and then crossed over letting me pass. I maneuvered the car around and started to head towards the exit. Again the white cow stepped into the drive once more blocking my path, once more looking into my eyes, then with purpose she crossed giving me access to leave. It is written that drinking from the Boyne gifts a person second sight. On processing my encounter with Boann, which of course means Sacred White Cow, at her very birthplace, I drink deeply from the fact that she looked me in the eye twice and I hear the reverberations of second sight.

Chapter Ten

RED DRAGON BLUE DOOR

Tangles of brambles, tumbling vines, shimmering moss, and shaggy old hedgerows guard ancient secrets in the hills, dales, valleys, moors and wild shaggy places dotted on Bridget's gnarled windswept spine. Forlorn forgotten tracks if foraged reveal mystic memories in the swirling vortexes of a vibrant past.

When one is willing to be a witness and not a tourist, gentle rambles and muddy bog stained scrambles amongst the bracken and boulders, reveal mysteries on the breath of a gentle wind and a rain soaked shower calls forth the ancient song of the earth, and for those who sink their roots deeply, magic is found everywhere. A memorable mosey down winding lanes, through the groves where pixies play, and the sidhe dance, where the veil is oh so thin, offers a unique glimpse into a resilient and respectful wonderland. All of the Celtic lands offer unique gifts, some of the places are so well guarded, that many mortals miss them. Some are hidden so locals don't even know the way, or locals keep, what they affectionately call the 'Excuse Me's ' (tourists), as far away from these ancestral gathering places as possible keeping sacred by leaving spirits undisturbed from the graffiti and litter stained stamp of the masses. Others lay forgotten as pilgrims flock to the shopping malls to stuff more emptiness into the gaping holes of unfulfilled expectation lost loneliness and fearful unworthiness that has the western world in a vice grip of the wounded wasteland. I feel fortunate and blessed to have been invited by locals and the nature spirits to explore the edge of the world with an assembled bouquet of related souls, as hollow bones, prayerful participants and omnipresent observers we pilgrims get to share ancestral symphonies as we fall into a fresh fulfilling depth of our own magical universal story.

In preparing myself for pilgrimage I always head to make relationship with the land and make myself known to Spirit. Since my first voyage with a small group of travelers in 1999, I now have 9 established routes in England, Scotland, Ireland and Wales. I reference these countries not in order of importance for no place or person is more important than another, only in order of where I first stepped in initiating the pilgrimages. I have still to incorporate the Isle of Mann and Brittany into the fabric of my walks and I am looking forward to connecting with their places of power as my journey continues to unfold.

In 2004 I embarked on a sun drenched stroll on the Isle of Anglesey and amongst the Peaks and valleys of North Wales. Wales has often brought me a fair share of down pours and on this occasion I received not one drop of drizzling sky juice. I was tickled pink on that scavenger hunt unearthing the wealth of riches of Yns Mon, the Great Mother, the mysteries of Merlin and the haunts of Llewelyn ap Gruffydd who many call the last Prince of Wales. His death in 1282 at the hands of the English troops led by Edward 'Longshanks' heralded a switch in the proclamation of this ambiguous title. Llewelyn had made his strong hold in Gwynedd the central seat being the Welsh built castle of Dolwyddelan. This stark functional square tower sits majestically on a rocky outcrop set against the bleak rugged backcloth of Moel Siabod, the translation of Moel is bald, bare or heap in England the word becomes Mel and means island. This is a fitting description of this barren hill deep in the heart of Snowdonia.

Llewelyn's grandfather Llewelyn the Great built this rectangular stone keep that his grandson fortified with a stone curtain wall enclosing the courtyard. It was here that Llewelyn lived, loved and tormented his Father in Law, John 'Lackland', Prince John of Robin Hood infamy and father to King Edward 1, who he harassed equally as well until 'Longshanks' littered Wales with castles galore in a campaign that ultimately defeated and slaughtered the rebellious efforts of Llewelyn. Dolwyddelan rises up as a beacon, a silhouetted shadow of the former glory of this fortress' story, a stronghold that controlled a strategic pass through the kingdom from Merioethshire to the Vale of Conwy that finally fell to English forces in 1283. It was the 'Butchering' Edward who stripped the Welsh crown and formal independence away from this regal land. You can rip and strip a title away from the people yet the blood of the Celts, like the ancestors before them lives in the spirit of the land. Edward conferred the title Prince of Wales on his son Prince Edward who later became King Edward II of England. According to legend the King gave an oath to the Welsh people that he would bestow the title of prince upon one born on Welsh soil who spoke not a word of English and then proceeded to produce his heir who was indeed born at Caemarfon Wales while the King conducted his campaign and he spoke not a word in any language as an infant.

This story has its origins in the sixteenth century and may be purely mythical, the aristocracy would have spoken Norman French rather than English it certainly is not out of character for Edward I to have thrown this type of 'assault' to rub in Welsh wounds. With the conquest of Wales another piece of exclusion needs to be addressed. The flag of the United Kingdom holds the St. George cross of England which dominates the center, the red cross on a white background, behind which stands the cross of St. Andrew, Scotland, a white diagonal cross on a blue background, and the cross of St. Patrick, Northern Ireland, a red diagonal cross on a white background, but where is the cross of St. David, Wales, a yellow diagonal cross on a black background, or the more commonly flown red dragon on the white and green background? The story of the development of the flag commonly called the Union Jack although it is strongly contested that its true name is simply the Union flag, has its roots not with the English but with the Scots. It was King James VI of Scotland who ascended to the English throne as James I of England and amalgamated the two designs to form a united flag. A proclamation was issued on April 12th, 1606 which read "All our subjects in this isle and kingdom of Great Britain and the members thereof, shall bear in their main top the red cross commonly called St. George's Cross and the white cross commonly called St. Andrew's Cross joined together according to a form made by our heralds and sent to our Admiral to be published to our said subjects". The result of this unification was met with disdain from both the Scots and the English. The English were upset at the 'muddying' of the white field with the Scottish blue and the Scots were rightly affronted at having the St. George's flag superimposed on St. Andrew which in no small measure was a statement of which country thought more highly of itself. The Scots offered many alternatives and even went to the extent of flying a converted flag when the king visited Dumfries in 1618, they had reversed the flag so St. Andrew's design was on top! In 1801 the flag of Northern Ireland was incorporated into the design and became what it is today. The contention with the name is traced back to the 'Union' flag being flown originally by Admiralty and Parliament and inherited the 'Jack' reference because it was hoisted up the bowsprit of the ship which is known as the 'jack staff'. Another alternative has been offered by 'His'torian David Starkey who claims that the flag was named after the king that introduced it, James 1 of Great Britain, the title Jack comes from the Latin translation of James which is Jacobus. All this being said, where is Wales? The official answer to this is Wales did not warrant an inclusion as in 1606 when the flag made its debut Wales was not a Kingdom it was a Principality. Henry VIII was on the throne in 1536 when the innocuous Act of Union was passed making Wales, in effect a province of England, Ouch!!! I do not have Welsh blood in me and my Celtic blood boils at the injustice of this, here lies another example of St. George trying to slay the dragon.

If the Welsh flag, the Celtic dragon were to be added where would it be put? The answer has to be in the center! How cool would that be? And of course England is not about to let Wales be at the center, yet in the Celtic story it was the center and still is. Yns Mon, Anglesey was the Druidic center for the whole Celtic world, from mainland Europe and across the Isles Druids flocked to the Great Mother, this small flat island, off the North Western shores of Wales, to study.. And in looking at the land mass tat makes up the Britsh Isles and Ireland, I say Wales is still the center. I infer here specifically to Yns Mon. If you take Southern Ireland and the United Kingdom and push them together the center, the heartbeat, the heartland is the Druidic Isle of Yns Mon, hidden like the dragons in the mist, just like the red dragon is hidden in the red of St. George's cross, blanketed by the blood of the English and given life by the blood of the Welsh.

It is Wales whom amongst the Celtic lands have led the way in maintaining and promoting their heritage. The Welsh language, Cymraeg or y Gymraeg is widely spoken and in certain parts of the North and West, principally Gwynedd, Conwy, Denbigshire and Anglesey it is English that is taught as the second language in schools today. All through the mountain passes and rich coastal terrain road signs welcome visitors in consonants and syllables that tie an untrained tongue into a magnificent Celtic knot. One pilgrim made the infamous mistake of asking Margaret our landlady on Anglesey for the full English breakfast. She was kindly and forcefully reminded that the lavish feast of foraged fruits, the sizzling rashers and lashings of mushrooms, tomatoes, and gourmet sausage, no gristle filled bangers served here, were of Welsh origin. Margaret is another model example of Celtic hospitality. The five star mansion which is their home and work place has a sweeping staircase, high vaulted ceilings, antique furniture dripping from each plush room and yet has the feeling of an abode well lived and laughed in. The family sitting room is a communal gathering place offering sweeping views over Anglesey's ironed apron to the high peaks of Snowdon beyond. On arrival a cozy fire dances in the ample hearth place, tea flows and Welsh cakes never fail to hit the spot. It is in those distant far off mountains that Llewelyn the Great laid the foundation of an indomitable spirit.

My first trek to Dolwyddelan was in the dying embers of a bright May eve. I had scaled the castle track that leads to the house and entrance gate to find the castle closed and no-one home. With a heavier step of despondence I began to trudge back down with the promise on my lips to return in the breaking light of day when my adventurous pixie nature nibbled at the edge of my mind and I swung around and pushed open the gate. So the castle was closed it didn't stop me walking up to it and around the towering Keep. Moss drips and drools from the spindly limbs that twist and obtrude from the vegetation clinging to the thin banks of the tumbling brook that cascades in a small waterfall as it snakes down the mountain pass. I continued my ascent and explored the crumbling remains of a second tower probably added by the English invasion. It was the solitary sentinel with her intact battlements that called to me. I slowly mounted the stone steps that lead to the thick haggard panels of the aged portal wedged shut and securely fastened to keep the public out and the reveling spirits in. My hand spontaneously groped for the heavy latch and lifted it and Llewelyn lit a fire of wonder in my heart as he welcomed me in. Blooming marvelous, Celtic hospitality never dies!!!

I peeked into the large banquet hall, I stood in the massive hearth looking up to the sky above, I explored the alcoves and stole up the spindling staircase that lead onto the battlements, repaired in Victorian times. The sweeping mountain vistas are a stunning reminder of the artistry of creation. I danced a merry old jig around the top of the tower, to be invited to share the twilight in the solitude and silence was overwhelming. I could feel the ancestors gathering as I put my voice on the wind and began the painfully enriching tale of Gelert.

The Tale of Gelert

Prince Llewelyn awoke eagerly to a bright March morn. In the grips of Imbolc the thought of Spring was rapidly changing into the realization of the Crone's demise and the Maiden's fullness with warmer winds and softer skin. The sun shone brilliantly in its sky blue cloak, a few thin wisps of white speckled on the collar and cuffs of the expanding horizon, a day to throw open the doors and leap into the possibility of change. Llewelyn grabbed his hunting robes and bounded down the stairwell calling for the horses to be saddled and the chase to begin. The hunting party took hold of their reins and Llewelyn cast his eye on the missing piece, his faithful wolfhound Gelert was nowhere to be seen. "Gelert boy, come on raise your lazy bones the hunt is on?" Cried an expectant Llewlyn. Gelert was a prized gift, brought by his beautiful bride Joan, daughter to King John of England, as part of her dowry. The bond between master and mutt was as strong and as bright as any of the Celtic weaves gracing the most treasured manuscripts in the finest libraries, to say they were inseparable was an understatement. As Llewelyn's voice echoed off the castle walls the sure footed long limbed Irish wolf hound failed to appear. "Come on boy, you know how much you love the hunt. Here Gelert or we'll leave without you". Gelert indeed loved the hunt, his large Irish paws and generous jaws were the terror of the wilderness for many a mile. "Last chance Gelert, we're leaving" roared Llewelyn in increasing frustration. There was still no sign of the agile hound so with a few choice words muttered under the breath Llewelyn and his retinue headed through the hills.

Although the maiden had dipped her fingers in the waters and released the frozen bite of the Crones grip on Winter the old hag was not defeated yet and what appeared to be an opulent day for hunting was just mirage hope, cabin fever had driven Llewelyn into the hills and before long his horses were bogged down in mud and the deer scattered safely in the shadows of the setting sun. Bedraggled and despondent the party cantered back into the courtyard. Lleweln's temper was rife. He slid off his horse and stormed towards the warmth of the hearth. There to greet him, tail hanging limply between his legs was Gelert.

"Oh now you turn up you grizzly mutt, couldn't make it for the hunt could you? Lazing by the fire all day whilst we froze our bollocks off. Perhaps if you had been out there fortune would have prevailed, but no…" Llewelyn's rant fell on deaf ears as Gelert pushed past him limping and painting up the spiral staircase. "Don't you go disappearing on me," chastised Llewelyn "I've not finished with you yet."

He flew up the flight of narrow stones to the floor above. He was about to unload another tirade of abuse when Llewelyn took in the sight before him. Gelert stood huffing and puffing, dripping and drooling, his shiny coat clotted and matted with blood. Llewelyn's keen eye took in the bloodstained flagstones and traced the trail to his son's nursery. The room was destroyed, the crib overturned globs of fresh blood stains seeped into the shredded torn furs the look in the eyes of the savage wolfhound told the horrific truth of the tale.

"You fucking mongrel, you evil fiend, you killed my son." Prince Llewelyn grabbed for the hilt of his sword and ripped it from the sanctuary of its leather bound scabbard. The sharp blade glimmered in the dying light of the day and the Prince's blood bubbled and boiled with an intensity matched in his menacing eyes. "You killed my boy!" he hollered in anguish. Gelert's sad eyes looked urgently for his master's recognition. Llewelyn's sword plunged from high, pierced through the strangled death yelp into the silenced heart of the treacherous dog.

"How could you kill my boy?" wept an uncontrollable Llewelyn as he sunk to his knees and his fists involuntarily beat the warm bloody corpse of Gelert looking to smash it into a pulp. It was in the depth of this darkness and despair that a light flickered in an adjacent room, the glimmer of life sparked from a tiny cry whimpering from an infants lungs. Crawling past the stiffening cadaver of the slain hound Llewelyn found his unharmed son. The boy was alive and well flanked by an enormous slumped figure of a mighty wolf. The wolf's shaggy throat gaped open spewing the blackest blood on the cold stone floor. Gelert had saved his son. A ferocious fight to the death won by the limber powerful wolfhound. Gelert had matched his jaws and speed against the most forceful of foes and he had not been found wanting. Gelert had protected the life of his boy at the risk of his own life and Llewelyn had repaid his friends love and trust by striking him down in blind rage.

It was with a splintered heart that Llewelyn carried the lifeless remains of his best friend and built a cairn to honor his life and mourn his death. He vowed that day that never again would he strike out in his anger and rage, he would instead breathe in the presence of the moment to make an informed decision. A village grew up around Gelert's grave and to this day carries his story on the winds, the village aptly named Beddgelert is a stones throw away from the hauntingly beautiful remains of Dolwydellan.

The Treasure of the Tale

The name Gelert is a cymricized variant of Kelert, Kilart, Kylart and Kelarth and deliciously is of unknown meaning and origin. Does Beddgelert house the remains of Llewelyn's trusted friend or is it the resting place of a 7th century St. Gelert who lived in a cave near what is now known as the Holy Well of St. Celer in Llandysul, Carmarthenshire?

Did Llewelyn ever have a dog named Gelert? Did it really save his son?

This story is found in many forms around the world. The mystery is to be found in the authentic truth of the tale as it related to us in the present moment. The story offers a timeless universal truth questioning us to live in the present moment. How often are we blindly dragging ourselves through the perceived edges of a frayed past or a glittering future? What do we do with our anger? How do we treat those closest to us? Why is it that I can be so much more patient with a stranger than a friend or family member? Why do we strike out and create wars in our own backyards? Llewleyn as we discovered earlier means Lion or Shining One, how are we the king, or as a Lioness the huntress and Queen of our own castle? Where are we rushing the seasons of our own life?

Don't just gloss over these questions, sit with them for a while, journey on them and see what nuggets of truth are hidden within the layers of your story.

The Irish meaning of Llewelyn, Lugh is oath, and I made my oath on those ramparts to share this tale that is embedded in Welsh folklore on each visitation. With a sense of direction and fulfillment I spiraled down the staircase and out onto the undulating land. I strode buoyantly down the path and stopped dead in my tracks. Looking right at me was a shaggy old Irish wolfhound. Our eyes met and then it leapt into a thicket and disappeared behind the veil. My eyes swelled with tears connecting to the thread of the story illuminating the worlds between the worlds.

For a poet's view of Gelert's story I feel the inclusion of Hon. W.R. Spencer's 1811 version is well worth reading and reciting.

GELERT

The spearman heard the bugle sound,
And cheerily smiled the morn,
And many a brach and many a hound
Attend Llewelyn's horn.
And still he blew a louder blast,
And gave a louder cheer -
Come Gelertl Why art thou the last
Llewelyn's horn to hear?
Oh where does faithful Gelert roam?
The flower of all his race
So true, so brave, a lamb at home
A lion in the chase.
'Twas only at Liewelyn's board
The faithful Gelert fed;
He watched, he served, he cheered his lord,
And sentinel'd his bed.
In sooth he was a peerless hound,
The gift of Royal John -
But now no Gelert could be found,
And all the chase rode on.
And now as over rocks and dells
The gallant chidings rise,
All Snowdon's craggy chaos yells
With many mingled cries.
That day Llewelyn little loved
The chase of hart or hare.
And scant and small the booty proved-
For Gelert was not there.
Unpleased Llewelyn homeward hied,
When near the portal seat
His truant, Gelert, he espied
Bounding his Lord to greet.

But when he gained his castle door,
Aghast the chieftain stood.
The hound all o'er was smeared with gore,
His lips, his fangs, ran blood.
Llewelyn gazed with wild surprise:
Unused such looks to meet,
His favourite checked his joyful guise
And crouched, and licked his feet.
Onward in haste Llewelyn passed-
And on went Gelert, too -
And still where'er his eyes were cast,
Fresh blood-gouts shocked his view.
O'erturned his infant's bed he found
The blood-stained covert rent,
And all around the walls and ground
With recent blood besprent.
He called his child - no voice replied!
He searched with terror wild.
Blood, blood he found on every side
But nowhere found his child.
Hell bound! My child's by thee devoured
The frantic father cried,
And to the hilt his vengeful sword
He plunged in Gelert's side.
His suppliant look, as to earth he fell,
No pity could impart,
But still his Gelert's dying yell
Past heavy o'er his heart.
Aroused by Gelert's dying yell
Some slumberer wakened nigh.
What words the parent's joy can tell
To hear his infant cry.
Concealed beneath a mangled heap
His hurried search had missed.

All glowing from his rosy sleep

His cherub boy he kissed.

Nor scratch had he, nor harm nor dread

But the same couch beneath

Lay a great wolf, all torn and dead

Tremendous still in death.

Ah! What was then Llewelyn's pain

For now the truth was clear.

The gallant hound the wolf had slain

To save Llewelyn's heir.

Vain, vain was all Llewelyn's woe

Best of thy kind, adieu!

The frantic deed which laid thee low

This heart shall ever rue!

And now a gallant tomb they rise

With costly sculpture decked

And marbles storied with his praise

Poor Gelert's bones protect.

Here never could a spearman pass,

Or forester, unmoved;

Here oft the tear-besprinkled grass

Llewelyn's sorrow proved.

And here he hung his horn and spear

And oft, as evening fell,

In fancy's piercing sounds would bear

Poor Gelert's dying yell.

The only way to experience joy is to know sorrow and the only way to know sorrow is to experience joy.

The Celts were never afraid of journeying into the depths of their darkness to find their light. Our Neolithic ancestors built Cairns and stone circles aligned to the sun and moon, on the western coast of Yns Mon a blustery headland juts into the Irish Sea housing an unusual ancient treasure more akin to Ireland than Wales. Above the sandy cove of Trecastell Bay is 'the Giantess 's Apronful', Barclodiad Y Gawres, a cruciform passage grave built in the same design as those on the Emerald Isle and similarly celebrated with deliciously decorated carvings. These etchings emblazoning the inner sanctum are a one of a kind for Wales.

The other intriguing aspect to this enticing tomb is its alignment to the north, which excludes any involvement with the sun, so why are there intricate carvings in this structure? What purpose does it serve to build the opening to the north?. I love a good mystery and my adrenalin was pumping as I tramped along the winding trail towards the cliff's edge. My heart was racing in delight having snagged the key to enter the ritualistic heart of the mound. The Wayside Stores in Llanfaelog, Rhosneigr have been the guardians of the key for a number of years and for a small deposit you could pick up both the key and a lantern, though it is always advisable to carry your own torch with fresh batteries to illuminate the nooks and crannies, in this case to feast on the hand chiseled lozenges, chevrons, zig zags and spirals that await you in the grave. Unfortunately due to recent vandalism the chamber was inaccessible for a while, but as I write Cadw the 'storical' environment service of the Welsh Assembly Government have contracted with the Wayside Stores to manage the chamber, one of their employees will accompany you on your visit. My ascent was auspiciously welcomed by a merlin flying overhead, the sand martins, oyster catchers, whinchats and wagtails are a bird watchers paradise. Other than my winged companion the promontory was deserted. A bracing wind added to the grayness of the morning sky lent an extra eeriness to this stark headland. The passage grave is both beautiful and ugly in the same breath, having sprinkled offerings and removed the heavy padlock I slipped inside the fortifications and leaving my flashlight in my pocket my eyes adjusted slowly to the light and dark of this musty tomb. Negligent visitors had left candle wax and tea light holders scattered on the earthen floor, a frustrating aspect of following in the footsteps of someone else's ceremony. Lest we should forget 'spiritual littering' is still littering, don't do it! Restoration to support the chamber from inevitable collapse is plainly evident in the reconstruction of the roof, an unsightly concrete dome screams of the duck tape mentality and technology of our civilized modern world and yet it is a thankful protector of the exquisite rock art and hauntingly atmospheric serenity found in the murkiness of the interplay between light and shade. Dank fusty dampness lingers on mildewed breath while tantalizing rushes of fresh salty brightness drift on the driving winds through the protected sheltering of the concealed entry way.

I collapsed contentedly with my back to one of the standing stones of the inner sanctuary. Here was the sacred fire pit, the place that excavators found the remains of a magical brew, a stew of eel, toad, frog, mouse, shrew, hare, grass snake and wrasse layered under a sheet of pebbles and strewn with limpet shells. I closed my eyes and imagined the gathering of an ancestral clan, the cremated remains of an honored chief placed in the south west chamber, a fire blazing in the center, potions cooking, whispers wailing, chanting, singing, a ceremonial calling of a collective kin. As my mind seeped into the compelling story I was aware of voices excitedly chatting outside the confines of the cairn. Two men were laboring their way toward the entrance, their thick accents betraying their birthplace, a distinctive Liverpudlian lilt resonated on the wind, "Your going to like this, it's an amazing monument, pity its always locked, shame you can't get in."

There was the sound of feet scraping on the loose earth and stone outside the iron gates. I had fortuitously bolted myself in so I would not be disturbed as I connected with the spirit of place. However I had not locked the door.

"Look," said the other Scouser . "There's no flaming padlock, the door's open" he exclaimed in amazement, "do you think we should go in?"

"Absolutely," chuckled his companion. "We're invited." the bolt screeched and clanged, the door hinges moaned swinging eerily open, and the two pals dawdled on the threshold working up the courage to walk into the darkness. I sat absolutely still completely obscured from their view, masked by the massive stone that was coolly pressing into my back.

"You first," stammered the deeper tones of what proved to be the older of the two men.

"Alright," stumbled his anxious friend, then giggling to release his tension he evocatively gurgled "Is anybody there?"

I couldn't resist, the pixies yelled play! So with the most haunting voice that I could conjure, I screeched cackled and chortled, "I am".

The two Scousers jumped out of their skin, I waited for a couple of beats feeling the electric charge surging through the vault and then I sprang out from behind the stone with a beaming grin. They shrieked again until the realization of my prank oozed into their bones and then we all fell into raucous laughter. It was with great joy we examined the decorated patterns on the stones and shared our thoughts and ideas about this sacred site, I left with a skip in my step a twinkling in my eye and laughter in my soul knowing that the ancestors had enjoyed the crack!

As I have eluded to, many of the ancient ceremonial gathering places are hidden, behind the veil, a hedgerow, a bush, off the beaten track, at a rocky coastline, in a farmers field, or on an isolated hillside, where no signposts or people made stairways or handrails exist. Sometimes locals keep their knowledge of the land hidden and sometimes the land keeps its treasures guarded from local lore. I remember fondly my journey to discover the ornate stone circle of Moel Ty Uchaf, I had a photo of this almost perfectly symmetrical circle that is nestled on a tall hill between Clwydd and Llandrillo in Northern Wales. I easily found the location of the nearest village and eagerly headed off to seek solace in this magical stone ring. I was not at all surprised to find myself driving way beyond the village with no indicators that the circle existed.

Unperturbed I turned the car around and after a fruitless search on the other side of the village I wound down my window having spotted a local sitting on his garden wall. The wizened face, of an elderly gentlemen, peeked from under a flat tweed cap and with a kindly smile shook his head and told me that he knew of no megalithic structures up on the hill but there was one on a nearby farm. He pointed the way down a lane and gave detailed instructions on how to get there.

I instinctively knew that I was on a wild goose chase. I was looking for 'The High Bare Hill,"
which is what Moel Ty Uchaf means, and yet I drove the way the old man had suggested toward
the lower valley floor. Back and forth along narrow lanes I went feeling the disappointed and
frustration etching at the corners of my consciousness. On the third time of passing a farm I was
thankful to see that the farmer was heading my way in his tractor. I pulled into his driveway
and felt a brush of optimism as he jumped down and lumbered toward me. I looked into the
round jovial weather beaten face of a man in his mid forties who had an air of satisfaction with
the world and was obviously connected to the earth because he was content to be in the present
moment and had as much time as needed to help wayward traveler. I stammered over my best
pronunciation of Moel Ty Uchaf, trying to get the full back of the throat hock to not desecrate
the name entirely. He repeated the name Moel Ty Uchaf many times and I was delighted that
my guttural rendition matched the farmers, however pronouncing it correctly was getting me no
closer to my destination. The farmer shook his head and shared firmly that there was no stone
circle up on the hill. He professed to know those hills like the back of his hand, they were after
all his childhood playgrounds and the only stone structure he knew of was the one on the farm
below. It was then that I whipped out my ace from up my sleeve, the photo of the land clearly
showing the stones on the hill. The tangible evidence of the picture clearly shook the man, his
face contorted in bemused wonderment. He seemed in a dazed trance as if he would turn into a
stone pillar himself! Then shaking his puzzled head he pointed to a diagonal formation of fields
and matched the two, land and picture, he could evidently see the reality of what lay before him
yet he was unable or at least for now unwilling to come to terms with the existence of another
stone circle within walking reach of his farm. He sighed deeply gazing forlornly into the distant
hills. There was a desperate quality to the way he murmured the deep desire to head into the
hills to find it himself. He even took the trouble to find a pen to write down the name of the
mysterious circle that danced on the horizon beyond his horizon. Still a little shaken, he advised
me to head into the village to the white house with a blue door and seek out Heffin Phillips, for
if anyone knew the way to the circle, Heffin would know.

So with grateful thanks I left him still staring into the familiarly unknown and headed into
the village to knock on the white house with the blue door. Imagine my bemusement when I
drove into a village with a bunch of white houses with blue doors. I must have resembled the
baffled farmer as I scratched my head and pondered which door to try first. I concluded that one
was as likely to yield success as the other if I chose incorrectly all I had to do was ask for Heffin.
I knocked on one door no answer, then another still no answer, and then a third, as is the Celtic
way, the number three holds so much magic, not for the first time today! A thin bespectacled
man opened the door and shook his head he was not Heffin, however he knew where Heffin
lived, but before I went on my way to seek out Heffin he asked if he could assist. A wide grin
came on his face at the name of Moel Ty Uchaf. He confided that the place was easier to get to
than find. He gave directions to a road and a track, he then told me to climb up the hill until I
was on the top of the ridge and go left and as far as my eye could see there would be nothing

there, but to keep going anyway and suddenly as if out of the mists, as if raised from the earth in that moment the circle would magically appear.

I followed his advice and sure enough The High Bare Hill opened up and shared an exquisite treasure where panoramic views sweep across the valley and the sidhe dance their dance with rippling laughter echoing on the wind amongst the ancestral stones. Although I never met Heffin Philips, I felt a connection to him in discovering Moel Ty Uchaf and I eagerly looked up the meaning of his name. I drew a blank on the name Heffin, yet I was intrigued to find that Phillips means friend of horses, a friend indeed to this inquisitive Steed!

Chapter 11

The Land Tells its Tale to Those Who Listen

My first visit to Scotland was a whirlwind adventure where I accompanied my good friend Steve Walding on a madcap journey to the Isle of Lewis. Steve worked for a health food company as a salesman and in the Spring of 1991 he took on a role that no-one else in the company wanted: for three nights and four days he became a delivery man. His company had a contract to erect a candy and nut stand in a small grocery store on Lewis which is roughly a 1,200 mile round trip excursion! It would have been cheaper to ship the small unit but the store insisted on a representative of Steve's company assembling it in person. So we trundled up north in a large box van that chugged and sputtered and groaned when you pushed her beyond 60 miles an hour. He didn't need to twist my arm too hard offering me all my meals, two nights sleeping in the back of the truck, where there was plenty of space, a twenty foot by nine foot container loaded with nothing but the slender framework of a stand that when constructed would measure no more than four foot tall by three foot wide, the fringe benefits included one night bed and breakfast accommodation on the Isle itself and a tipple at the pub each night, all I had to do was keep company and share the wheel.

I was 27 years old and had never crossed the border into the ancestral lands of the Davidson and Innes clans, but now I was going home. Driving through the lowlands into the Highlands was exhilarating and a brief stop at Culloden the site of the last battle on British soil brought a lump to my throat and a tear to my eye. It would be another ten years before I would return to stand in the same spot and another five years before I fully understood the significance.

From the desolate moorland just outside of Inverness we drove to Ullapool and took the ferry ride to Stornoway on Lewis. We arrived on the last ferry and after a good nights rest and a full Scottish breakfast we went to the grocery store to do our work. It took about twenty minutes to set up the candy and nut stand and then the rest of the day was ours to play. We spent a remarkable day of tranquility amongst the standing stones of Callanish. This was before the days that 'His'toric Scotland laid a path around it to cope with the increasing amount of visitors that flock to this awe-inspiring site. We sat in the circle for hours soaking up the atmosphere. This laid the foundations of traveling to these nemetons as a witness and not a tourist. I watched a handful of people arrive during my five hours at the stones, they marveled at the view, Callanish stands on a rise with sweeping views of mountains and lochs, they snapped their photographs desperately trying to capture the magnificence on film and fled the scene in pursuit of their next dramatic shot. In the space of minutes they had come and gone and Callanish had kept quiet, the Shining One that skips down the avenue on a midsummer dawn must have cackled whole heartedly at the absurdity of the fleeting tourists.

The seeds planted that day took eight years to root and it was another two before I walked the land in Bonnie Scotland to find the routes to wander with a pilgrim band.

I have since crossed the border many times with many good people in tow. I remember in 2004 a man of Hawaiian Scottish descent clambering into the passenger seat as we headed to Inverness. Mark MacLean informed me in a gentle voice that he would be no trouble. He was accompanying his wife who was 'into this kind of thing', he loved her with all his heart and wanted her to experience a spiritual journey through his ancestral lands that he felt no connection with and no real desire to connect to. I invited him to be open to the journey and welcomed his presence and participation in our circles and endorsed his right to the freedom to choose his own path. I am always amazed at the shifts that happen when in the magical vortexes of these ancient sites and just as my mother had claimed to not believe in faeries, Mark's insistence that this was not his gig left me salivating to find what would occur. Scotland sat Mark down on his behind and made love to him.

Our first port of call was the Clava Cairns, three burial chambers that sit amongst standing stones in a moss green faerie wood a stones throw away from Culloden Moor. I have sat at this spot at dawn, at dusk, in the darkness of the night, in the rain, hail, snow, and full sunshine and it always conjures a new part of its evolving song. Since 2000 BC the stone people have honored the passing of the generations of Scots and travelers who have sauntered into this otherworldly realm. If you get into your roots and stay awhile the place will empty of frivolous traffic and the interplay of light, the sweet whisperings of the grove and the deep hum of the primordial stones will move you. Mark felt it, I saw him shift even if he was unaware of what, why, how or when it took place, but I saw him arrive and connect with something bigger than himself that was part of himself.

Mark's wife shared with me that he had fully owned his Hawaiian roots and rejected his Scottish. Great combination don't you think? A tropical Celt! As we traveled to Mull and Iona a raw truth swept through the cobwebs in my mind and it clearly dawned on me that Duart Castle greets you, standing proudly on a point, to the left of the portside, as the ferry sails into Craignure. Once we had settled into our Bed and Breakfast in Fionnphort I asked Mark if he knew of Duart Castle. He looked up excited and revealed that he had just read that the castle was the seat of his ancestors, the MacLean Clan.. I asked Mark if he knew that Duart Castle was on Mull which immediately piqued his interest and he smiled saying that he had just read that fact and was wondering how he could get there. He looked flummoxed when I told him I would take him and the rest of the pilgrims too. He shook his head sadly and said "We can't go, it's not on the itinerary."

"Mark," I gently chided, "It is now."

"But that's not fair to the others they wont want to go," he sighed.

"Want a bet?" I giggled, "Who wants to go and see Mark's Castle?" I called to the other pilgrims.

"I do" was the resounding response. I am not particularly fond of castles with other people's furniture and pictures neatly arranged within, I much prefer a desolate ruin where most folks don't go and my imagination can play with the silent stones tumbled, tossed and covered in lichen, but on this occasion my heart was full as I watched Mark beaming with the discovery of his kin. He even bought his clan colors and ordered all the trimmings to go with his kilt!

I am often asked which pilgrimage is the best one? Should I go to Scotland first, or Ireland, what about Wales, and where is Cornwall? My reply never alters, "My favorite pilgrimage is the one that I am on!" I could as easily pick between these wonderful lands as tell you which of my children I love the best. The countries, like my children, are very different and yet they have similarities and they are all beautiful. There are, however, some harsh desolate places in Scotland that tug and pull at you, their wild majesty weeping jubilant laughter and blood stained tears.

It was April 2006 during a snowstorm that I gathered the pilgrims in Eileen MacLean's front room at Eiland View bed and breakfast. Eileen had stoked a welcoming fire and we had all tucked into one of her delicious breakfasts, Eileen like her mother in law Margaret who lives across the way know the meaning to offering Celtic hospitality. Their beautiful abodes are within a hike of Culloden Moor and on a blustery morning with flurries falling thick and fast we jumped in the minibus and headed to the battleground. There had been some resistance to going I have experienced this before with people feeling that they do not need to visit a site of war. I tell them Culloden is more than battlefield it is where everything changed in the story of Scotland.

On April 16th 1746 the Jacobite rebellion was scattered after an ill fated forced march to Nairn the night before had left the Scottish Highlanders tired and weary, Bonnie Prince Charlie led the clans onto Drumossie Moor, a boggy marshland, at Culloden and a massacre took place. The Jacobite rising of 1745 supported the claim of the House of Stuart to the throne of the British Isles wishing to restore the Stuart line by placing James II's grandson Charles Edward Stuart on the throne deposing the Hanoverian line and removing George II. They came close to their task marching all of the way to Derby in the midlands with London beckoning and King George II preparing to flee, the Scots changed course and returned to the highlands. They had been only 127 miles away from the capital. My understanding for this was that the army was thinning because highlanders were missing home and deserting and they were reportedly facing a three pronged attack by a far superior numerical force. In hindsight had the Jacobites stayed intact and continued marching their army would undoubtedly have thronged with those sympathetic to the Stuart cause. There were many in England and Wales who would have been motivated to get off the fence and join the rebellion.

The French were preparing to send ten thousand troops into Southern England to aid the Jacobite campaign. This was not to be and in the December of 1745 the five thousand or so

Highlanders headed north into the hills. Things still might have turned in the Scots favor had a series of calamitous events not taken place. Starting with the disastrous night march to Nairn, designed to surprise the Duke of Cumberland and the Jacobite army, reaped nothing but sore feet, aching limbs and a dent to morale. The strategy on paper looked good. It was the Duke of Cumberland's birthday and if the enemy were reveling and too intoxicated to defend their position, the Scottish force would drive through them and claim a sweet victory. However the sustenance offered to the rebels was a single oatmeal bannock, which was hardly enough for a mouthful let alone nourishment to carry a grown man on a grueling march into a strenuous battle. Worse still, the English were ready and sober soldiers guarded the line leaving somber bedraggled clansmen retracing their steps through the cold darkness across boggy taxing terrain. Exhausted starving and chilled to the bone the insurgents collapsed to rest and sleep off the calamitous slog of their nighttime trail. Sprawled in ditches crammed in outbuildings or off in search of food the Jacobite army was unready and ill prepared for the arrival of their foe and even though reports were received of the pursuing Hanoverians, Bonnie Prince Charlie's troops were still in disarray at 11am when the two camps were in sight of each other.

A line was hastily formed with about 5.000 men gathered under the flags of the Jacobite cause. The next perplexing decision was the site of the battleground itself. The strength of the Highland charge, the ancient Celtic war cry and mad dash at the enemy swinging axes, swords, maces and clubs had been the ferociously terrifying tradition of ages past. The sight of the kilted clansmen tearing towards you their faces contorted in primordial screams, their hair whipping in the wind and their glinting weapons swinging with your name written on their blades was enough to send bowels into overdrive and legs to desertion. The success of this howling stampede lay in the Celts choosing the upper slope, having their enemy struggling uphill to meet them as they ran hell for leather at the rival ranks. Culloden Moor offers no such advantage. It is a flat desolate bog, hard to walk over let alone run at speed, and the only benefit befell on the gathering foe for they had in their possession heavier artillery and their canons were deployed to devastating effect.

Lord George Murray an experienced veteran in the ways of war counseled Bonnie Prince Charlie to withdraw but the youthful leader insisted on the fight. In retrospect a large contingent of people argue that if the Highlanders had taken to the hills and fought a guerrilla style campaign with night time raids drawing the enemy into ghostly glens and using the hidden hills to disappear into the mist then the outlook may have been different. Shots rang out around 1pm as a driving mix of sleet and rain hammered in to the Highland faces.

The Duke of Cumberland had organized his 9,000 men well and had opted to use grape shot rather than a single cannonball meant that forty to fifty missiles whizzed through the air scattering and killing the clansmen by the score. With no instructions to charge, the frustrated rebels finally took the battle to the British Crown. It was the Mackintoshes who led the right wing in a frantic frenzied race breaking through the Government troops front line only to be skewered on the bayonets and riddled with holes from the second lines musket fire.

The left wing led by the MacDonalds is reported to have delayed their charge and when they did make their move they had a further distance to travel over much more difficult mud and marsh, hence the line broke and the fragmented force was cut down. The brave attempt to break their enemies formation fell sadly short and the piles of bodies slumped over each other. It was a mass of dead and wounded Highlanders - an army decimated in an instant. By two o'clock the battle was over, barely an hour had passed and yet countless souls had passed. The losses on the Hanoverian side were around 300 dead and wounded whilst the Jacobite army estimated numbers between 1,500 and 2,000 dead. The wounded were slaughtered as they lay dying on the field. The Duke of Cumberland's infamous nickname of 'the Butcher' was notoriously gained as he sent his men to leisurely slay the defeated injured rebels on Drumossie Moor, some meeting their maker with their throats slit two days after the battle had ended. Raping, pillaging and murder continued for several days with indiscriminate hangings and the victors scorched the Highlanders homes raped the women and forced families into starvation as over 20,000 head of livestock were driven off for sale, the profits split by the conquering soldiers.

The Battle of Culloden, however, was and was not a Scottish defeat. The Crown's force included The Royal Scots, the St. Clair's, the Scots Fusiliers, now known as the Royal Highland Fusiliers, the Scottish Borderers, the Semphill's and the Argylle Militia, on the Jacobite side standing shoulder to shoulder with the Highland Clans were French Regular Troops. So Scots fought Scots and the Crown won the day. However it was a costly loss for the Scottish. Not only did it defeat the Stuart's claim, a line tracing its ancestry to the Dark Age Gaelic Kingdom of Dal Riata and beyond, it is the haunting place where the Highland clan culture sang its last song. With the fleeing of Bonnie Prince Charlie from Scottish shores and his failure to ever return the rebellion bit the dust. Hardship was to follow as the British Government enacted several laws that effected Scottish life especially for the Highlanders. The judicial and military power of the clan chiefs was crushed as the hereditary right to govern justice on their own lands was stripped away the clan chiefs who had supported the Crown were richly compensated for this loss whereas the clan chiefs who had supported the rebellion had their lands seized and sold the profits being used to promote trade and agriculture in Scotland, in short sheep became more valuable than people. The Highlands were garrisoned by Government troops with roads and barracks protecting the Crown's footing in bringing Scotland to heel.

The wearing of clan colors was forbidden the kilt was banished unless worn in service in a regiment of the British Army and the pipes were silenced. Many of the rebels that were rounded up and captured were put to death at Carlisle, York and Kennington Common with the highest ranking rebel lords being refused a pardon and being executed on Tower Hill in London, thus enforcing the nickname of 'Butcher' to the Duke of Cumberland. Those fortunate enough to escape death were herded on to boats and were transported and banished to the 'New World'. This was the beginning of the 'Scottish Trail of Tears' known as the 'Highland Clearances". It is with the rich tapestry of the changing face of the Scottish story that I lead pilgrims to the path of honoring the dead and listening to the strands of the song so that it might be remembered and contrary to what is written earlier here the Highland Clan Culture's song will sing again. So on a day akin to April 16th 1746 with a blizzard swirling in the air I pulled into the car park at Culloden and braving the elements we made our way onto the hauntingly desolate moor. Even when there are throngs of people I find an eerie stillness and solitude amongst the mounds and marshland of Drumossie. Culloden never fails to stir my soul and on previous occasions the poetry of the land rushed through me, and my pen scribbled words that echoed my thoughts, my knowing.

Culloden Speaks 2002

On Culloden's dank and boggy moor

I sit in the centre of an ancestral war

Amongst roots moss heather green fir

I sink into Sovereignty my cauldrons stir

What do I run from? Why do I hide?

When do I fight in truth and when with false pride?

Do I have the courage to step inside?

Do I manifest beauty or is my brilliance denied?

Authentic questions are my weapons of choice

In answering them I claim my voice

So I lay down my busyness my desire to always win

I release lingering fears of intimacy and embrace my being

The truth of my soul the song of my heart

The radiance of my story the voice of a poet

I spiral into my centre sink my roots deep in the ground

Honoring my Kingdom the Sovereignty I've found

Ancestors rest in peace for you all live in me

My laughter joyful song and playful mirth lead us all to VICTORY!

Culloden Speaks 2004

Sweet song of memory

the winged chorus sings to me

the earth wet with tears seeping into her body

as the blood of our ancestors has before

all for what, a noble war?

May I stand as strong as the Rowan tree

bringing light and life to history, herstory, my story the mystery.

The unseen beings in their finest green

Whisper gentle remembrance to Culloden's screams

And as the cleansing wind kisses the field that once ran blood red

Rays of dancing sunlight ignite a fire in my head

Calling from the past of a bright tomorrow

That all life grows through joy and sorrow

That to live my life in truth today

I too must walk a warrior's way

Stand my ground face my fears

Step into my darkness taste my tears

As my light shines dawning my day

I am who I am in an authentic way

Bless this land for its poetry

Thank you ancestors for your gift to me

I swear an oath upon this hallowed earth

To sing my rich song for all it is worth.

Culloden brings up both laughter and tears and always invites me to glean a new piece of the story. As the driving sleet whipped into my face mingling with the salty tears that ran freely down my shivering face I found my spot, a place that always calls to me, where I lay down and put my whole torso into the soggy earth and I taste the land and breath her in to my willing body. It was with frozen fingers an icy nose and cold numb toes that I stumbled into the visitors center seeking a bowl of hot soup to warm my cockles and thaw my bones. Most of the pilgrims were nestled inside, but a couple were still braving the blustery winds and showering sleet.

One of the women in the party by the name of Karen caught my eye and exclaimed how powerful her experience had been. She was evidently moved by the majesty of Drumossie Moor and she confided that the spirits of place had shared an essential secret of her ancestral past. "My clan was on this field," she claimed with wide eyes and glowing cheeks. Her family name is Evans, which I told her sounded more Welsh to me but I escorted her into the gift shop where we perused the bookshelves looking for confirmation of her discovery. Daunted by the task we cut to the chase and asked for help. The person we were told would know the answer was Hugh Allison who was at lunch and was immediately sent for. I tried to explain that we would wait until he returned but the staff member assisting us was having none of it. Within seconds Hugh appeared not at all put out but excited to share his knowledge, another fine example of Celtic hospitality. He scratched his head on hearing the name Evans and also remarked on the Welsh connection as he reached for a book rifled through it and nodded with satisfaction verifying Karen's intuition that indeed an Evans had been on the field that day and had been among the survivors fleeing the battle scene after all was lost. Karen's face beamed with delight and she looked at me and thanked me profusely for bringing her to a place she thought held no special significance for her. I looked into her teary eyes with heartfelt gladness for how Spirit works and the magic that continually draws us to these thin places. I looked across at Hugh and asked about the Davidson's. I knew that our clan had formed part of Clan Chattan the clan of the cats and had been on the field that day. Interestingly the clan chief was serving on the side of the Government so authority fell to his wife Lady MacIntosh who opposed him and raised troops to take the battle to him. The fighting spirit of Lady Anne Macintosh also known as Anne Farquarson and Colonel Anne echoes that of the mighty Queen Boddicea, She chose MacGillivray of Dunmagalss to lead the combined forces of several clans under the umbrella of Clan Chattan. Their fateful charge was met by the annihilation of all but three of its members.

Hugh confirmed that the Davidsons died that day and it was with a shiver down my spine that he shared where they fell. The place upon which I always lie down and weep, close to the Well of the Dead, is the site of their demise. Tears fell freely as if the Well of the Dead was rising up in me, overflowing and pouring forth, as I understood the significance of why I go to keen in the same spot each time I visit the haunting graves of the Highlanders last charge. Both Karen and I received more than we expected in honoring the story of our ancestral roots.

As you are well aware I love to explore the meaning of names, Karen means Pure and Evans is a gracious gift of God. She certainly was gifted graciously a pure piece of wonderment to weave into the fabric of her bones. Hugh means mind heart or spirit and Allison means noble kind and truth. His bright mind and kind heart helped us to find the spirit of truth about our noble clans.

The Duke of Cumberland's name was William Augustus, which translates into the great and magnificent protector led by will and desire. He protected the crown against the Jacobites which is from the name James which means he who supplants and the leader of the rebels, Bonnie Prince Charlie looked to supplant George II, Charles means free man and the Prince got off the field that day and indeed fled to freedom, his name Stuart means steward or manager and he was the leader that managed to order his troops into a futile dash to death on that infamous day in April of '46. Macintosh means son of the chieftain and it was the MacDonald's whose name means chief that lagged behind as the son of the chief perished on British bayonets. So the son of the chief, the Macintosh's died first and the chief the MacDonald's followed suit. With the son and the Chief dead the symbolic death of the Highlanders rebellion was complete. Lastly the name of the King was George, which means farmer, and Scotland's Highland Clearances began as sheep became more valuable than people and the land was stripped from the chief's and converted into farming lands for the supporters of King George. I find it uncanny how names can so easily tell a story!

Chapter 12

ALBA

Many treasures of Alba are unearthed in the Kilmartin Valley. From the Hill of Dunadd to the Templewood stone circle, this remote vale on the West coast of Scotland is arguably the most impressive antediluvian site in Scotland and mayhap the whole of the Isles. Over 350 ancient sites litter a six mile radius, from Pictish carvings to burial cairns, hill forts to standing stones this tranquil megalithic paradise is sheltered in groves, laid open and bare to the sweeping winds and hidden along winding trails and thick dense woodland. As well as the relics of the old village, which if you blink you might miss, Kilmartin has a notable museum, a fabulous graveyard aside the parish church, the best banoffie pie I have ever tasted courtesy of the Kilmartin hotel where for several years Laura and Martina have provided exceptional service to a hungry and weary traveler. And the piece de resistance is the warm welcome and hospitality of Isobel and Tom McLaughlin of Rosebank Bed and Breakfast. These two delightful souls epitomize the meaning of Celtic hospitality and have made me feel like I am part of their family.

I brought my first group of pilgrims to Kilmartin in 2002 and it left a memorable impression and a yearning to return to touch the soil of this ancestral heartland. I recall my first trek up Dunadd on a May morning as the sun rose over the sleepy valley reflecting the expansiveness of this jewel in Scotland's crown. The steep ascent winds up to a platform with sweeping views across the valley, there is one more tier to climb to reach the top but before you take that final clamber to crest the peak of this ancient kingdom you are met by a substantial stone that looks uncannily like a giant foot, this is the coronation stone and is a prominent landmark in Scotland's rich story. An observant eye will pick out the fading boar etched on the side of this stone, the boar is a powerful totem to the Isles both for the Celtic tribes and those that lived before.

The boar totem is a symbol found in both story and artifact. A boar emblem is portrayed on the earliest silver coins of the Corieltauvi (Coritani) in Britain and are known to be connected to the Hallstadt culture and dated at 1100 BC. The antlered god Cernunnos is shown attended by a boar on the Gundestrup cauldron and on coins from the La Tene period dated 500 BC. In Ireland the otherworldly boar Orc Triath was the possession of Brigit the Dagda's daughter and is synonymous with Twrch Trwyth in the legendary Welsh saga in which Arthur hunts the boar so that his cousin Kilhwch can win the hand of Olwen. St. Kevin of Glendalough's encounter with a wild boar being chased by a hunting party and seeking St. Kevin's protection. The White Boar of Marvan inspired this herdsman, physician, messenger and musician to write music and poetry which has connections to St. Brigit as St. Broccan scribed in a poem :

A wild boar frequented her herd,
To the north he hunted, the wild pig;
Brigit blessed him with her staff,
And he took up his stay with her swine

The poem echoes the Goddess Brigit's relationship with Orc Triath. A gleaming white boar is used to lure Pryderi into an enclosure, which he cannot escape, from the Mabinogi, and Gwydion is transformed into a boar by Math in the fourth branch of these famous Welsh sagas. The boar is associated with strength ferocity hospitality and feasting. The carnyx a Celtic long handled boar headed war trumpet to bellow the aggressive charge of a boar like strike are just a few of the threads that endeared this once flourishing beast of dense woods to the indigenous people of the Isles.

So as I watched the sun kiss the earth where the kings of Alba made oaths of sovereignty to the land I traced the thin outline of the mighty boar and looked to the footprint that is carved conspicuously toward the front of the stone. An indentation in which Fergus Mor, son of Erc, placed his foot as he became the first king of Alba around 500AD. Behind the inauguration stone is a carved basin etched in a nearby rock that looks like it would have been part of the ancient rites of the kings mating with the land.

Dunadd simply means the Dun, the hill fort by the Add. The river Add serpentines across the valley floor, which would have aided the rise of this place of power so close to the Atlantic Ocean. The Dal Riata who had sailed from Ireland made this their stronghold, the seat of power and was the site of early coronations and the birth of the people we now call the Scots. Kenneth MacAlpin united the kingdoms of Dal Riata under control of the Scots with the native inhabitants known as the Picts. It is believed that Kenneth son of Alpin, King of Kintyre was born of Royal lineage from both parents. His mother as a Pictish Queen offered her son an opportunity to rule through matrilineal succession practiced by the Picts. So in 845 AD he accepted the title of Rex Pictorum and was crowned king of Alba moving the coronation ceremony from Kilmartin to Scone in the heart of Pictish land where future kings were crowned atop Moot Hill over the Stone of Destiny, believed to have been used in biblical times by Jacob as a pillow at Bethel. It was moved from Syria to Egypt and a fleeing King Gathelus took it to Spain before one of his descendents took it to the High Seat at Tara in Ireland until the Dal Riata brought it to Iona the druids Isle and then on to Argyll. The stone was then forcibly removed by the notorious 'Hammer of the Scots' and thorn of the Welsh, Edward I who placed it in Westminster Abbey in 1296 AD and supposedly every King and Queen of England from Edward II on has been crowned upon it. Legend has it, however, that this may not be so. Suspicion has it that the monks of Scone replaced the Scottish artifact with a forgery that Edward I carried off in triumph. It is interesting to note that the Coronation Stone is geologically similar to the sandstone commonly found in and around Scone. Ten thousand people celebrated the return of the stone to Scottish soil on St. Andrew's Day, 30th November 1996. One other footnote to the story of the stone is its disappearance from Westminster on Christmas Day 1950. It was stolen by Scottish Nationalists and though returned the following April some have questioned whether they returned the actual stone or a forgery. I love that there could well be three Stone's of Destiny floating around, very Celtic!!!

Our pilgrimages to Skye and to Iona via Mull end up in the Kilmartin Valley, the original Scottish capital, the heart center of the Neolithic people who dug their roots into the soil, who recognized the shape of the land and the natural forces that dwelt there. The river Add snakes across this ancient Valley of the Dead. I giggle as I write river for the pilgrims from the USA scratch their heads and in baffled unison they echo 'this is a river?' Our serpentine tributaries are deemed to be creeks or streams Stateside yet these weaving arms welcomed traders from all over the world. In the River Add's case the branches from sea to land twist and turn for miles which allowed Gaulish traders a short cut into Alba. This gateway was a bustling center, a true capital, akin to Glasgow or Dublin today. Much like Tulsk in Ireland, the valley is often overlooked as people rush to Oban or Inverary for here the magic remains in the fabric of the land and in the megalithic paradise that is weaved in the rock structures that date back 5,000 years. The road through Kilmartin like the river Add, zig zags through the sleepy village and if you blink you may miss it. For those who stop awhile and sample the soup at the museum's restaurant, (the mushroom is the best on the planet!) will feed more than their bellies.

The land nurtures the soul in a blanket of reverence to those who went before. Over 350 ancient monuments are scattered within a six mile radius. If you walk out of the village on the Oban road and step through the gateway on your left you begin a gentle stroll through this linear cemetery. To the North beyond the Glebe Cairn lies Upper Largie and to the South the Nether Largie, North, Mid and South Cairns stretch in alignment to Ri Cruin. Templewood stone circle is set amongst the lush green grass and teeming spray of vibrant flowers and abundant moss clinging to the standing guardians of the tree people, the Nether Largie stones, Dunchraigaig cairn, Ballymeanoch stones, henge and cairn and the Pictish carvings of cup and ring marks that sprawl magnificently across the bedrock of Baluachraig. All of these strikingly powerful nemetons radiate a tranquil peace if you are in your roots and spend time with the spirits of place. Individually the structures may easily be dismissed as being diminutive compared to the giant stones at Avebury, the enormity of Aengus' temple of love at the Bru na Boinne Newgrange, or the easily recognizable features of the Merlin's Dance at Stonehenge, yet collectively these dotted structures emanate a depth of story etched into rock and forged into land. Stretching beyond this lazy morning amble to the North stands the relatively new block work of the 1565 AD Carnasserie Castle, and to the South are the impressive outcrops of Achnabreck with their spiral, multiple rings, peltas, ringed stars and parallel grooves. Here lies the largest gathering of ancestral art work in Scotland and within spitting distance for Fingal the giant and other carvings that abound at Ormaig.

The piste de resistance is the hill fort of Dunadd, the crowning glory, the home and capitol for the Irish immigrants of the Dalriadan dynasty. This high rocky knoll that dominates the surrounding landscape is a natural breast and it was here at the teat that the ancient kings came to swear Sovereignty with the land. On the lower of the twin summits imprinted on the inauguration stone is the Boar, the footprint and set back is the hollowed basin.

Our culmination to our wanderings in Bonnie Scotland take us to the 176ft climb upon the sacred mound of Dunadd and we place our foot where kings have placed theirs and taking a piece of earth like the ancestors of old, we cry our oaths onto the wind. We pledge how we will live our lives for the next year and a day.

The words of J. J. Lafferty sing in my ears and pluck the heartstrings of my soul:

DUNADD

As I stood on rock where the crowned kings of Dalriada stood, Christian was not how I felt
wind eerie and singular reinforced the sense of mystery
the sacred that dwelt there in the shifting light.
Totemic boar etched in rock a bridge to the otherworld spiritual guide and nourishment this
fierce wild untamed essence drawn on to imbue mettle in those he faced.
Here the newly crowned took on his tenacity and courage.
A place for regal foot where the king vowed to continue the culture of his people and hold
sacred the gods our people swore by until Dalriada like Tara passed and the grieving wind
now blows the grass around the hill of Dunadd.
Ogham language of mystery script of trees lines of the Druid the dance of meaning in a
meaningful place,
The centre now shaped to the margins as the world moves and the wind weaves the grasses
and kisses the script incised on the crowning rock of a faded kingdom.
On this height I was connected as stone, plain, stream and keening wind conjured a moment
of grace a gift of continuity to me. By the gods my people swear by, I pledge the same.

Where Dunadd 's song has its roots in ancestral calling, the valley floor calls you to return to the silent rustlings of the dead. Dunchraigaig and Ri Cruin Cairns are wooded copses with fluttering faerie wings and spinning sprites darting behind the veil weaving magic on the shifting breath of a moody wind. On the Oban road just north of the village stand the intact ruins of Carnassarie castle with winding stairwells to two intact towers and a sheltered dank dark room to shield a pilgrim on a blustery day. I love this spot for its ambience and the fact that you can climb the tumbled ruins at any time day or night there is no admission charge no security no turnstiles, no obtrusive paved walkways and thankfully no vandalism. Carnassarie is one of the more modern gems of the valley dating to 1565. There is something romantic and freeing in the knowledge that you can stand on the battlements on a mystical full moon, in the drizzling rain or a pounding thunderstorm and you may meet a horde or two of tourists but if you're willing to be the witness and stay awhile, you will experience the castle as your own as you listen to the whispering ghosts of eons past.

Chapter 13

Giants & Faeries & Sheep Skulls - Oh My!

My first visit to Iona was after the autumnal equinox. In late September 2001. I began building a relationship with locals in Fionnphort and Iona. Tourists are known to some as 'excuse me's', 'excuse me is this where I get the ferry? Excuse me how often does it run? Excuse me where do I park my car? Excuse me'..... I was delighted to be told by Jane, who was the Island's nurse for many years before she and her husband Ian sold Shore Cottage, the penultimate house before the ferry ride to Iona, and headed to Brittany to live on a barge, that I and the pilgrims were not considered "excuse me's." Arriving in the depth of autumn has its consequences. The swells of the relatively shallow Straits of Iona are crested with white caps and Davey Kirkpatrick's boat is firmly anchored in port with no trips to Staffa,, but the mid size Caledonian ferry that holds about three cars and a boatload of passengers runs regularly, yet I was amazed to find that even the ferry could be put to rest for the day due to the sea gods stormy temperament. I do not do well on boats and I was grateful that the crossing from Mull to Iona is within leaping distance of Fingal the Giant, and the highest point Dun I stands proud and tall in front of the abbey that is clearly seen from Mull's shore. I was even more pleased when the hatch was lowered and we were given the all clear to go ashore. 'Wait, wait, now' cried a helpful ferry worker I rushed and his good deed was met by a surging wave that lashed up my leg and leaped at my armpit. I was soaked, blessed by the cold salty waters, as I made my first step onto Innis nan Druidhneach the Isle of the Druids.

I was cold wet and feeling forlorn initially as I strode the familiar tourist path toward the Abbey. It was when I went beyond the steps of the familiar that Iona opened up and sang her song to me. It is beyond the multitude of stories, for Iona is full of rich tales. It is buried in the fabric of the rock and when we sit and listen she attaches strong chords to our heart that will make lovers of us forever.

This enchanted nemeton for Druidic studies later became St. Columba's Isle as the Celtic Saint looked for a place where he could settle and no longer see the shores of Ireland. St. Columba was thrown off the Emerald Isle in the 6th Century and some believe wrote the Book Kells while sequestered on the holy Isle of Iona. The island is about 3 and a half miles long by a mile and half wide. Though the scenery is easy on the eye there are many more prolifically beautiful landscapes on the mainland, yet Iona has a unique feel. It is said when the Isles are swallowed by the sea, Iona will still stand strong. Here the spirit of place is thinner than thin, the archaic rock strata is more than 2,900 million years old, some of the oldest on this planet. The green and white marble stones are found scattered on the beaches of remote coves on the southern side of the island. Scouring the tide line on these beaches will reward you with polished gems kissed and washed smooth by the countless tides.

It was on a quest day in 2002 as the heavens opened and Taranis, god of thunder, ripped the fabric of the sky hurling a torrential downpour on us wandering souls, that I came across a huge chunk of rock, green and glowing.   Green stones are said to be the most magical in the Celtic world and this one was shouting at me. I stooped down and picked it up. It was as big as both of my fists combined. I have always held great conversations with the rock people. When I am fully in the moment and I truly listen, the natural world opens its doors and invites me in to see beyond the appearance of what lies before me.

A number of years ago I was on a shamanic training weekend at Kirkridge in Pennsylvania, USA where a megalithic park has been built at Columcille. Interestingly the founder of the park, William Cohea Jr., was influenced by his stay on Iona. Even more intriguing is that there are no standing stone formations on Iona, just the whisper of the magic that emanates from its core, its soul. One who steps foot on this transformative Isle will experience shifts whether conscious of them or not. As St. Columba reportedly shared, "Behold Iona a blessing on every eye that sees it, one who does good for another here will be repaid a thousandfold." And so it is that William Cohea Jr. was blessed to bless others by offering a space for 'tired sinners and reluctant saints' to visit and share their ideas and experiences in Eastern PA. This fed the development of stone circles, a labyrinth and peaceful trails that imbue the meaning of Colum Cille's name, the older version of the name Columba which means Dove.

It was close to Samhain one year that I had made my way to this modern yet old sanctuary in the Appalachian mountains where I wended my way to Bridget, one of the bridges that cross the sparkling stream. I flopped in the betwixt and between on this linking thread, my head lying on the hard boards my body curled up gazing at the autumn colors and breathing in the delicious scent of the season. I watched the smooth flow of the current caressing a rock and I spoke out loud, as I often do when alone in nature,

"It must be lonely and frustrating to be a rock being stuck in one place, not having legs to wander and see the world, being overlooked by so many people."

"Well you noticed me didn't you?" Replied the rock. That got my attention. "And who says I don't have legs? Its all a matter of perception, I am visited by the stream each and every day, the trees, fish, birds, insects, deer. fox, frogs and occasionally even people stop by to share a tale and when they are listening hear my story. As a rock I am never lonely for I am part of the Universal story and just as you are a storyteller so am I. Just as you are a dreamer so am I. My imagination grows from the tales that the blackbird chirps, that the dog barks and the stream gurgles, and I spread my wings for I am the eagle, I stretch my legs for I am you and I am part of the mystery, the story, its beginning, middle and end for its end is merely another beginning and now you and I are connected even though we already were and my story goes with you and yours is already part of the stream, the bark, the soil, reaching the edge of the world beyond the rocks of Iona beyond the boundaries of thought, beyond the limits of the unlimited."

All of what the rock told me I had known before, in this remembrance I sank to a new level of understanding and I giggled because in this adventure we call life there is always more, like the Dagda's Cauldron of plenty, we live in the midst of prosperity in each moment, when we celebrate all that is rather than focusing on all that isn't.

So as I ventured over the southern crevices of Iona's rocky swampy dips and hollows that are so much more challenging than the sandy coves of the northern shore, the green rock pulled me to my knees and asked me to dance. Amidst the pouring rain I clutched this mini megalith of a two fisted stone and clearly heard the invitation to carry it with me and work with it. This was close to the beginning of my day and a mineral this large was going to cause the straps of my backpack to cut and dig into my soaking wet shoulders. The stone also gave clear instructions, telling me that if I chose to carry it with me it was to be passed on in time through my lineage. Anyone who has slipped, slid and been turned around by the shifting bogs of Iona's thin landscape will appreciate that an extra 5lb load is not undertaken lightly, more importantly the responsibility of caring and sharing the magic of the green stone which seemed heavy would ultimately carry me and my family for eons to come.

It has been mind boggling getting my head around the age of the rock formations on Iona. Although 2,900 million years old is just a number, I have increasingly taken this knowledge out of my head and placed it in my body to help me feel the timeless connection to the strands of creation.

The pink granite of Mull is but 300 million years old a babe by comparison. The energy on Iona is at a high frequency of enriching loving essence. A clear field of tranquility, you can feel the thinness of place aboard the ferry on the approach to the Eastern shore, and the vibrational pull of the Island is tangible. No wonder 48 Scottish kings are buried here. To stand atop Dun I and look out to the small land masses of the Dutchman's Cap, the Treshnish Isles and Staffa not to mention the looming mountains of Mull is to commune with the angelic heavens while rooted in Biera's brew. A cairn stands at the top of Iona's highest hill and beyond the stones laid in honor of the ancestors is Tobar nah Aois, the Well of Age, which is said to contain youth restoring water, if you bathe three times at sunrise you'll be transformed! Is this the Well of Eternal Youth? Biera returns every year to the floating Island of the West to bathe in the pool of water that brings sprightly youth and each day she grows older so she can once again pick up her hammer and at Samhain imprison Bridghid until the maiden dips her hand in the rivers of Imbolc to continue the on going cycle of life death rebirth. What is interesting about the well is that it is almost invisible until you are right upon it, I imagine that people climb Dun I each year and miss the well or stumble upon it in sheer delight. The more challenging walk of the south side of the Island leads to St. Columba's Bay. Here is where the Saint docked with 12 followers and when they could see Ireland no more, they stayed. The beach today is full of Cairns, strategically placed stones that take on many meanings to a witness, I love the golden egg shaped stones in a boulder nest that becomes the home of a giant eagle for me. There is also a well laid labyrinth that offered a gift of two snails making love. The glistening juice of their love potion spread beyond my outstretched hands and as I quested there in July of 2009 I received the bequest to remember patience, especially in the matters of the heart.

Iona always has a new side to show you and Mull is no second rate sister to the crowning glory of the graveyard of kings. The pink granite hides treasures of her own amongst the folds of her pleated skirt. I was gifted the way to the Cave of the Dead some years ago and crawling into it always leaves me in awe. The bodies of the dead kings were carried across the Ross of Mull and rested in this cave before safe passage could be found over the Straits of Iona and the body buried in the ancient earth. Why was Iona chosen as the final resting place for the leaders of the people? One obvious observation is its western location, an island in the place of the setting sun where the kiss of death comes each night before wielding in a fresh new dawn. The cave itself is well hidden and on my last visit was inhabited by several spiders and a toad. After journeying to the bones of our grief we crawled out of this birthing chamber where Kenneth MacAlpin and Macbeth, amongst other notable kings, had lain. One exuberant pilgrim marched fully clothed into the sea and swam like a selkie in pure delight of transforming grief into a resurgent breath of life.

There's a grassy mound above the white sand that stretches to the clear ocean where sea otters frolic in the morning mist and the seal people feast on the plentiful supply of pollack, mackeral and ling. It is on a desolate shore such as this that I often weave a tale of Selkie magic.

The Tale of Mary

Close to a pink granite cove that tumbles in humps and bumps all of the way to the sea lived a crofter by the name of Angus, a hardy man, salt of the earth, as craggy as old Mull rock. His wife Margaret was his steadfast companion and together they worked the land, tended sheep and set nets out in the deep blue sea. The land was rough and hard and the few sheep were set to wandering so Angus spent most of his time bobbing up and down on his small boat doing what he liked best, fishing. The greatest joy in their lives was their beautiful daughter Mary. From the moment she was born a warm glow flickered brightly in their small cottage. Mary was free spirited always singing with a bounce and skip to her step that brought a tear of joy trickling down proud parents cheeks. Mary was Angus' constant companion in her early years, setting the nets, picking out fish to give to her mother and the rest were taken to market. She threw herself into her work without complaint or reservation and her proud parents were fit to burst.

As the years flipped by Mary grew as beautiful from the outside as she was within. Unaware of her striking features she soon attracted the attention of the village boys and the tongues wagged freely in a small place where everyone knows each other's business. Mary oblivious to village gossip would saunter past the pub, post office, general store and the local houses to the edge of the village where her Uncle Lachland lived sequestered in a tiny shack by the sea, his boat tethered to an old post, oars slung inside and more often than not Lachy was to be found smoking his pipe rocking in his chair to the time of the lapping waves. Mary loved her eccentric old uncle and would make the short trek to see him often.

By the time she was sweet sixteen Mary was rowing her father's boat out to a small island about a half mile off shore. Angus and Margaret never blinked an eye at their daughter's escapades for she would always get her work done first and her spare time was hers to do as she chose. All was well in the world and nothing would burst the bubble of bliss unless a watered seed took root in a tangled garden.

Margaret was in the grocery store routing through the canned goods on the bottom shelf when two of the local busy bodies entered the store and began a tirade of gossip. Margaret, hidden from view may not have taken any notice of their malicious tongues until Mary's name entered the fray.

"Och I fell sorry for the parents of poor wee Mary. Margaret and Angus are such nice folk" rattled the weasel thin woman with a pinched face

"To think they bore such a misfit in the world.

"Your right there," squeaked her confidante. "Mary's a real oddball, she goes rowing off each day in that boat, heading for that desolate bit of rock out at sea."

"I know, bloody weird if you ask me. She's always on her own, doesn't mix with the other kids, never had a boyfriend, doesn't come to the Calleigh's , she's touched if you ask me," sneered the bony tittle tattler.

"It's a crying shame indeed, such nice folk to have such a queer daughter, poor Margaret, poor Angus" sighed her eager companion. Margaret kept low the shame washing over her, her throat constricted and her breathing shallow. The bell rang as the door closed behind the judgmental duo and Margaret inched her way up, her head held low as she walked within her lost thoughts to their humble abode.

Angus was resting his weary bones puffing on his pipe when Margaret sluggishly crossed the threshold and gazed into the blazing hearth. "What's eating at you Margaret you've got a face like a wet cabbage?" he gently probed.

"Bloody wagging tongues that's what" snipped Margaret.

"What on earth are you on about woman?"

"Your daughter that's what" and Margaret went into a mad tirade of all that was said about Mary and how peculiar their daughter was for rowing to an island rather than socializing at parties and hanging out with the village kids.

"Woah, stop it now Margaret. We have the kindest, brightest, most beautiful daughter in the whole wide world. We can thank our lucky stars that she is not gallivanting around with every Tom Dick or Harry. Would you rather she was skylarking about and jumping in the sack with some village halfwit? Would you rather her be bringing a wee bairn into the world with no means to feed or support it? Would you woman? The lass is doing no harm, now leave her alone and be done with it."

Margaret glared at her husband her jaw set and her thin mouth twisted "Angus, there is something going on here that we need to get to the bottom of. I want the truth. She's been rowing out to that isle nigh on five years. Och we've turned a blind eye and we can do so no more. She needs to spend time with people, learn to socialize and fit in" "Why Margaret Munroe you're worse than those tongue waggers in the village. She is probably reading a book or searching the rock pools, what harm is she doing? She likes her own company like Lachy, there's nothing wrong with that."

"A fine mess she'll be if she ends up living alone like Lachy with his weird ideas and ways, and don't give me that look Angus, you know as well as I do that he's one slice short of a loaf. Now get yourself to his tumbling shack and borrow his boat and find out exactly what Mary is playing at."

Angus saw the steely resolve in her pale blue eyes and reluctantly swung his jacket over his shoulder and muttering loudly stormed out of the door.

Lachy was found with his bodhran in hand crooning an old tune with a whisky glass by his side and his pipe smoked clean. He looked up with soulful eyes at Angus and nodded to the bottle and uttered liltingly, "help yourself to a dram man."

"Not today Lachy, I need to borrow your boat."

"Why? What's wrong with yours?"

"Mary has it."

Lachy looked imploringly into Angus' eyes "Tell me you've not been listening to the gossiping fools in the village. Oh Angus leave her be man. Mary's a gem, spying on her will bring you no joy. Do us all a favour and pour yourself a dram."

"I need your boat Lachy." Angus stood firm, Margaret's essence chiseled in his jaw line.

"Then take the dashit thing you damn fool and away with you.

Angus heaved on the oars skimming speedily across the calm waters to the small island and moored up beside his own boat. He followed a forged path beaten down by Mary's tread up and over a steep knoll, the highest point of the desolate isle. From this vantage point he glanced over at a sandy beach where a large rock sat prominently at the edge of the incoming tide. He feasted on the sounds of the gentle waves lapping on the shore, the humming buzz of a bee zipping amongst the abundant flowers growing wild and free, and laughter, a distinct peel of joy drifted on the breeze. He stealthily crept towards the screams of delight and was amazed to see his daughter frolicking with a seal, a large gray seal. He stood transfixed watching the two of them roll around in the sand playfully wrestling, with Mary giggling and carrying on, the seal grunting and Angus beaming a smile as warm as the sun watching his daughter having such fun.

Angus settled and watched for a while before edging his way undetected to Lachy's boat. With a glad heart he rowed home to share his tidings with Margaret.

"Good news: he called as he strode up the pathway to his front door where Margaret stood waiting anxiously.

"You saw her?" she asked warily.

"Aye I saw her and we have nothing to worry about."

"What's she up to reading, wading, drawing?" she probed

"She's playing."

"Playing at what?" demanded a flummoxed Margaret.

"She has a friend on the island, a seal, she probably reared it up from a pup and she goes out each day to feed it. You should have seen the two of them Margaret, it was if they were dancing in the sand."

"A seal?" Margaret rasped in horror

"Aye a big gray seal, they were having the time of their lives and…"

"I knew it," screamed Margaret, a look of abject horror sweeping across her face. "She's enchanted by one of those sea-people. Our daughter is finished, ruined. I've heard tales from my Grandmother telling how the Selkie prey on our kind and whisk us away never to be seen again. A gray seal is uncommon Angus, it has bewitched our Mary. If you don't get rid of the beast the sea folk will claim our daughter."

"What do you mean 'get rid of it', I am not interfering, I'm not going to…. Margaret I cannae do it."

"Yes you can its for your daughter's sake, we'll ne'er see the likes of her again if you don't do it."

"But Margaret"

"No buts Angus. You will take care of it you'd best heed me if you want to see your daughter again."

And so the argument raged on Margaret getting more forceful as Angus' defenses weakened until in total surrender Angus agreed to go out first thing in the morning and shoot the seal.

When Mary returned that evening she was in buoyant mood. She skipped into the cottage and flung her arms around her dad and kissed his balding head then she turned and hugged her mother. She helped cook the dinner, wash the dishes and after a couple of hands of bridge she slipped off to bed. When the sun peeked through her window the next morning she heard the latch of the front door creak as someone, probably her dad was headed out to fix the nets. She jumped out of bed to get herself ready so she could try to catch him.

Indeed it was Angus who has skipped breakfast and was headed, gun in hand, down to the boat and off to the island. He climbed the same knoll and looked at the large rock on the sandy white dune and he loaded his gun his eyes never straying from the gray seal sunning itself in the bright morning sun.

Mary had one foot out the door when Margaret stopped her. "Mary dear you have jobs around here today. The cow byre has been poorly neglected I want you to scrape and whitewash a nice clean place for the cow."

"Sure Mother I'll get right on it." Mary turned and went straight to get the tools needed and threw herself into her task.

As the first lick of paint soaked into the knotted wooden post Angus raised his gun and looked keenly down the barrel at the passive seal. The suns welcoming morning beams glistened off the tranquil water, Angus could hear the quickness of his breathe and the thumping of his racing heart as he loaded the gun. A harsh voice in his head scolded his cowardice for bending to Margaret's will. This seal is not harming anyone he rationalized and then he heard his wife's shrill screech warning him he'd lose his loving daughter to this magical sea being and with his sight on the monster who would steal his babe he gently squeezed the trigger. The aim was true, the bullet smacked through fur and blubber ripping the silence from the moment and gulls screeched to the crack of gunpowder echoing on the dawning day. The seal reared up and fell. With great effort it heaved and dragged its bleeding body into the healing salt of the ebbing tide. Angus watched horror stricken as the fin footed creature slipped beneath the waves and disappeared in the depths below. He involuntarily dropped to his knees his mouth open aghast. A sweeping feeling of desolation washed over him, his heart seemed to lodge in his throat constricting the anguished scream that desperately fought to be heard. He stared in stunned silence for a long time eyes fixed on the blood soaked sand. A bubbling sense of guilt, grief, anger and shame stirred, frothed and splattered in his aching heart, his mind twisted in the image of slaughter. It was as if he had murdered a dear one. The sick sensation was as raw as if the bullet had penetrated the heart of his wife or daughter. In a daze he groped for the fallen gun and with heavy steps he trudged back to the boat. The sense of loss consumed him in the gentle hand of Manannan Mac Lir and the primordial scream of sorrow hovered on his lips until he forcefully swallowed the burning angst and shoved it into the recesses of his disturbed self. Reaching land he hauled the boat ashore and skulked his way home. Shoving the gun into the back of his closet he turned to see the quizzical face of Margaret.

"Did you get the seal?" jabbed the old woman.

"Aye and I feel awful"

"You look it man, pull yourself together, it was for the best. For goodness sake it was only a bloody seal."

"Tell that to Mary," muttered Angus. "I feel horrible, we shouldnae have done it Margaret. It was …"

The door burst open and in bounced a resplendent Mary. She sensed the heaviness in the room and strode anxiously over to her Father. "What's wrong Dad you look terrible?"

"I'm fine Mary just a little… well I'm fine".

Mary's Mother turned away so as not to meet her daughter's eye.

"Are you needing to pull up the nets soon Dad?"

"Nae lass, the tide will not be going out for a while so I am going to have myself a smoke." He slumped in his chair and fiddled with his tobacco pouch.

"Cow needs milking and then I'll be done unless you've got more on the list.

"Nae Mary you've done enough, milk the cow and be done with you." Angus sighed.

"Is it alright if I take the boat out when I'm done?"

Margaret shot a frantic look towards her husband who raised his hands up in surrender and croaked "Take it Mary, take it whenever you want you didnae have to ask me again lass the boat is yours at anytime.

Mary milked the cow brought the milk in and set the basins for the cream. "I'll see you soon," She cried as she grabbed her jacket and thrust a sandwich in her pocket and with a dazzling smile she sauntered off.

"There she goes off again and if you did the deed Angus she'll come home sadder and wiser."

Angus didn't acknowledge his wife's claim. He cut a forlorn figure by the hearth smoking his pipe for all it was worth, a sinking feeling of loss engulfing his dark thoughts.

Mary's arms had grown strong from the years of rowing and tending of the Croft, so in no time she was pulling the boat up out of the cresting waves. Just as the sea swells rose and fell, so Angus puffed and toked on his pipe, gazing despondently into the dying flames.

Margaret called him for dinner later in the day and he still did not stir and nor did Mary return home. Margaret started fretting, "Has she returned to milk the cow? It's that time again."

"No," Angus murmured, "Mary's not come."

"Take yourself down to the village man and see if she's there will you? Check to see if the boat is in."

Angus returned shortly with a glum look. "No boat," he called.

"If there's no boat then she's still out on that blasted Island. Its no use crying over spilt milk, go and get her Angus, take Lachy's boat. She needs to cut the ties with that desolate place once and for good," ordered Margaret turning on her heels and busying herself with cleaning the kitchen counter for the third time in an hour.

So Angus went and took Lachy's boat, not stopping to ask permission, just untying it from the mooring post and with due haste he rowed for all he was worth across to the island. Pulling himself in beside Mary's boat, he scampered up the knoll. He clambered to the place where he had shot the seal and his eyes were drawn to the blood splattered on the side of the big rock, traces of his morning visit illuminated by the setting sun. He scoured all of the terrain visible and nowhere did he see Mary. He walked the entire circuit of the small island, once, twice, thrice he circled this sanctuary of Mary and still she was nowhere to be found, not by bush tree or rock. The heaviness in his soul seat choked a heartbreaking sob, tears that had lingered dangerously on the edge of release finally cascaded down his wrinkled cheeks for the tide was on the ebb and the blood caked on the rock was dry and Mary was gone. Through the salty stream flowing freely from his sad eyes he caught a movement in the water but a stones throw away. As he gazed into the West two gray seals popped right out of the water. They seemed to hang in mid air for what was but a moment and time stood still, Angus felt them, saw them, they met his eyes and looked deeply into him, then with a flip and a splash they were gone, disappearing into the blue beyond. Another knot turned sharply in his stomach and a feeling ever so queer that he would never see Mary again washed through him. He climbed into his boat left Lachy's there tethered to the shore and he rowed home. He returned to his spot by the fire and overfilled his pipe.

Margaret came and sat beside him and stared into the newly built fire asking, "Did you find her?"

Angus puffed long and hard and with steely eyes glaring into the darting flames he said coolly, "No, I didn't find her, I didn't see her. I searched the whole Island 3 times and Mary is gone. Mary is gone for good, we'll no see Mary again."

And they waited, and they waited, and they waited for the entire days of their lives, but Mary never returned.

The Treasure of the Tale

The Selkie are huge part of the Celtic culture. There are Clans to this day that claim direct lineage from the seal folk. In this beautifully haunting tale, Mary grows up in the acceptance of her parents and with a freedom of spirit. It is not until Margaret overhears other people's version of her family's story that she becomes incredibly perturbed to the point of spying on Mary and disturbing Mary's natural order. When do we let others influence how we see and treat family, friends, neighbors, and or associates in our world?

Angus does not want to spy on Mary but his defenses wear down and he goes after her. How do we try to fit in to society and agree to do things even when it doesn't feel right? Where are we pressurizing someone else to do what we are not prepared to do ourselves? Where are we pressurizing someone to do/be who they are not?

Lachy is an interesting character with his Bodhran, pipe and whisky. Is he someone who is dancing to the tune of his own drum? Or has the bottle got its grip on him? There is certainly something of the wise elder in him as he is someone who knows that Mary is best left be, that Margaret and Angus would be better served by tuning out the village gossip and yet he to succumbs to following the crowd by allowing Angus to take his boat. Where are we like Lachy, walking with wisdom and then falling down by not following through, allowing someone direct access to that which will harm them? Angus sets the Seal in his sight and shoots it although his gut instinct is to walk away. Where are we pulling the trigger when we know better? Neither Margaret nor Angus have the courage to tell Mary what they have done. Where are we hiding from owning our decisions? Where are we owning our decisions belligerently and where are we owning them gently?

Mary follows her heart by joining the Selkies and lets go of all that tries to hold her hostage. "Where are we willing to let go and be our vision and when are we holding on to that which holds us hostage? Margaret is in fear that Mary is alienating herself, that she is not part of the community, that she doesn't fit in. Where through fear do we create that which we are trying to avoid?

Finally lets take a peek at the meaning of the names in this story. Angus means 'One Choice.' Iti s interesting that he is offered a life changing choice in the story and his one choice dramatically affects the conclusion of the tale. Margaret means 'Pearl' it is interesting that she fails to see the Pearls of Mary, she lacks the patience to let the sand transform to the richness of the gem, she sees sand through the villagers eyes where she once recognized the pearl that Mary is. Lachland is in two parts Lach means 'Lives Near Water' which is exactly where you find Lachy and Land simply means 'Land'. He is the land which lives near the water. Mary has several meanings of note including 'Wished for Child." Margaret and Angus look at Mary in her youthful exuberance as the greatest joy of their lives so indeed she was a wished for child. How do we treat the greatest joys of our life?

Another meaning is 'Rebel' and Mary is absolutely a rebel, a feminine after my own heart! A third meaning is "Star of the Sea' and it is interesting to note that she gives herself to the sea. You can imagine the parents losing their 'star' and even looking to the 'anceSTARs' for their beloved Mary. The last piece is that Mary means 'Sea of Bitterness' and I can see Angus and Margaret staring at the waves with their bitter tears welled up inside of them.

The Tale and the Land

I am so grateful for being introduced to the land where Selkies swim. On Mull, off the Cornish Coast at Bollowal Barrow, and at the Tomb of the Eagles on Orkney the Seal people have made their presence known to me. The cove of the Cave of the Dead offers spirit of place to both honor the Selkies and then crawl into the carved out space where forgotten kings are remembered, honored in sovereignty with the land, the ferryman is paid again with offerings of coins that I scatter on the earthen floor which I am sure the local children gladly apprise or mayhap they disappear for faerie behind the veil.

I have become extremely discerning where nature calls. I have rocks, feathers, twigs and treasures that are part of altars, cairns, and anchors to support my journey, and I used to pick up a bundle of calling treasures wherever I went. I now understand that I can appreciate the beauty of the moment without the need to take it home in my suitcase. It was a lesson shared through the roots of faerie stirred on Iona unfolding dramatically outside the Cave of Women on Carsaig Bay Mull in 2007.

The road leading to Carsaig gives a hint of the challenges that this rocky precipice offers. The first time I drove down there in a tiny rental made me acutely aware of bringing a minibus down the winding potholes that twist and turn up and down, spiraling to a sweeping rock strewn bay. There is space for a handful of cars to squeeze into the hedgerow and the minibus pushes the boundaries to their max. Sweeping views are afforded from the pier built by prisoners in the Napoleonic wars. A little wooded lane to the west passes a manor house and draws one to the rocky cove where you need to negotiate tricky terrain, crossing streams, slick surfaces, gorse bushes and thin paths that take you up and around where scrambling becomes a necessity and the drop off edges will get the heart racing for fear of falling. There is initially some assistance offered in the form of wooden planks to help cross some of the muddiest boggiest pitfalls, but these soon disappear and you are very much left to pick your way carefully and purposefully across the crumbling cliffs of seriously eroding sedimentary rocks underlying Mull's volcanic heritage. I have forged my own path here alone and with pilgrims, in all my visits I have seen only a handful of hardy walkers, their dogs, the thrilling flight of golden eagles and the wispy beards of feral goats that guard the pass. The views are majestic the walk is wild and the cove calls its song through a spectrum of dimension, hauntingly beautiful, imposing, intimate, harsh, soft, a juxtaposition of so many elements that contradict and compliment in a single breath. For the most dedicated hikers the reward of the Carsaig Arches, a natural rock formation carved by Mannanan Mac Lir awaits, and for those who sense it the Cave of the Nuns provides a mystical interlude. I learned to plan pilgrimages to this untamed inlet on 'free days' a choice for pilgrims to go off on their own and explore more of Iona's hidden secrets or jump aboard the bus and experience the untamed freedom of raw serenity that Carsaig croons, whistles and roars. I have hiked this trail with people in their upper sixties and I have recommended that much younger travelers spend their day on Iona's soft welcoming northern or western shore. Carsaig is not for everyone, a body that says yes, boots fit for the task and a willingness to clamber, shuffle, slip and laugh humbly are pre-requisites to an adventurous day. I had first found the cave by feeling it on my solo visit where I keened for my pet cat who had crossed the spirit bridge while I was away working with pilgrims in Cornwall. On a stormy October afternoon I added salt to the sea as I wept for the bundle of warm fur that would no longer dig claws into my chest and sleep under my chin with a motorboat purr of pure affection. As I released my grief on that day I searched for the cave that can only be seen when you walk up over the ridge and look down into it. It is well concealed and so easy to miss. I passed it and felt a shift in my energy field, which I promptly ignored. I love spirit's patience with me! I never got as far as the Arches on that blustery autumn day and as I retraced my steps somewhat despondently having failed to locate the cave or the arches my senses went on high alert and I stopped in my tracks. It was in the same location where I had felt my energy shift before and I let myself follow instinct to climb to the height of the rocky ridge and I was rewarded with the sight of vines dangling and water dripping at the mouth of a wide long cave. Many graffiti marks are carved into the wall some dating back to the nuns who made their home here after a mad dash escape from Iona during the reformation. Some carvings were supposedly etched in the 6th century however it is hard to pick out the old from the new as crosses and dates litter the walls. To the back of the cave there is a piece dated from 1633. This sheltered chamber is capable of holding up to 300 people, and it is with admiration that I view the nuns clambering up the sheer rock face from the swirling sea below and living amongst the breathtaking cliffs in what is commonly known as the Nuns Cave and sometimes by its older name Uamh na Cailleachan, the cave of the old woman, the hag, the Cailleach. Maybe it was my tears for Hazel, my black feline friend that obscured the rock giant that guards the cave, for on my second visit to Carsaig I was struck by the gigantic face of the caves guardian. A natural sphinx boldly jutting out to call you to climb and see beyond the perceived horizon and enter the womb of the old hag. The first time I sat with pilgrims around the glowing embers of a scavenged fire I was gifted an eagle feather that lay at my feet and showed itself to me as I spoke the words, "Before the eagle married the owl, there lived a wise woman of immense power, her name was Cerridwen." I had not planned to share the tale of Taliesin that is so irrevocably linked with Wales and by association Cornwall on the fringe islands of the Scottish Highlands. It was the Cailleach who stirred the cauldron and coaxed her story and that of the Merlin from my reluctant lips and so it was that on my third visit to the cave I met the fullness of her birthing process as I integrated aspects of the tale, Merlin, magic, fae enchantment and the power of the stone people into the fabric of my being. Two days earlier I had met the pilgrims for the telling of Rose before they wandered in love and trust to Iona's calling. To support their quest I offered them a card from the Sacred Circle deck a wonderful Celtic set beautifully illustrated by Paul Mason and written by Anna Franklin. I was shuffling the deck in my room prior to our gathering and one card leapt from the deck and I knew it was mine. I picked it up looked at it and decided to put it back in the pack and pull a different one with the group. Needless to say as we stood in circle and I shuffled the cards one flew from my hands and landed face up so all could see, it was my same card. "That one is mine," I chuckled. "I drew it earlier and now I need to own it." Everyone else took a card and went on their way.

I thought after the pilgrims returned the individual quests were done, however, I was wrong. Three days later it was my turn and I was going to quest with a group in tow. Five of us, the number of Sovereignty. Three feminines representing the Maiden, Mother and Crone and two men representing the two god consorts, although that had not dawned on me as we sidled down the steep slope toward Carsaig pier. The cave is about a two mile trek and we ambled, scrambled found moments to rest and time to crank up the heart rate as we merrily trooped to stoke our fire. With driftwood gathered, the flickering flames reflected the dazzling light of the day and took the chill of the dampness from our bones. We began to do some deep insightful work to release what holds us hostage, to identify who we are in that moment and vision the vastness and endless possibilities of our dreams. As we prepared to focus on this journey I once again heard the voice of the hag and the story of Taliesin dripped into the flaming cauldron so we could all drink the brew and find our three drops of inspiration. Every time I tell a story it goes deeper, revealing new pieces and teaching new lessons. As I spoke the final poetic revelation the "I am Taliesin,'" I embodied the words, feelings, soul threads and I expanded and contracted as Gwion Bach, as Taliesin merging, shifting understanding and being, and as I write this I look at the words I've written and I change the tense from embody to embodied and I see I'm body and I'm body died and another piece of the Merlin is born within, for my renewal, transformation and subsequent rebirth were being stirred by the old one as she, unbeknownst to me, prepared to eat me.

After the laughter and tears of self-discovery we sauntered into the birthing light sparkling luminously on the sea and my step was brighter and lighter. We thought about continuing on to the Arches and decided to picnic instead. We lunched with a freedom of spirit glowing as brightly as the Beltane sun and a rock called to me. It was a gleeful, shimmering, twinkling stone that flickered a thousand lights glistening like a glazed donut deliciously tasty and mine, most definitely mine. It was so glitzy with a hint of danger, would I have listened? I was consumed with it and when two of the women came to see it, I felt annoyance that one of them touched my stone. I withdrew it away sharply and put it in my pocketsies for my keepsies!

As we traipsed past the cave entrance on the two mile hike to the pier, Susan, my partner at that time and I were separated from the others and we had a chance to playfully flirt as committed partners are prone to do. As we picked a path she had a glint in her eye as she commented on my legs.

"You just like what's attached to my legs," I teased.

"I do," she beamed, "And you know exactly what I am talking about."

"Yes I do," I snickered and together we both said "ankles."

On the very word ankles, I was taken down, my right foot rolled and my ankle popped. I lay sprawled on the rocks. In my embarrassment I tried to leap to my feet and hobble on regardless. A shooting pain surged through my slender frame, my body overheated and I threw up my leisurely lunch. I felt my head spinning and the dizziness took me to my knees. I crawled towards Susan and collapsed in a heap at her feet. Her concerned voice echoed in my ears and the other pilgrims came running. It was crystal clear what my next move was, there was a burning hot rock in my pocket, a shimmering gift from faerie that I had coveted and it needed to be returned home. The youngest pilgrim Megan, a wise one beyond her youthful years of 20, took the shining stone and carried it to the cave. With deep breaths and the release of the stone my body temperature stabilized and I tried to stand. The two-mile challenging hike now became a full blown pilgrimage as my right ankle swelled and the realization that I could not put weight on it sunk in. So for four hours I crawled, hopped and when possible I leaned on pilgrims, climbed on their backs and took much needed rests as we slowly made our way through the shadowed rock face into the last embers of the brilliant sunshine. The piggy back rides were rare for the trail is treacherous, thin and winding. Rocks of all shapes and sizes were strewn in our way. The new born babe needed to crawl before he ran. As my wrists tired and my knees numbed we came across a hawthorn tree, a fae sapling clawing its way out of this ruggedly striking landscape. "I need a clootie," a cloth prayer tie, I cried. I normally have a couple on me to make prayers when needed, today my clooties were in the minibus. One of the pilgrims reached into her bag to retrieve one of hers when it became painfully obvious what I needed to do. I always invite people to rip up a favorite shirt, one that is past its sell by date, yet is hung too for nostalgia, to give it another life, an opportunity to carry prayers for self and others. I tell people to choose a shirt that holds value to them as it gives value to their prayers. I was wearing an old faithful, a shirt I had owned since my college days in the early 1980's, of course it took writing this very sentence to gather another thread, the shirt is of a waning moon which represents the hag, the crone. I had always carried clooties in my pocket. I had never ripped the shirt off my own back as the pilgrims of old would have done. So I tore away and produced 5 strips one for each of us pilgrims to anchor our prayers through the soil. the sea, the wind and the passion of our own fires. With renewed energy blazing within me I slithered onwards. There is one hillock that gets my heart racing when I am in fine fettle, crawling up the narrow ledge took my breath away and at its height my cell phone rang. It was bizarre in the middle of nowhere, I had strong reception. A call from the USA none the less. It was from my friend Rhianna who owns and operates a mystical, spiritual store called the Dreaming Goddess in Poughkeepsie. She was meant to be meeting me with a group of her friends in London to go to Cornwall five days later. Her call was to let me know that her then mate Jim a gentle giant and wisdom keeper would be there leading the group in her stead, but she would not as her son had been in an horrific motorbike accident and was in the intensive care unit. As I reflect on this aspect of the story I receive new insights years after the event. The fact that I had a cell phone on me, a rare occasion on pilgrimage indeed and turned on for that matter whilst out on the rocks is quite a phenomenon in its own right as I am not Mr. Technology! I am still amazed that I had reception and that a call came through. Writing helps me process some of the essential secrets that make up the recipe for my life and looking at the details of the story. I went to the meaning of the names. Rhianna is from Rhiannon meaning Goddess, Great Queen, or Nymph. She is the goddess who rides the White Night Mare. Her association with horses is a constant in her story as is her link with Epona, so is it any wonder that when the Great Faery Queen, goddess of the Steed, needed to reach through the veil she would be able to contact him. Rhianna's last name is Mirabello which means beautiful viewpoint, an interesting opportunity to find dual meanings. Carsaig Bay is a beautiful viewpoint, the scenery is amongst the finest in Scotland. I was also invited to explore the beautiful viewpoint of my life story through many layers and levels. Jim means he who supplants and Rhianna told me Jim would be taking over from her.. Tyler, Rhianna's son, carries the name of a worker on roof tiles, Tyler's accident took his legs from under him and he was forced to go on a journey to explore his higher self, he was raised to his own roof as I was being raised to mine, my legs had been taken from me, Tyler and I were being encouraged to explore our cauldron's of wisdom. Five of us went into the hags womb, one named Susan which means Lily which translates to Unconditional Love in the Celtic world which is what the number 5 represents when we are in Sovereignty with the land, Megan means Pearl, Gwion Bach transforms from a grain of sand to a shining pearl, from a boy to man. Our life journey is in finding the pearls of our story, seeing the richness in all of life, as Peggy Dylan, my teacher from Sundoor teaches, 'take your pearls into the dreamtime, At the end of the day count your blessings so they can weave into your dreams!' Oh and that brings us to Rhianna the Great Goddess whose shop if you recall is the Dreaming Goddess! I love how all of these connecting threads weave through our stories.

The Great Queen had contacted me, the Old Hag had spoken and the maiden, Megan, the pearl, had revisited the Crone's womb and returned the shining stone, the faerie treasure. Kathryn means pure and this was a pilgrimage of purity as our last member, Tor, carried me on his back when possible. His name means thunder, turtle dove, and is the name of the rough outcrop in Glastonbury, home to Gwyn ap Nudd, King of the Faeries and the Gateway to Anwynn and the Underworld! I immediately connected the turtle with the USA and my journey in the land of the first people of North America, and I was surely the shell as he carried me on his back. The dove connects with Iona and of course St. Columba whose name means Dove. Put all of this goodness into the cauldron with the card I drew and the pot gets even richer. The page of cups had leapt from my hands on Iona, The card is reflection, the mirror., here was my mirror to reflect on how

I walk in this world. The card depicts a young man on his knees holding a chalice, the cauldron. He is by the hazel trees that drop nuts into the pool of wisdom as a salmon leaps consuming the nuts and connecting with the man. Gwion Bach becomes a salmon as he flees Ceridwen, in the story of Taliesin. The salmon is the totem animal of the East which represents rebirth, abundance and prosperity. It pops up in the Celtic birthing stories;

Tuan Mac Carrell shapeshifts into a salmon and is caught and eaten for dinner by the lord's wife, she consequently gives birth to him and he brings to fruition the story of Ireland's roots, remembering the generations of the story and carrying it into his rebirth.

Anna Franklin writes "Fintan was the Salmon of Knowledge in Irish lore. Originally he was human and survived the great flood hiding in a cave in salmon form for centuries gaining wisdom and knowledge of all that went on in Ireland. The giant Finegas hunted the fish along the banks of the Boyne for seven years eventually catching it and setting it to roast watched by his pupil Fionn Mac Cumhal. Fionn burned his finger on hot flesh and placed it in his mouth and thus acquired all the knowledge of the salmon."

I had gone to my knees, and like Fionn, Tuan, Gwion Bach and others in the Celtic world,, I had sipped from the womb, the cauldron of the hag, to take a perceptive reflective journey for spiritual renewal and rebirth, to step more deeply as a Spirit Walker, to claim the power of my inner Merlin and celebrate the totem treasure of the South, the Stone, and the aspects of the South which are the story, music, poetry, dance and laughter, to celebrate my story, my poetry, my music, my dance and my laughter as the true King, in Sovereignty with my own life.

I am still integrating the pieces of this remarkable journey, after crawling the rocky headland of Carsaig, I made a fleeting visit the following day to Oban hospital, we had returned to the mainland that morning and while the pilgrims ate lunch I shot in and out of the accident and emergency ward and within half an hour I was on the road again with a set of crutches for physical mobility in middle world and my own knowing that it was a faerie illness. My recovery was aided by regular reiki magic as two of the pilgrims worked on me daily in Scotland and then when I picked up the new group in England I received the attention of a third pilgrim, making three, giggle, it is the Celtic way!

Andrew as we know means Strong and Manly, so I also needed to crawl and walk into a new phase of my manhood. It is time to stand in the truth of who I am. There has been a deep healing in my psyche and the integration of walking with my inner Merlin is still unfolding in my life. More importantly, I keep on stirring the cauldron and I love tasting the brew, which is tangibly more flavorful.

To stand on our own two feet, to dance in alignment with the masculine and

Feminine takes remarkable courage. The meaning of strength shines from a

true story I was once told by a beautiful woman who believes above all in the power of

love.

Faith is the bird that feels the light and sings

while the dawn is still dark.

Anonymous.

A MOTHERS TALE.

In my capacity as a storyteller, I get to share some of the world's greatest tales. Occasionally, someone gifts me a story. One that is ripe for the telling, again and again.

I remember a woman, let me call her Elizabeth, telling me about her family's journey. It had a profound effect upon my life.

Elizabeth went to the doctor for a routine exam when she was eight months pregnant.

The doctor's response was a bitter pill to swallow. "Your baby is dead, you will give birth to a still born."

The words callous, dismissive, hard and hurtful were the dark scratchings that crashed into her ears. Her heart pounded, her mouth twitched, a grimace of pain contorted her pretty face. Elizabeth's gaze was fixed firmly on the Doctor's stern glare. Slowly her eyes were clouding over, she felt the tears welling up, spewing forth in an uncontrollable surge of grief.

"Look on the bright side, one less mouth to feed." The Doctor's matter of fact tone chilled her bones to the marrow. The stinging bite to his casual indifference momentarily froze the whirlpool of torment surging inside her. Elizabeth fought desperately, blinking back the tears, struggling to stem a tidal wave of emotions that threatened to consume her. It proved to be as helpless as trying to damn Niagara Falls with matchsticks. The flood gates opened and a torrent of salty tears danced sorrowfully to the beat of her shattered heart.

"Get a grip woman, it's not the end of the world." His haunting words echoed through her mind, the room was quickly closing in on her. It was as if a knife had been plunged into her stomach and was twisting sharply in her gut.

Elizabeth gasped for air, and as quickly as thunder follows lightning, the grief was struck aside. A sudden jolt kicked life back into her breath. A sharp blow knocked the Doctors energetic knife from her stomach. Her baby lived. The tears now fell freely. Warm, wet tears of joy.

It was on June 16th 1963 that Elizabeth went into labor. It was a time when men generally stayed away from the delivery room. Her husband was about to wear out the carpet threads with his incessant pacing. It was also a time when home births were more common than they are today. So in the same bed that she conceived this child, she prepared for the delivery. As night crept slowly toward morning, the contractions intensified. Pain threatened to rip her slender body apart. She could see the anxious expression of the midwife. Something was dreadfully wrong. Elizabeth felt herself sinking, her thin tender voice, strangely edged and coarse, cut through the moonlit stillness, in a barrage of guttural howls.

"Don't push, don't push, push, push," the swirling emotions threatened to

overwhelm her. She gritted her teeth and dug her nails into the soft flesh of her palms. Her milky white skin felt on fire. She was blotchy, sweaty, and ready to burst. She gave one almighty push that seemed to split her insides in two. In that instant, the fierce unbearable torment threatened to break her body, and then it was over. The desperate pain simply vanished. A dramatic shift that brought relief, tranquility and an absolute understanding that heaven was here, right here, right now, on earth.

The baby's transition into the world was as difficult as the midwife had ever witnessed. She wished fervently that they had been in hospital and that they had access to drugs to numb Elizabeth's evident pain. She had prayed continually for baby and mother's survival. Even when the ordeal was over, when the baby finally emerged from the womb, the midwife could still not feel the excitement and relief of delivering another child into the world. The frail, weak, body of this scrawny boy had emerged feet first, his skin was a blotchy purple, streaked with black. The midwife carefully unwrapped the umbilical cord that had been constricting his throat. Her reaction was instant, she said a prayer for this child who had come from God, and would return to God, before he ever saw the light of day. Wrapped in a bloodied white sheet the dying infant was handed briefly to Elizabeth. The boy was incredibly fragile, he had been pronounced dead prior to the birth, and now was given but hours to live.

Before the sun rose and the dawn chorus celebrated the arrival of a brand new day, Elizabeth spoke to her son. She told him that he could do anything that he chose to do that he was going to live a remarkable life. As she gazed lovingly at the scrunched up face, and tenderly stroked his soft wrinkled skin, she saw greatness. Elizabeth's spirits rose, she looked at her son with absolute faith, and continued to promise that life would unfold in special ways for this small bundle of treasure. Her positive energy still emanated from her long after the exhaustion of birth had given way to sleep. As the darkness was replaced by the bright light of day, her son, small and frail, proved the doctors wrong again, he lived.

Was it the strength and love of a mother that made a huge difference that night? While the doctors and the midwife had seen impending death, Elizabeth saw joyful life. The celebration was short lived, however because the boy was born with a deformity. The bones in his legs were underdeveloped. An eerie creaking sound emanated from his joints, and he was destined to never walk. As other children crawled, he shuffled on his bottom. As other toddlers took their first steps, he continued to scoot around on the cheeks of his backside. It was with mixed emotions that Elizabeth digested the findings from the doctors that examined her child. Her son would never walk, but he would live. Elizabeth struggled with the reality that her boy would never run, jump, tumble and fall. Her other son always amazed her with new feats of dexterity. As neighboring kids ran freely outside playing childhood games, Elizabeth consoled herself with the undeniable fact, that her youngest child was a happy soul, forever smiling, and chuckling, as he discovered new wonders of his world.

Tony, Elizabeth's husband, worked on the building site. The money was meager and the family survived on small rations heaped with a lot of love. Elizabeth was chatting to the next door neighbor on the front steps of the house when Tony came walking towards her. His lean muscular figure, bronzed from the days spent out on the roof rafters, glowed handsomely, as he strode purposefully home. Their eldest son, John, who had full mobility of his limbs, pushed past his mother, and his footsteps could be heard bounding upon the pavement as he ran to meet his dad. Elizabeth was momentarily distracted before focusing her attention back to the neighbor. Then out of the corner of her eye, she caught a sight of her husbands face. It was an expression that she would never forget. Joy and light radiated out of the man, love shone, and tears flowed freely. As he reached out to swing their son in the air, she saw him hugging their youngest child. It wasn't John, it was their youngest boy, the boy they said would never ever walk. He had jumped up and ran. Elizabeth and Tony wept and jubilant tears eagerly spilled for their youngest son Andrew, and the miracle of a dream come true.

The Treasure of the Tale

Forgive me Elizabeth if I have embellished this story in any way. I have filled in the gaps to paint the picture of your courageous story. I know for a fact that this is a treasured truth. I am sure you have surmised Elizabeth is my mother, and I am the little boy whose bones creaked, the boy who was pronounced dead, too weak to live, and was never going to walk. I have so much to be thankful for.

I am blessed. I thank Spirit for the use of my legs. I am so thankful that I can skip through the fields, hike up a mountain, and dance with the freedom and grace of a butterfly. I thank my parents for their absolute belief in me to achieve whatever it is I set my heart and mind upon. The midwife who delivered me bumped into my mother about ten years ago. She asked my mum "How is your boy, the one in the wheelchair?" My mother shared gleefully that I had got up and danced and have been doing so ever since, sharing tales about my travels and adventures that my strong legs have carried me on.

I'd like you, the reader, to take a moment now, and choose a part of your body to concentrate on, say you chose your hands, take the time to really see them touch them, explore them. Now with all sincerity say, either out loud, or in your mind, "Thank you hands..."

Did you do it? I hope so. If you didn't, give it a go. I know you might be wondering what on earth is this all about! Let me explain: Have you ever said thank you to your hands? Of the thousands of people that I have invited to participate in this exercise, only a handful had ever thanked their hands before. Ask yourself what do your hands do for you? When we start to look at the countless tasks performed by our hands each day, we will realize how thankful we are for them. I have met people in this world who tell me they have nothing to be thankful for, "You just don't know what its like to be in my shoes Andrew." They are right, I don't know what it's like to be in anyone else's shoes, but I do know that all of us have so much to appreciate for this is a great day to die!. We are all more powerful than we have ever given ourselves credit for. One of the largest problems that our society faces today is that most people continually give their power away. Part of the Carsaig experience was to illuminate how I needed to reclaim my power. One way to start reclaiming our own power is in accepting our own unique gifts, and adopting an attitude of gratitude in life. Next time the gray skies are looming over our heads, and we feel nothing ever goes our way we need to remember what we have. Often people don't appreciate what they have until they lose it. Recalling the sentence 'The grass is always greener'..... do you still say 'on the other side?' Well if you do I say no, no, no. The grass is always greener when you water it! For anyone whose ever experienced a drought, with the grass, brittle and brown, you will know to pray on rain. As Voltaire said 'cultivate you own garden', and he wasn't talking about tomato plants, its all about our own inner garden. So many people spend their whole lives wishing they were somewhere else, desperately trying to get to the other side. The simple truth is that it doesn't matter where we move, we will not be happy until we find contentment living in our own garden, the temple of our body. Celebrate the fact that we have a physical body, a vibrant mind and a playful soul. Sense the sunlight that is in every one of us.

My mother had a choice when I was born. She could have fallen into self pity. She could have bought into the darkness, yet she focused on the light. I received unconditional love while I was in my mother's womb. That love remains as strong today as it was then. Although there have been times when my mum has told me she didn't like my behavior, she always followed this by affirming that she loved me, and always will. Words that I now hear myself saying to my children. Its difficult to like everybody all of the time, but its simple to love them. I said simple, it is just not easy! If we simply offered everybody unconditional love then we'd all clearly see heaven here on earth! One of the challenges I have faced in life is learning to accept myself and to give that unconditional love to me! I challenge you to love yourself unconditionally. Step by step, moment by moment. Louise Hay invites people to look into a mirror, deep into their own eyes and say 'I love you, I really love you'. If that is uncomfortable, she beckons them to do the same but say ' I am willing to learn to love you.'

For some this can still be difficult, so she encourages the words 'I like you, I really like you.' Or to help people get started, 'I am willing to learn to like you. These aren't just words on paper, this is word magic, thought magic, an opportunity to live life on purpose. And remember it is not just saying the words, it is connecting those words to feeling so we truly feel the love for ourselves. Its time to put down the book, go look yourself in the eye, and try this out!

Did you do it? Or are you still hiding from the beautiful you?

Not all children receive the depth of love from their parents that they deserve. Some children who are deprived of this gift seek it elsewhere, from siblings, extended family, friends, teachers or religion. Some just have an inner resolve that illuminates all darkness into light, and others follow their parents down the same rocky road, and repeat abusive behaviors throughout their life. To discover the light we have to travel through the darkness, discover our own shadows and thank them for helping us to get where we are, and then be prepared to release them. This is no easy ride, for we must peel the layers, and like the layers of an onion, we will shed tears as we reveal our own truth. To know joy we must also know heartache and pain.

The reality of my own journey, as a child who proved the doctors wrong, did not sink in until I was in my mid twenties. Today as I look back on the events that led to me running up the road to meet my dad, I am struck with the triple aspect of my birth. The doctor confirming I would be 'still' born, the fears that I would not live through the night, the confirmation that I would never walk. A typical element in all great Celtic tales is present, three pieces to shift and change the transitioning story.

As I have traveled through this life, I have come to understand that no one is born a winner or a loser, however, we are all born choosers. We all choose each and every response to our situation. Life indeed can be a long, hard slog or it can also be a wonderful uplifting adventure. The best part of all is that we are free to choose.

In 1993, just after we emigrated. I was sitting in a laundromat, in the small town of Red Lion in Pennsylvania. I was thinking of some of the differences between the States and England. The fact that most of my friends considered Red Lion a great name for a pub! How none of my electrical goods would work in the States. I had sold them before moving over. In the British Isles everything is run on 240 volts and in those days you could not get an adaptor to bring it down to 120 volts. Consequently my washing machine and tumble dryer were a thing of the past, and I was forced to cart the weekly wash down to, as we'd say back home, the laundrette. As I waited for the wash cycle to complete, a woman struck up a conversation with me.

"Your not from around here are you?" Her statement was full of pride and satisfaction on having identified that I had an accent. It always amuses me when people come up to me and say 'you've got an accent,' don't they realize that they have one too!

We chatted for a while and then she asked "How long have you lived here?"

I replied that it had been barely three months since we'd arrived. She then looked at me incredulously and uttered, "That's amazing.

Confused I asked her to explain what was amazing. Emphatically she asserted "You've been here three months and you've already picked up the language, that's what's amazing."

I somehow managed to keep a straight face as I assured her we didn't speak German in Britain. I am always reminded of this story when someone affirms that we live in the communication age. This is the information age, but when it comes to communication, we so often miss the mark.

In the aftermath of my incapacitation from the sparkling tumble at Carsaig, one of the locals shared with me that there was more on Mull than most people knew. Along the coastline are many caves and one of them is amongst the most priceless gems in Scotland. Tucked into a hidden cove that is both challenging to find and tough to traverse is a cave that is in pristine condition with Pictish carvings by the score. It was on my last voyage to Mull in July of 2009 that I went in search of this ancient treasure and as in all great Celtic tales there are stories within the story of getting there.

We had boarded Davey Kirkpatrick's boat that morning from Iona and after passing the sun bathing Selkies we had crossed a fairly calm sea to arrive at Staffa for our pilgrimage into Fingals cave, a well known spot for seekers of Puffins, lovers of the sea and as in my case cave dwellers. I have harbored a romantic notion of spending time living in a cave! I was feeling particularly buoyant as I stepped across the individual pillars of basalt rock towards the gaping mouth of this cathedral cavern. The sky was glistening a rich shade of deepest blue, the sun god beaming as his season of Lughnasadh crept across the horizon, with a skip in my step fed by the tranquil seas, I led the pilgrims carrying my newest walking stick. A leprechaun carved into the head of a sturdy hawthorn branch with carvings and paintings of a rainbow, a sun, the eye of Balor, a spear, and the protective spirit animal, the one I was working with at the time the staff was carved, the courageous boar, all emblazoned on this magical faerie staff.

Upon my head sat another new acquisition of my continued voyage into my own eccentricity, a beautiful couple Paul Hersey and Jennifer Murphy of Organic Armor out of Ashville North Carolina who have rightly been described as tailors to the gods, goddesses, warriors and priestesses of our world. They had cast their magic on a custom designed hat for me, again honoring the story of Lugh with Balor's eye, a sun, rainbow, flames, oak leaves for druid knowledge and the horseshoe signifying both the Celtic heritage in relationship with Epona and the spirit of the horse and of course my own name Steed.

I was bursting with the anticipation of discovering a new cave that afternoon and with the practiced grounding that gives me roots and wings I brought myself to the greatness of the present moment. A sturdy silver link chain brings explorers to a halt within several feet of the opening to Fingals Cave the ledge continues to run practically the length of the deep opening of the Mother's womb. A journey at ones own personal risk takes an intrepid adventurer on to the unprotected exposed shelf. In the moist depths of this vaulted grotto of the giant Fingal whose cave and isle we had stepped deeply upon we lifted our voices in song. Here the mystical acoustics of our lilting melodies hauntingly swept and reverberated on in and around air rock and swirling sea. It is no wonder that Mendelssohn was inspired when he visited Fingals Cave in 1829 to compose his symphony number three, the Scottish symphony, writing the overture De Hebriden, the Hebrides. Accompanied by the sound of rattles our voices harmonized with the Oran Mor, that deepest note that connects us to all beings, a ceremonial gathering in the mother's womb where we became instruments of acknowledgement of the oneness that we truly are.

The unique rock pillars are the result of volcanic activity and the varied sizes of fractured columns provide higgledy piggledy stepping stones forming depth and dimension according to the speed of which the lava cooled. There are other basaltic column structures in the world the closest being the Giant's Causeway in Northern Ireland. Scotland's connection to the Emerald Isle is prevalent in the 'storical journey of the Dal Riata and the merging of nations with the Picts, the gods and goddess' followed with the likes of Fionn mac Cumhaill (Finn McCool) who becomes the legendary Fingal. The story of the Scottish Giant Benandonner being bested by Fionn echoes the Irish influence in carrying the medicine of their stories to Scottish soil.

Fionn mac Cumhaill from the shores of Ireland would hurl an insult across the Moyle Sea and Benandonner a rival Scottish giant who would spit back a retort equally offensive. Tired of trading slurs Fionn challenged his foe to a battle of strength and eagerly got to work building a bridge of basalt columns stretching across the sea to Staffa. When Fionn spied Benandonner on the tiny isle the sheer size of the giant sent Fionn trotting home his weary limbs were in no fit state to battle against the bulk of Benandonner. When the colossal Scot shook himself from his slumber he saw the pillared causeway that Fionn's sweat and toil had built and being that Benandonner was inept at swimming, his route to Ireland had been blocked up until now, with several strides he was on the northern shores of his enemies land.

Word of his arrival rippled through the land and Fionn's wife Oonagh felt the vibrations of the stomping boots pounding the pathway to her door. With a swiftness that belied her cumbersome frame she whipped a bonnet and nightdress from a drawer and wrapping Fionn in a blanket the transformation from man to babe was done.

Benandonner stormed through the door growling for Fionn to fight him.

"Sh" hushed Oonagh, "I just got the wee tot off don't you go waking him he's a sickly child, nothing like his father Fionn. If its himself your wanting take a seat for he'll be home for his tea in a jiffy.

Benandonner scraped a chair across the floor and winced as a loud bawling screamed in his ears.

"Now look what you've done you half oaf, you've woken the babe."

"What do you mean half oaf women?" croaked Benandonner, "Well you being half sized like, you are so much smaller that the average male giant, now my Fionn what a man is he, so tall his head scuffs the ceiling, Oh for goodness sake you pitiful child will you not throw your toys from your crib."

Oonagh shot a disapproving glare at the child who had tossed a massive rock from its cradle. "Be a love and pass the sickly little imp his pebble will you?" she screeched at Benandonner who bent down and lifted the huge boulder, a substantial rock that was very manageable to move yet a babe tossing such a heavy weight with apparent ease was frightening to the burly Scot. Before Benandonner could place the boulder back a whizzing thump resounded on his head sending him spinning to the floor, dazed he saw the infant swinging a hefty tree branch as a club,

"Oh you are a sweetie playing with the young 'un like that such a fun sight being that the child is so feeble and probably won't make it to adulthood. You wouldn't believe he's from the same stock as Fionn. Here, have a steak. I thought Fionn would be home by now and he likes his steaks well done not burnt so here." She tossed one to the baby who grabbed it and gnawed into for all that he was worth, making light work of tearing the meat apart he licked his lips and curled up in a satisfied ball with a trembling belch. Benandonner reached for his steak, which was actually a brittle rock about the size and shape of a juicy steak. Benandonners teeth cracked down on the stone and a splintering pain shot through his jaw.

"What are you like you little half pint, you make more noise than that deathly child, if your not enjoying your steak leave it for Fionn he will gobble it up cold.'

Benandonner shot a look at the babe who was preparing to throw the boulder from his cot again, his mind raced thinking that if a sickly bairn could eat through the toughest steak, wield a tree branch and toss a boulder with such effortlessness, then what would the father be able to do? Benandonner staggered to his feet and mumbled something about needing to get home before dark which made no sense because at the height of the summer solstice it doesn't get that dark on Staffa. A violet sky gives an almost betwixt and between quality of day and night. Benandonner fair skipped across the causeway kicking over some of the bridge so Fionn would not be able to follow, leaving Oonagh to take back the bonnet and nightdress, for Fionn to acknowledge his wife's strength of mind and his willingness to take her lead.

Treasure of the Tale

I love the role Oonagh plays, her quick wits saves the day. It is amazing how perspective drives our truth and how our beliefs are bound tightly by our thoughts. Benandonner is convinced that the unseen form of Fionn is an insurmountable obstacle judged against the strength of the supposed babe and he runs away. How often do we run away because we have bought into someone else's version of the truth rather than having the courage to explore our own? Fionn builds a bridge to confront Bennandonner. What bridges are we currently building in our lives and between whom? Are we building bridges of confrontation or resolution? Fionn means fair haired and the resplendent sunshine shone its fair rays onto Davey's boat as we pulled into the port of the holy isle Iona. Oonagh means holy or pure. We had journeyed to Staffa which is old norse for staves or pillars. Where do we stave off the truth of our story? Where do we stand strong as pillars of truth taking responsibility for our journey? How do we purify ourselves in a blemished world? What are we doing physical, mentally, emotionally and spiritually to cleanse our fields, our living space, our environment? I found no meaning of Benandonner and if you break it up Ben means son, ann means grace and Donna means lady so the lady and her son gracefully outwit the brute of this giant of Staffa, the son of Scotland being replaced by the son of Ireland, of Dana the Great Mother herself, as the Irish Dal Riata's tales merged with the Picts and the Scots were born anew.

The Tale and the Land

So we can plainly see this fun tale has its roots in the occupation of the Dal Riata. Fionn came with them and at some point Fionn became Fingal and in doing so takes up occupancy on Staffa supplanting the indigenous giant Benandonner.

After a brief stop on Iona for a gathering cauldron, a circle for us pilgrims to share our experiences, I boarded the ferry and went in search of an unmarked path across the Sound on Mull. I am indebted to a local who lives in a small village on the road to Craignure, whose name I will keep in my own medicine bundle so that he is not inundated with people asking for the directions, which are a wee bit like turn right at the first dandelion and left at the third clump of nettles and watch out for the rabbit hole! Not only is the track that leads toward the coastal path hard to find, the problem was in selecting the correct inlet, there were several sandy and rocky beaches to choose from, with difficult routes to clamber and climb down and then up again.

The walk alone is food for the soul and I had a picnic lunch to fuel the body, although my eagerness to find the cave was hampering my desire to sit and be in the moment of a delectable lunch. I was hungry and my concern was for the tides of time. There are only a handful of occasions when the pilgrimage moves to meet the dictations of the ticking illusion of time and today was one of them, the last ferry waits for no man, woman or for that matter pixie. The last ferry to Iona on a Sunday sails at 6pm and it was already 3:30pm and I had not yet descended the cliff face. I chose a cove that looked promising and began to scale the thin ledge that dropped towards the sea. My heart pounded both in keen hope of discovery and the adrenaline pumped in fear of a fall. I breathed into my roots to become one with the earth and shuffled down the rock face in growing confidence. Jubilantly I took my first steps on the rock piled beach and my alarm clock flew out of my top shirt pocket and the battery promptly disappeared. The back case of the clock is broken and the battery dislodged and promptly vanished without a trace. The hands stared up at me fixed at 3:42 pm. I know that, as I still have not replaced the battery and the hands have been fixed in this position since. I smiled as I realized that the numbers added to nine: three times the three levels of being.

After scouting around the right hand side of the beach clambering rocks and craning my neck to see as far right as possible I drew a blank. No cave and no time. The thought of the ferry leaving without me pushed me back up the cliff face and I trekked to the minibus leaving the cave calling its presence on a distant breeze.

High on the bluff set back on a winding trail sits a house and as the man was in his garden I approached with the dreaded 'excuse me' on my tongue. I was hoping for guidance to find the cave and the Scot who faced me weighed me up quickly and nodded in confirmation that my search was on the right track. "If you had just gone left there is a thin strip of sand that leads up to the cave that sits high up in the rocks, a real beauty, well hidden, not many people know about it, be sure to visit the beach just down the way, it is the best beach in Britain and I live next to it" he smiled in delightful satisfaction.

With the news that I had been close my spirits rose, I would offer the group a Mystery day, for those who chose to accompany me in search of the carvings and cave, we would return in two days and continue our search, even if the cave remained hidden the beach would be a beautiful place to weave some of our profound experiences from our time on Iona.

With a bus full of songs we retraced my steps and trucked down the bumpy lane, all but three of the pilgrims expectantly boarded the bus in high spirits for the adventure that lay ahead. Our voices lifted high with joyful merriment guaranteed to get the ancestors giggling, they were already gathering and we pilgrims would not disappoint!

We hiked to the spot where the trail ceases and the scrambling begins. In the full blaze of a cobalt blue sky I asked the pilgrims to connect to the land, their roots, to the heavens and their hearts and ask for guidance to whether this climb was right for them. One brave soul owned her voice and in her full power chose to support our climb from the cliff top, which gave permission to two others, leaving six of us to climb, four of us were steady and like goats made our way to the boulders below. Two of our party with courage and a willingness to be helped were coaxed and supported emotionally and physically down the steep descent. One had been terrified of heights and was ready to face the fear and move beyond it, processing work that had flowed through her on Iona when she cast away her fear by placing it into an Iona stone and then casting the stone into the sea to be cleansed by Mannannan Mac Lir.

This is the tradition of casting out the pebble in our shoe. How often do we wander through life's garden with a pebble in our shoe? What is your pebble? On pilgrimage there are traditions of carrying a stone and throwing it into the sea that stretch from Scotland's tip to Cornwall's coves. I have carried stones out onto the causeway that links the Cornish mainland to St. Michaels Mount at low tide, come high tide the causeway is swallowed up by the sea god's heaving crested mane that swirls and rolls into Marazion's shoreline.

It is one thing to put the words on the wind, but it is another to put the word magic into practice, and to move through the terror of doing it.. A classic example of moving through knowledge into wisdom. The Universe is sure to provide an opportunity to face our trepidation and the pilgrim in question was ripe for the testing. The other lady is a sixty year old whose knees are weak so she shuffled and breathed deeply accepting hands and allowing her feet to be moved at times to the next ledge below as she inched her way to the waiting rocks below.

I eagerly picked my way across the stones to the left hoping to see an open cleft up in the cliff face. Within a few steps the movement caught my eye something the rest of the group had already seen, two adders basking in the sun now slithering their way into the world below. In my whole lifetime I have only ever seen one adder before and that was on Lizard Point in Cornwall many years previous when my blood brothers Mark Gooden and Paul King had joined me in a madcap adventure to the South West of Cornwall dressed up as the Pirates of Penzance. We strolled around the ports and coves dressed in full pirate togs one weekend and on a clamber up the cliffs south of Helston I had reached my hand up to grab a ledge and on pulling myself up an adder was coiled up three feet to my left hand side. Now two of the underworld serpents whipped and slid into the dark shadows. These phenomenal beings teach us about our transformation knowing how to shed their skins, they are symbols of life death rebirth connecting with the roots of the underworld carrying both the poison and the antidote these majestic magicians represent healing and when we imbue the graceful flow penetrating swiftly and slowly through the dark and light spaces within and around us we can adapt ourselves to the constant changes with authentic power peeling away that which no longer serves us and truly letting it go.

So as I picked my way over the rocky beach towards the left hand side of the cove, I swept my eyes in eager search and the memory of looking with soft eyes flooded into me we so often don't look we overlook, so I scavenged around softening my field to no avail, every crevice, plant, and sea worn rock gave not a hint of a glimpse of the sacred treasure that we sought. I even made my way to where another cove loomed beyond the pillar of rock and the clear cool sea that gently lapped at the craggy shore.

In a jiffy I stripped down and plunged into the sea. The large jagged rocks provided seclusion and with anticipation I waded to the concealed inlet, my bare feet hobbled over the spiny spikes and at times skipped over the sea kissed, smooth rocks that abound on a coastline that boasts both the pointy sharp uneven face of rock and stone with the beautiful expanse of fine white sandy beaches, diverse terrain within a stones throw from each other. Scouring the dips and hollows again bore no fruit and reluctantly I trudged and tottered my way to my clothes with the realization that this was not the right cove after all.

The satisfaction of seeing the snakes and helping the two pilgrims walk, crawl and shuffle their way through their fears was a striking addition to the story of our day and the cave tugged at my heart strings, I knew she was near.

We took a much less hazardous route to the salt and breeze licked expanse of soft fine sand, bleached with the elements and glittering from the fullness of Lugh's shaggy mane beaming in the cloudless sky of radiant blue.

Undaunted I headed to the rocky coastline bordering the shore and again hidden from view I stripped off and swam around the protruding rocks to once again stand on the rocks that I had examined diligently for signs of the elusive cave. I was struck later by the Celtic three as this was the third time I had been on this beach. Now I was satisfied that I had left no stone unturned, so I swam to my clothes and was soon striding towards the group who were all feasting on a variety of goodies from smoked salmon to stinky cheese.

Discussion abounded to whether the cave was closed on Tuesdays, and of course it was Tuesday!, or whether the mists would dissipate to reveal the sacred loins of the rebirthing chamber. I heard one of the pilgrims share, "Maybe Andrew needs to find it on his own." Close, but not on my own.   I was going to discover and experience the birthing of this hidden womb with Susan. Again in retrospect I saw the number connection. I searched first on my own, then with the group and the third expedition was yet another piece of magic in the winding tale and trail of an amazing day.

We chose to veer off the trodden pathway and picked up a trail to the next cove along from our morning escapade and quickly found ourselves traipsing through potholes, stingers, and bog land, echoes of the Rose story from quest day flickered on the wind. Our hearts were pumping as the full dawning that this was the cove penetrated beyond my thoughts to shiver in my pores. My cells were vibrating in exalted bliss. We both thought we saw it straight ahead to the right. As we came in striking distance, the shadows rolled off the side of the cliffs teasing us with false expectation and with carefree abandon we swung ourselves to the left and were greeted by a slim stretch of sand that had lay hidden behind a clawed fist of rock that sprawled toward the sea. Following the strip of gold, our eyes rested on the gaping tear of the jagged lair that rose above us burrowed into the cliffs of Mull.

Walking into this undisturbed sanctuary filled me with the ecstatic journey and the dance of my field twirled, floated, leapt and expanded with undiluted joy. The cave is pristine, the carvings untouched. The graffiti ravaged age of dominion over has not tarnished the sovereignty of this priceless gem. At the very end of the cave is a natural altar. I have no idea when another human being has stood in this spot. Very few have witnessed the ancestors mysterious art work glowing on the walls of the darkened dank womb. More sheep have sheltered here over the years as bones and aged droppings covered the dusty floor.

I laid my day bag, a Greenman shoulder bag, on a stone to the right of the cave and took out Norbert, my pet dragon who is the pilgrimage mascot. Norbert learnt to be a gypsy dragon real quickly within his first five months of being with me he had visited Wales, Scotland, England, France, USA and then Ireland! Norbert loves caves, when I had waded and swam through the sea earlier Norbert had come with me. Now he was in his element, as he is prone to say in pilgrimage circles, "Norbert was born in a cave and he learnt to make love to the land!" With Norbert flying in one hand and my rattle shaking in the other I was jiggling and wriggling in gratitude to the ancestors and spirit guides for bringing us home. The safety of the Mothers belly held me, nurtured me. I felt the reverberation from the old hags cauldron way below my feet sending waves of recognition and connectedness through me and to all beings.

It was with reluctance that I placed Norbert on top of my Greenman bag and prepared to go and find the others. Susan breathed in the gentle calmness of place and shared. "I would like to stay here with the cave while you go and get the group, is that okay with you?" Knowing I will visit the cave many more times it was a great gift to offer her time alone in this protected haven.

"Yes that's okay," I uttered with a tinge of coveting flowing in my cauldrons. There was definitely a small part of me that wished I could stay too the peacefulness called to my spirit to nestle in and I needed to go and get the pilgrims. The group was waiting patiently, expectantly. It is in these moments, in all moments that we need to be clear why we are doing something. This day I was here to serve the pilgrims not myself and with that realization the exit was easy.

I moved with bounding gleeful steps and I worked to subdue my exuberance as I came across the sand toward the gathered pilgrims. The Pixie in me wanted to be part of the delivery. They knew I had intended to ask the Scot who lived close by for directions so I declared glum faced, "We did not find him," then with a giggle and a caper I flashed a brilliant grin and chuckled out, "We did find the cave."

Squeals of delight erupted and a rush of energy rose as bags and belongings were hastily gathered. I bent down and swung Susan's back pack onto my shoulder and I heard one of our band cry,

"Does any one want to take these otherwise I am leaving them here?" The pilgrim in question has a delightful trait of exploring where her heart calls and finding unique stones, pieces of glass, intricate wood sculptures and on this occasion two sun bleached sheep skulls.

"I'll gladly carry them as an offering to the cave," I beamed thankfully, thinking of the sheep droppings littering the floor. I swept up the cauldron bones of wisdom in my left hand and we began our climb and my thoughts drifted to the story of Kate Crackernuts,.

Kate Crackernuts.

Kate was an exuberant young teenager with a love of life, an infectious energy that couldn't help but put a smile on your face. Her new stepsister, also called Kate, looked at the sprightly girl as a kindred spirit, a reflection of her own spry nature. Two peas in a pod, friends for life and princesses to boot. Kate's dad the Regent had invited her stepsister, Kate's mum a neighboring Queen, to live in the luxury of their sumptuous abode. All was well, the King and Queen were in love, their girls got on like a house on fire but the Queen wanted to make sure part of that house burnt to the ground. She had taken an instant dislike to the prettier Kate. Her Katie was rather plain looking but this young nymph was a stunning beauty. Her Kate was going to come first and the teenage hussy would be relegated to a second hand footstall if she got her way and she was renowned for getting precisely what she wanted.

"Come here you straggly little imp," the Queen smirked at her step daughter Kate and then reached out her spindly fingers and grabbed the pretty girls cheek. "My daughters name is Kate and there is room for only one Kate so you are going to get a new name... let me think."

Before she could spit some debasing name on the wind her daughter Katie crooned, "I don't have a middle name but Kate does and its Anne. We can call her Anne if its okay with you Kate, Kate Anne, Anne?"

"That would be fine with me," the newly named Anne squeaked plucking herself from the clutches of the Queen and heading to safer waters beyond the Queens malicious gaze. Of course when in the presence of her new Beau she was all sweetness and light "My Love your daughter is delightful, what an inspiration,. She came up with the idea of calling herself Anne so as not to have confusion with two Kate's in the house. How selfless, just like my beautiful husband who lives to spoil me. She rolled into his eager arms and planted a sensuous kiss on his keen lips.

Besotted with and bewitched by his Queen, the Kings interest level in Anne dwindled while his Queen's interest in the girl grew.

Slipping into the town on the night of a new moon the Queen's henchmen led her beyond the walls to the very edge of the looming dark forest where the henwife sequestered herself in an intriguing curvy cottage, this mystic grandmother mixed the potions and weaved spells and would do the Queen's bidding or burn at the stake, a simple choice for the cackling hag who told the pompous monarch, "Send me Anne at sunrise and make sure she fasts."

Anne was used to being given extra tasks to do so the Queen whipping her covers from her and throwing cold water in her face before the sun had woken up the day was no surprise to her. A jingling pouch was thrust into her chest and she was bundled towards the castle door. She shook the sleep from her eyes and grabbed her cloak, for it would be cool making her way to the henwife's house at such an early hour.

"Get a bakers dozen of eggs you lazy sack of horse shit and hurry about it, no breakfast for you until you bring back the eggs to cook. " The jagged shriek of her stepmother's words still stung her ears as she bustled through the castle and took the short cut through the kitchen to the west gate. With the speed of an arrow and the grace of a swan she whipped a piece of crust from a freshly baked pie and munched merrily as she bopped, weaved and even cart-wheeled her way to the old crones door.

"Come in lassie and pick the lid off the simmering pot here." Anne grabbed the hot saucepan lid using the hem of her sleeve and looked inside at the bubbling water. "Tell your stepmother to keep the pantry locked next time," screeched the wise one.

"Here take those eggs, cross my palm with that purse you brought with you and bugger off," she squealed.

The next morning the Queen escorted Anne to the West Gate without going through the kitchen and kicked her into the dusty main street leading past the town square and out to the farm fields with her stepmother's shrill demand that Anne should bring 'it' back from the Henwife.

As Anne skipped by a group of children working the land she stopped to say hello and went on her way nibbling on a freshly picked pea pod. Eager to find out what the 'it' was Anne poked her head around the henwife's door and inquired excitedly "What do you have for me?"

"Lift the lid from the pot and you will see," growled the old one the wrinkled brow of the frustrated crone furrowed as she watched Annie remove the lid and stare confused into the rising steam.

"Tell your stepmother the pot won't boil if the fire's away," howled the hag who was steaming by this time in a rare tempest of dark fury. Anne made a mad dash for the door and hoped the information about the fire being off somewhere was the 'it' she had been sent for and would appease the Queen leaving Anne to sleep in the following morn. Before the cock had crowed thrice Anne found herself being frog marched down the town street by the Queens guards with the agitated monarch kicking up the dust as she led the abducted princess to the wise ones door.

"Open up witch and give this pretty little creature the gift we have prepared for her."

"Is she ready?" whispered the hag. "Are you ready this time or have you sent her to me full again?"

"Yes she is ready," howled the Queen.

Anne stood under the scrutiny of piercing eyes shooting daggers into her turned back. Slowly she lifted the lid to the bubbling liquid spluttering on the boil, in the blink of an eye her head toppled off into the pot and a sheep's head rose out of the water and plunked itself solidly on Anne's shoulders. Job accomplished, the Queen pushed Anne roughly out of the cottage and she was left to find her own way home as locals gawked at the misshaped figure of the sheepheaded girl.

The Queen, like a cat with the cream purred affectionately in the Kings ear stirring the Sovereign's scepter. Meanwhile her own daughter Kate gently wrapped her stepsisters head in the finest linen, took her by the hand and led her out of the kingdom to seek their fortune. Their steps echoed through the towns, forest, across mountains, meadows and swamps until in a moss covered, wild flowered dell led the two weary travelers to a round castle door. Kate knocked and after quick negotiations she agreed to trade lodgings for her sick sister for a peck of silver and a nights work for herself.

Her job on one hand had the appearance of ease and on the other as life threatening. Kate who had a bundle of courage listened fervently to the earnest tone droning in her ear "The King of this castle has two sons one who is wasting away, on his deathbed he is, no one has been able to ascertain what is ailing him and the curious thing is that whoever stays overnight with him vanishes, never to be seen again."

Kate walked to the Prince's chamber and settled at the foot of his bed watching keenly for any small interaction. The Prince lay pale and sweaty in a comatose state. Kate moved to wipe his brow and she gently crooned as the clock ticked its way to the midnight hour. As the chimes struck the Prince threw back the covers jumped out of bed and strode purposefully to the stables where by he whistled for his hound and he saddled his favorite horse, mounted her and trotted off toward the woods without once recognizing the presence of Katie. The young Princess quick of wit and physically fit was on the Prince's tail the whole way and without invitation or deliberation she hopped up behind the riding prince and galloped away from the dell towards the tree line. As they galloped through the greenwood Katie reached out her hands and plucked nuts from the trees stuffing them in her apron. Over creek with twists and turns the steed and hound took a well forged mysterious path carrying their quarry to a clearing where a burial mound shone in the gleaming moonlight. The Prince reigned in, drew his bridle waving it as if it were a magic wand he cried "Open, open, open Sidhe mound let the young prince in with his horse and hound

"And let his lady in too," called Katie from behind. The mound opened up and swallowed them inside. Immediately they entered the bright candlelight of a magnificent dancing hall, colors abounded and an assortment of gaily dressed fey swarmed around them, grabbed the Prince and led him to the dance. The music rippled and plucked at the heart strings calling feet to hop and sway as the rhythmic bodies spiraled through the night. Katie darted for cover and found herself peeking in on the dance from behind the door. The Prince threw his body into the melody of music and tore up the floor gyrating and twirling until he could spin no more and collapsed in a heap on the floor then the eager shining ones would fan him until they revived him and then they coiled him up and released him to spring whirl and topple once more.

The limp Prince wasted and worn from being ridden hard all night buckled and bowed to the screeching cry of the rising cock crowing, the explosion of sunlight on a brand new day. With a renewed vigor he sprang to his feet and Katie only just jumped into the saddle in time as the hoof beats drummed a trail to the castle stables and when the morning sun had finally risen to a bright height Katie was found sitting by the fire cracking nuts in the Prince's chamber while he lay sprawled and seemingly lifeless in his comfy bed.

"He did well and if you wish me to stay another night with him I need a peck of gold for my trouble and food and lodging for my sister and myself.

The second night followed the pattern of the first with Katie plucking nuts and including herself by calling, "And let his lady in too" as the mound grabbed and gulped them from the cool night air. With the faerie ball in full swing Katie's attention shifted from the manic dance of her sickly young companion, she knew exactly what was going to happen to him, to the antics of a fay babe playing with a wand.

"Careful pet that wands special," croaked the wizened face of a leathery bat like woman with bristly hair and a toothless smile. "Three strokes from that healing stick would make Kate's sister as bonnie as she ever was."

Hearing this Katie rolled a nut towards the wee tot whose attention swept upon the nuts that kept flickering and spinning across the floor, chasing the rolling shells that pinged this way and that, the babe dropped the wand and began gathering nuts by the score. Katie reached out her hand and whipped the wand into the folds of her apron. This time when the cock crowed she was waiting by the mare and took great delight in tapping Anne's sheephead three times to transform the woolen bleating into the chiseled beauty of her sister, with great satisfaction she sat back in her chair and cracked nuts by the fire.

Kate's terms for a third night of watching over the Prince included a marriage proposal and acceptance to her sick patient. As Anne was now being wooed by the exhausted Prince's younger brother he proved a useful ally in talking the King into accepting whatever demands Katie made. Again Katie collected nuts and called for entrance behind the trance like figure of her weary guide. Leaving the Prince to the mercy of the toe tapping dance weavers she once again noticed the fay child who tonight was playing with a birdie.

"Careful pet that's a precious winged one you have between your palms," squawked the twitching frame of a raven like dark one who jerked and jolted to the staccato tempo of the Fae Ball. "Three bites of that birdie will bring full health and alertness flooding back into the Prince."

Hearing this Katie juggled the nuts and rolled them tantalizingly close to the babe's reach, within no time the birdie was forgotten and the dance of a new game absorbed the fascinated tot until the cock crowed. Meanwhile the birdie was neatly stored in the pocket of her apron. This time her return to the castle was not consumed with cracking nuts, instead she plucked the feathers from the bird and cooked it. The aroma of the savory snack aroused something deep within the sick prince who stirred and mumbled, "I wish I had a bite of that birdie."

Katie duly obliged and the Prince rose up on his elbow and crooned, "Oh if I just had another bite of that birdie." With two morsels delectably chewed and swallowed he sat upright and affirmed, "Oh if only I had a third bite," and the taste of which restored him to his true nature, energetic, curious and healthy.

When the chamber doors were opened, all saw the happy couple laughing, cuddling and cracking nuts together. With Anne and the youngest Prince madly in love and Kate and her new found love besotted with each other a double marriage ceremony was announced through the land where the sick son married the well sister and the well son married the sick sister and they lived happy, died happy and never ever drank out of a dry cappy.

Treasure of the Tale

The sheep heads that I carried had invoked the memory of Katie Crackernuts, such a weird and wonderful tale. Begging questions such as; Where are we like the queen? Where do we judge someone on their appearances and victimize them, or on the other hand offer preferential treatment to them because of it? Where do we insist on someone taking on or being something they are not? Are you noticing some of the echoes in the different Celtic tales?

I'll never forget being turned off French language at an early age because the French teacher decided that we were all going to be called by our French names so I was labeled Alain, French for Alan, why not Andres for Andrew? We already had an Andrew in the class and it would be too confusing for the teacher to have two, hence I was Alain and as a result, I switched off! Where do we switch off instead of owning our voice and standing in the fullness of our power? The teacher offered me an opportunity to speak my truth, I hid and so I take responsibility for a poor vocabulary in French!

The Queen maliciously hurts Anne, which begs the question; where do we hurt people to get what we want?

When and where do we hold double standards? Is there a difference in the way we talk to someone directly and about the same person behind their back? Why do we feel the need to gossip?

Who is the Kate/Anne that scratches my skin and brings out the spiteful monarch in me?

The Queen uses sexuality to get what she wants with the King so how and whom do we manipulate in this way?

The hag asks Anne if she is ready, the appearance of the sheep's head leads to an onset of sickness which she willingly walks into. Are we ready and willing to walk into the depth of our sickness/darkness to bring health/light to live more purposefully, more freely? If so, how?

What is my sickness?

How and where do I lose my head?

Kate asks to be included and gains entrance to the cairn. Where do we ask to be included? Where do we shy away from asking? Where do we include or leave ourselves out of the picture of our own stories.

Anne willingly lets Kate wrap a cloth around her sheep's head and follows trustingly; where do we allow others to help us? Who do we trust to help us?

Like the exhausted Prince, where and when are we dancing to the beat of someone else's tune and where and when are we frolicking to our own poetic melodies?

The Tale and the Land

All food for thought and the naked sockets of the bleached sheep bones recalled the time that I attended my first Celtic sweatlodge at Dunderry Park with Martin Duffy. My Irish brothers and sisters had reclaimed this indigenous practice to the Isles and knowing I was on the cusp of pouring I chose to honor my heritage and fly to Ireland to study to pour on the Green Road. That morning before my first Celtic lodge, had seen us wander Slieve na Cailleach the Hill of the Hag at Loughcrew. It was on a hailing December morning and I had picked up a sheep's head which I carried to Dunderry as my fetish, a Celtic bundle to offer to the fire to release that which was holding me hostage. I had picked up the head as a vessel of wisdom and that night before entering the womb I offered it to the fire to cleanse and light the creative sparks of my imagination while firing up my walk into the wisdom ways. Now in Scotland I would work with two other sheep's heads making my dance with them three as I offered these two skulls to the cave. In honor of Kate, which means pure and Anne, which means grace and favor I carried the skulls to their new resting place.

Access to the cavern is made more challenging at high tide, the inlet floods and the path becomes more rugged, scrambling and shuffling become the order of the day, so with this in mind I was keen to move the group to the cove as I knew the tide was turning. The elated travelers were already making light of the climb and I noticed that the majority of them were forging ahead of the snails in our pack. Snails are beautiful teachers and the pilgrim with the aged knees listened to her body and moved in time with its natural rhythms. I strolled beside her and uncharacteristically offered to carry her pack.

Her response was, "It's my shit to carry not yours" which was absolutely right and one I normally honor and adhere to and on this occasion I wanted to reach the cave before the easier pathway became cut off by the sea. Now with two packs on my back, hers and Susan's I led the group all together as quickly and yet fairly slowly, a cross between the snake and the snail we slithered to the rocks below. Not wanting to flood the cave with bags I suggested that we leave all extemporary belongings on a nearby rock. It was at this moment that my eyes became transfixed on my left hand, the skulls were gone.

"Did you see me pick the skulls up?" I asked in confusion as my mind raced through my journey over the cliffs.

"You definitely had them," someone responded.

"Maybe you put them down when you picked up Candace's bag," another offered. "I don't remember putting them down," I stammered. "I don't remember you putting them down either," someone called.

Baffled I opened up Susan's bag knowing I hadn't put them there and I looked anyway. I zipped it shut and then had to look a second time to be sure, it's a small bag!!! Letting go of the enigma, we skirted the giant stone claw and dashed by the encroaching tide. Susan stood framed in the doorway a French goddess with a joie de vivre smile, her rebirth looked as vibrant as mine felt. The group scurried to join her and after a prayer and offerings we toned in the space. Basking in the electricity of the mating ritual as we entered this hallowed womb, the death, the life, and the subsequent rebirth, my cup brimmeth over. Aware that Mannanan Mac Lir was riding the white foam Steeds of Rhiannon to bless our births and cover the claw I suggested we head out before the climb became too difficult. As the pilgrims began their descent and the subsequent climb, I reached for my Greenman bag that I had left behind when I went in search of the waiting group and was puzzled by its weight.

"What on earth is in here?" I exclaimed to myself and a sharp intake of breath revealed the two sun bleached sheep skulls sitting in the bag I had left behind in the cave. "Magic," I shouted. "Magic, I have the skulls."

A cry of wonder went on the wind and the skulls were placed reverently on the natural altar at the far side of the cave.

Transmutation? Alchemy? Magic? This adventure is etched forever and a day in the great tapestry of story. Is it possible that I did not leave the Greenman bag in the cave? Yes it's possible, my recollection is that I left it and when it was time to leave I had to go and pick it up from the spot I had placed it. If I carried it with me to retrieve the pilgrims I have no remembrance of it as I placed the two back packs on the beach or when I frantically searched Susan's pack for the skulls. Equally I do not recall taking the bag off when arriving at the cave with the group in tow. It also makes no sense to me that I would have carried it from the cave knowing I was returning. I always say to people do not doubt the magic. It comes in many forms, shapes and sizes and as a Celt I celebrate and love the mysterious wonder that the sheep's skulls brought to an already fully charged day. Part of the magic is in not knowing, it is a mystery! The numerology added further spice, Three times I went onto the one cove in search of the cave. Three independent times I searched, once alone, once with the group and then with Susan. It was three inlets that we stood upon. First the snake cove, then the sandy beach and finally the cave cove itself. Three of us entered the cave first, Susan Norbert and myself as Norbert would say, he 'made love to the land." I looked in Susan's bag twice and then the third bag, my Greenman bag, revealed the skulls, and of course there were nine of us who toned in the cave, like the fellowship of the ring, our vocal chimes honored the sanctity and sovereignty as we celebrated three times the three levels of being. Thank you ancestors, thank you Spirit Guides, thank you pilgrims, another Celtic three! SEA (Yes).

One of the greatest gifts of leading pilgrimages has been the constant necessity of doing my own inner work. To lead a group and hold a safe space for people to explore themselves intimately requires that I do the same. A luscious painful succulent challenging insightful journey of reclaiming the fullness of my soul has prepared me for one of the richest chapters in my growing story.

I drew the Wolf card last year to support my quest and I am getting to know Wolf intimately. The lone wolf is teaching me to howl at the moon as I go on a pilgrimage walking celibate for 13 moons. I laughed vigorously when it dawned on me that my oath for a year and a day of being intimate with myself through the 13 moons of transformation was my moontime! This solitary journey brings me closer to my pack, to my beautiful children who live with me and teach me each day the importance of being a father and to the depth of relationship where Sovereignty calls. I have such a deep understanding of aligning my 4 bodies, emotionally, physically, mentally and spiritually. I know that bringing these into alignment creates the 5th body, which is Sovereignty. So I wear my coat of joy and sorrow, of pain and ecstasy, of life and death and I am thankful for having faith in the rebirthing process. For holding the poets soul in the center of my heart as the mantra that the bohemians sing from the galleries at the Moulin Rouge rings triumphantly from my bones "The greatest gift you will ever know is to love and be loved in return."

Each visit to the Isles I feel the power of the ancestors standing with me and my tears flow on each parting, for leaving Alba, Eire, Brighid, Rhiannon and all of the folds of her patchwork skirts and ample bosom brings the joy and sorrow bubbling from the depths to ripple and gleam on the surface of my expanded soul and beyond, for the soil beneath my feet sings the Oran Mor through me and fragments of rock, earth, sea and keening wind permeate my being and lead me to the edge beyond the horizon to the center of the Universe. The Isles have left an unfathomable print upon my spirit that calls to me. I yearn to return and dance amongst the nemetons of my homeland again and again, to explore the forgotten places, to peek into the mystery with gay abandon and to take willing souls to these places of Spirit on sacred pilgrimage.

There are so many delicious questions to ask ourselves and in our willingness to answer them we glimpse the truest beat of our heartsong, it is in our willingness to follow our passion, to be the Peddler and follow our dreams, to awaken our inner Merlin and be the Taliesin of our own life story, to dance to the rhythm of our own drum and find the truth of our heart beat as wise old Bet so we can recognize our own 'luck' and open ourselves up to celebrating a remarkable life. A toast on each and every one; to living on our own edge, to stepping into the center of our own story as the authors and to being the heroes in the adventure of our lives! Power of a remarkable life on you, power of story on you and remember today is a good day to die.

A PASSAGE TO PILGRIMAGE.

For interested travelers looking for authentic soulful adventure that meets the needs of people of all fitness capabilities and ages email Andrew Steed at **asteed@andrewsteed.com**.

His web page at **www.andrewsteed.com** will share some information and often there are other opportunities for travel and workshops across the world that may not be mentioned.

Andrew is grateful for the experience and loving energy of Kat Naslas who is co leading workshops across the globe and some of the pilgrimages in the British Isles and Ireland and they are currently working on trails through Greece, Kat's ancestral heartland. To find out more about Kat visit www.katalysthealingarts.com

As well as joining a group of no more than 10 pilgrims you can also gather your own group of 5 or more for a customized adventure into the land, stories and the adventure of the Isles!

Be a witness not a tourist and wander/wonder well!